PRAISE FOR *What's Your Type of Car*

"Every book on type has a chapter on career, so you may wonder if there is really anything new to say on the subject. But there is, and Donna Dunning has said it. In the way she describes the types, in the way she uses checklists to establish your type, in the way she talks about career implications of the results—in many ways, she offers new and helpful assistance to anyone who wants to base a career on who he or she really is."

WILLIAM BRIDGES, PRESIDENT, WILLIAM BRIDGES & ASSOCIATES
AUTHOR OF *TRANSITIONS, MANAGING TRANSITION, AND CREATING YOU & CO.*

"Donna Dunning's *What's Your Type of Career?* is packed full of information about how our personalities mesh (or don't) with our work choices. It will help readers understand themselves and make authentic career choices that build on their strengths, skills, preferences, and values. This is a must read for anyone who uses the MBTI® instrument."

ROBIN A. SHEERER, PRESIDENT, CAREER ENTERPRISES, INC.
AUTHOR OF *NO MORE BLUE MONDAYS*

"The key to self-acceptance and dealing effectively with others is knowing our natural instinctive style. Donna Dunning takes us to a new level in exploring our type and relating it directly to career choices. This is must reading for adults in the career change and renewal process."

HELEN HARKNESS, PRESIDENT, CAREER DESIGN ASSOCIATES, INC.
AUTHOR OF *THE CAREER CHASE AND DON'T STOP THE CAREER CLOCK*

"Anyone who has taken the *Myers-Briggs Type Indicator®* (MBTI®) instrument will find these in-depth interpretations extremely thorough and highly relevant to careers."

RICHARD L. KNOWDELL, PRESIDENT, CAREER RESEARCH & TESTING, INC.
AUTHOR OF *BUILDING A CAREER DEVELOPMENT PROGRAM*

"This is the most thorough explanation of personality types you will find. Dunning provides useful terminology to express MBTI® typology, offers clarifying quotes and checklists, and suggests tips for action appropriate for each type. Extremely useful for ongoing career management."

PEGGY SIMONSEN, MANAGING VICE PRESIDENT, TALENT MANAGEMENT,
RIGHT MANAGEMENT CONSULTANTS
AUTHOR OF *CAREER COMPASS*

What's Your Type of Career?

UNLOCK THE SECRETS OF YOUR PERSONALITY TO FIND YOUR PERFECT CAREER PATH

DONNA DUNNING

Davies-Black Publishing
Mountain View, California

Published by Davies-Black Publishing, a division of CPP, Inc., 1055 Joaquin Road, 2nd Floor, Mountain View, CA 94043; 1-800-624-1765.

Special discounts on bulk quantities of Davies-Black books are available to corporations, professional associations, and other organizations. For details, contact the Director of Marketing and Sales at Davies-Black Publishing; 650-691-9123; fax 650-623-9271.

Visit the Davies-Black Publishing web site at www.daviesblack.com.

10 09 08 07 06   10 9 8 7 6 5
Printed in the United States of America

Library of Congress Cataloging-in-Publication Data

Dunning, Donna
    What's your type of career? : unlock the secrets of your personality to find your perfect
    career path / Donna Dunning.—1st ed.
        p. cm.
Includes bibliographical references and index.
ISBN 0-89106-154-1 (pbk.)
1. Vocational guidance. 2. Personality and occupation. I. Title.

HF5381.D88 2001
158.6—dc21

                                                                            00-064535

FIRST EDITION
First printing 2001

Contents

PART ONE: IT ALL STARTS WITH YOU

1 · Introduction · 3
2 · Introduction to Personality Type · 9

PART TWO: EXTRAVERTED CAREER PATHS

Introduction to the Extraverted Ways of Working · 33
3 · Responders: Act and Adapt · 35
4 · Explorers: Innovate and Initiate · 69
5 · Expeditors: Direct and Decide · 107
6 · Contributors: Communicate and Cooperate · 141

PART THREE: INTROVERTED CAREER PATHS

Introduction to the Introverted Ways of Working · 177
7 · Assimilators: Specialize and Stabilize · 179
8 · Visionaries: Interpret and Implement · 211
9 · Analyzers: Examine and Evaluate · 243
10 · Enhancers: Care and Connect · 275

PART FOUR: MAKING BETTER CAREER CHOICES

11 · Taking Stock · 309
12 · Shaping Your Career · 335

References · 355
Index · 357

PART ONE

It All Starts with You

CHAPTER ONE
Introduction

We spend a lot of our time and energy working. It is important to make sure that the work we choose is satisfying. But what makes it satisfying? Work becomes satisfying if it interests you and allows you to do the things you enjoy. Work that is interesting and enjoyable for one person may be totally unsuitable for another. Take, for example, Kent and Linda.

Kent says, "I find it very difficult to deal with details. I find them tedious, since they take my time and energy away from doing interesting things. I like to play with new ideas and do something that has never been done before. I enjoy continually changing and improving things."

Linda says, "The idea of continually changing things doesn't sit right with me. I have very high standards, and I like to do things right the first time. I want my work to be clearly defined, and I want to be able to follow through and pay attention to all of the tasks and details. Some people may think I am a bit too compulsive, but I really enjoy planning ahead and being careful and meticulous."

Kent and Linda approach work in very different ways. Because of their preferences, they enjoy very different types of work. For example, Linda might be strongly attracted to a project management position, where she could organize and deal with lots of details. Kent, by contrast, might find himself overwhelmed or bored doing the same project management work. He might procrastinate or get a poor work evaluation because he finds it difficult to focus on all the details. Kent might be most satisfied working as a designer or in a position that requires him to create or market new ideas.

You too have your own natural and comfortable way of working. If you take the time to clearly assess your work preferences, you will be able to identify types of work that will be personally satisfying.

TAKING ADVANTAGE OF YOUR NATURAL WAY OF WORKING

Whether you are just starting out, maintaining work you already have, looking for a change, exploring business ideas, or thinking of retirement activities, this book will show you how to find work that is both meaningful and rewarding. It will also help you understand how you are likely to grow and develop over your life span. This knowledge will help you manage your transitions, enrich your current career choice, and move into opportunities that will best suit your unique talents. The result will be a satisfying career.

We all have a most comfortable, natural approach to the world around us. From the time we are babies, we show definite preferences and ways of acting. At a family gathering, for instance, one child creates a show for all the relatives while another one quietly sits in the corner and watches the action. These personality differences have been the subject of intensive research for more than fifty years. As researchers studied and analyzed individual differences, it became very clear that we could reliably group people according to their personality types. From this base of personality types, it is possible to define and describe specific ways of working—different natural and comfortable approaches that people use when they are at work.

This book introduces you to eight distinct ways of working, each with its own natural approach to the world of work. The eight approaches have been studied, validated, and defined in detail through extensive studies. Research has shown us that people use one of these eight ways to communicate, organize, approach work tasks, solve problems, make decisions, lead, and be led. Research has also shown us that these ways of working can help individuals define the types of work and work activities that are motivating and satisfying. Of course, it would be unrealistic for any book to prescribe one specific ideal job for you. However, understanding which one of these eight natural approaches you use can give you a huge head start in finding work that comes naturally and is personally rewarding.

When you understand your way of working and find work that lets you do what comes naturally, the following attributes will come naturally, too.

Use Your Strengths and Skills

Everyone has unique strengths and skills. It is important to make sure that you arc working in the environment you prefer, doing activities and using skills that reflect your natural approach. You can focus on using and learning skills to help you do better what you do best. If you work with, rather than against, your natural approach, you will be satisfied and motivated. You will learn to appreciate how you like to lead or be led and the type of contribution you make as a team member. You can choose where and how to expand and enrich your range of skills and competencies.

Become More Aware of What Affects Your Job Satisfaction

We have all encountered people who are obviously happy and satisfied in their work. The waitress who serves you with friendly, helpful flair and the brick-layer who takes pride in creating a solid, straight fireplace are likely using their natural way of working. Perhaps they have other aspirations or goals in mind, but you can tell that they are engaged in and enjoying their current work. On the other hand, we have all run into people who are not suited to their job. That grumpy public official, teacher, plumber, or sales associate may be just having a bad day . . . or perhaps he or she is not doing work that uses his or her nat-ural approach. Perhaps some plumbers would be happier if they were design-ing software. Knowing your natural work preferences will provide you with a link between work and personal satisfaction.

Make Better Career Choices

We know that different people are motivated and satisfied by different jobs and activities. Understanding your natural way of working will help you choose suitable work. You can focus your job search and your ongoing work negotia-tions to ensure that your career choices reflect your personal approach as well as your unique skills and situation. Only you can decide whether you prefer to smell the roses, design new varieties of roses, grow the roses, or perhaps even paint the roses.

Be Better Prepared for the Changing Future

Change is continually forcing us to adapt. Almost everyone is affected by changes in the world of work. Businesses are being reorganized, jobs are being lost while others are being created, and advances in technology are changing the way we do our work. Our information society is requiring more and more workers to be effective lifelong learners. Thinking, learning, and using change management skills are becoming integral to success in any job. Understanding your natural way of working can help you adapt to the future.

Sometimes just staying the same can mean moving backward. Things are changing so rapidly around us that, if we simply keep our head down and do our work, we can lose ground! Thus, it is essential that we assess our situation, our options, and ourselves regularly and revise our career path from time to time. Then we can take action to keep us on track to where we want to go. By choosing and moving toward options that will make you more adaptable, you can effectively decide what information to learn and which skills to develop.

Identify Areas for Growth

Along with strengths, each of the eight ways of working will have types of activities that are not preferred by some. For example, highly imaginative people may find it very difficult to manage their budgets. A reliable and conscientious worker may not be highly flexible. Even when a person is able to find a satisfying type of work, he or she will have challenges and activities that are outside of the preferred way of working. As well as being able to find and work within your natural approach, you often need to expand and develop. Identifying your areas for growth will help you focus on the skills and strategies you need to learn to be more effective in all of the tasks and duties you perform.

Initiate Personal Growth

A person changes and develops over his or her life span. When you are starting your career, you are beginning to understand and test your preferences. As you develop and mature, you learn to use your natural way of working and compensate for your weaknesses. Over time, you may choose to gradually (or dramatically!) expand or move into new and different challenges, taking on activities and roles that you might have avoided earlier in life. This, too, is part of your natural way of working.

Our personal priorities, situation, and lifestyle also change over time. For example, changes in relationships, roles, physical and mental abilities, health, and location make it important to reassess our goals and priorities. Understanding your natural approach to work can help you make decisions that allow you to both adjust your career and life path and maximize your personal and work satisfaction on an ongoing basis.

Increase Your Self-Acceptance

It is very helpful to acknowledge that you have a unique way of working and to identify its associated strengths. Too often, we find ourselves performing work that might better suit our parents or others, rather than stopping and truly defining our own personal approach. Your natural strengths may be quite different from those of your family members, co-workers, and friends.

Understanding and appreciating your personal work approach and preferences is a helpful step toward self-acceptance. As a by-product, you will also become more tolerant and accepting of others when you recognize *their* way of working. You may find that some of your work conflicts with colleagues are simply differences in approach. Understanding and communicating these differences can be the first step to improving your working relationships.

Heighten Your Career Satisfaction

The most important result of learning about your natural way of working is that, with that understanding, you are more likely to engage in work that is personally satisfying. By increasing your self-understanding, you can choose a career direction and take more control in your search for satisfying work. Considering all the hours and years you will spend working throughout your life, it is essential to expend your time and energy on pursuits that will allow you to do what comes naturally.

How to Use This Book

In the next chapter, you will learn about *personality type*. Personality type is the theoretical basis behind the eight ways of working. Once you know your personality preferences, you will fill out a checklist to discover which of the eight ways of working applies to you. The simple exercises and checklists will help you define your characteristic way of working.

Once you have defined your approach to work, you can go directly to the chapter that specifically defines your characteristic way of working. There you will confirm your preferences and gain greater insight into what, specifically, makes a career satisfying or unsatisfying for you. The customized information in the chapter will reveal the secrets of career satisfaction. This information has been compiled from decades of research on personality and work preferences.

In "your" chapter you will see a summary of data from thousands of people working in hundreds of types of jobs. You will discover how others with your way of working have found career satisfaction. You will find lists of occupations that others who share your way of working have found to be rewarding and meaningful. The chapter will not only suggest specific types of work that will be rewarding, but also explain your characteristic work preferences, strengths, and skills. Helpful suggestions will be offered on how to use and develop your strengths. Areas for growth and improvement will also be highlighted, with tips and strategies to help you develop greater adaptability.

As you work through your chapter, remember that you are a unique individual and that your needs, skills, interests, and constraints will further define your personal choices. Read the information and customize the exercises to reflect on how you are the same as (and yet different from) others who share this way of working. Helpful exercises and summary charts will show you how to make the most of your exploration.

Once you have turned the magnifying glass inward and understand your personal approach to working, you can use that knowledge to make informed career decisions. The ongoing challenge is making sure you are choosing and heading down the path that will take you where you want to go. Often, because we are not focusing on where we want to go, we are surprised when we end up somewhere else.

In Chapters 11 and 12, a career-shaping process will help you apply your natural way of working to your current situation. In Chapter 11 you will assess your work needs and preferences to come up with a picture of what, for you, makes a career satisfying. In Chapter 12 you will learn how to generate suitable work options, complete career research, and make a thoughtful career decision. As a result, you will be able to manage your career progress and ensure that you find work where you can do what comes naturally.

CHAPTER TWO
Introduction to Personality Type

Personality differences are a natural part of what distinguishes us as individuals. For example, we know that some people are naturally more outgoing, meticulous, structured, or flexible. Various categories and frameworks have been developed to help us understand and appreciate these individual differences. The personality type framework in this book uses as a starting point the insights and writings of Carl Jung. Jung's approach looks at the ways individuals prefer to gather information and make decisions. Personality type also shows us how individuals prefer to orient themselves to and deal with the world around them.

In the last several decades, thousands of studies have been conducted in the area of personality type. The research includes a wealth of information on how our personality type affects our career choices and work preferences. Understanding our personality type provides a useful tool to help us choose satisfying work activities and environments.

Jung's theory of personality type has been elaborated and popularized through the work of Katharine Cook Briggs and Isabel Briggs Myers. This mother-and-daughter team created the *Myers-Briggs Type Indicator*® (MBTI®) instrument, an assessment tool for identifying personality type, which has thrived through more than forty years of research and development. The MBTI® instrument can be administered and interpreted only by a trained professional. If you are interested in using this tool, the Association for Psychological Type (APT) can refer you to an MBTI® specialist in your area.

Personality type is a nonjudgmental tool that looks at the strengths and gifts of individuals. This is a refreshing change from many other personality tools, which compare the so-called normal to the "abnormal." Knowing your personality type will help you apply your personal preferences in a positive way.

First you will need to define the characteristic ways in which you prefer to function and orient yourself to the world. These ways of functioning are grouped into four pairs. You will naturally prefer one element of each pair to the other. By choosing one preference from each pair, you can discover a four-letter personality type, one of sixteen personality types. Read through the preference pairs to identify your personality type, and check the box that best applies to you.

EXTAVERSION AND INTROVERSION

· 10 ·

This preference pair describes alternative ways of orienting to the world. Extraversion (E) is an external, action orientation and Introversion (I) is an internal, reflective orientation.

E: EXTRAVERSION	I: INTROVERSION
"Let's talk this over."	*"I need to think about this."*
Individuals with a preference for Extraversion tend to	Individuals with a preference for Introversion tend to
• Focus their energy and process information externally by talking and acting	• Focus their energy and process information internally, through reflection and introspection
• Dislike complicated procedures and working on one thing for a long time, especially if they must do so on their own	• Prefer quiet places to work and can work on one thing for a long time
• Learn and work best when able to share, discuss, and process information with others	• Learn and work best by having time to understand and process information on their own
• Ask questions and think out loud during activities or while working through a decision	• Tend to think before they speak or act; they may be uncomfortable when asked to perform or respond on demand
• Understand their world best by acting on it or talking about it	• Downplay their strengths externally, with the result that their abilities can often be underestimated

Everyone uses both Extraversion and Introversion to carry out day-to-day activities. However, one of the two will be more natural and comfortable. The one preference that best describes me is

☐ **E: Extraversion**   ☐ **I: Introversion**

Sensing and Intuition

Sensing and Intuition are two ways to take in information. Sensing (S) indicates a preference for more practical attention to facts and details. Intuition (N) indicates a preference for more abstract attention to patterns and possibilities.

S: Sensing

"Just the facts, please!"

Individuals who prefer Sensing as a way to take in information tend to

- Focus on individual facts and details before seeing underlying patterns or whole concepts

- Be most interested in the facts, as they are known now

- Prefer information and tasks that are organized and presented in an orderly, sequential format

- Work at a steady pace

- Become impatient or frustrated with complicated or future-oriented tasks that may take a long time to complete

- Like having their senses engaged as they work

N: Intuition

"I can see it all now."

Individuals who prefer Intuition as a way to take in information tend to

- Focus on what facts mean and how they fit together; they pay more attention to implications, possibilities, and relationships between ideas than to facts and details alone

- Become bored or impatient with details; they are more interested in understanding the "big picture"

- Like solving problems and developing new skills; intuitive types may become easily bored with routines and sequential tasks

- Jump around between ideas and tasks as they work and learn; they are likely to have bursts of energy rather than stamina

Everyone uses both Sensing and Intuition to carry out day-to-day activities. However, one of the two will be more natural and comfortable. The one preference that best describes me is

☐ S: Sensing   ☐ N: Intuition

THINKING AND FEELING

Thinking and Feeling describe information-processing and decision-making preferences. An individual with a preference for Thinking (T) would focus more on logic and analysis. An individual preferring Feeling (F) would focus more on personal values and effects.

T: THINKING
"Is this logical?"

Individuals with a preference for Thinking as a way to make decisions and process information tend to

- Focus on logic and analysis
- Deal best with objective data and cause-and-effect relationships
- Consider the pros and cons of ideas, information, and opinions
- Understand emotions and feelings best when they are introduced as facts and details to consider in decision making and problem solving
- Prefer calm, objective interactions

F: FEELING
"Will anybody be hurt?"

Individuals who prefer Feeling as a way to make decisions and process information tend to

- Be more interested in the effects of information on people than in things or ideas themselves
- Be motivated by other people and work best in an environment that provides support and encouragement
- View the atmosphere at work as being as important as the work itself
- Make subjective decisions; they are often good at understanding and appreciating the values of others
- Find objective, logical reasoning harsh; they may feel criticized by others who function in a logical, analytical mode

Everyone uses both Thinking and Feeling to carry out day-to-day activities. However, one of the two will be more natural and comfortable. The one preference that best describes me is

☐ **T: Thinking**   ☐ **F: Feeling**

JUDGING AND PERCEIVING

Judging and Perceiving describe two ways of orienting to and dealing with the external world. An individual with a preference for Judging (J) would tend to be decisive and prefer structure and control. An individual with a preference for Perceiving (P) would tend to keep his or her options open and prefer spontaneity and flexibility.

J: JUDGING
"Just do something."

Individuals with a Judging orientation tend to

- Make decisions as soon as possible to have closure
- Plan and organize their world
- Be tolerant of routines and structure
- Like roles and expectations to be clear and definite
- Be uncomfortable with change and ambiguity
- Complete tasks and move on
- Be organized and have a plan

P: PERCEIVING
"Let's wait and see."

Individuals with a Perceiving orientation tend to

- Defer judgments and gather more information
- Act spontaneously and leave things to the last minute; they may choose not to plan or organize tasks or time
- Prefer starting projects to following through with them
- Be flexible and adaptable
- Become frustrated by rules, routines, and closure
- Focus on exploring and seeking new information; they embrace change

Everyone uses both Judging and Perceiving to carry out day-to-day activities. However, one of the two will be more natural and comfortable. The one preference that best describes me is

☐ **J: Judging**   ☐ **P: Perceiving**

The four letters I have chosen as my personality type are _____ .

It is essential *not* to use personality type to categorize, label, or limit yourself or others. The descriptions given here are general, so not all statements will apply to you or any other specific individual. For instance, the preferences you express and develop are greatly influenced by your current situation and experiences. You may have ignored your natural disposition and learned the skills and attributes of an opposing preference in order to be successful. You also may be at a point in your life where you need to or choose to develop preferences you have not used much in the past. The characteristics and descriptors of personality type theory are provided as a guide to your self-assessment and understanding.

Each of the four-letter combinations represents a distinct personality type. There are sixteen possible combinations and, thus, sixteen different personality types. Your four-letter personality type is, however, more than the sum of your four preferences. Each of the sixteen combinations of letters represents a way of relating to the world that is different from the others. Thus, someone with an ISTP personality type will be quite different from someone with an ISTJ personality type, even though three of their four letters are the same.

WHAT'S KEY FOR ME?
Relating Personality Preferences to the World of Work

How have your preferences affected your career choices to this point? Think back to three activities that you have found satisfying and enjoyable. These activities can be from your hobbies, volunteer experiences, school projects, community involvement, or work duties. Then reflect on the personality preferences you have chosen. Do the activities you enjoy match the personality preferences you have picked? Here are a couple of examples to get you started:

I really enjoy talking to people and sharing ideas.
I can see now that those activities use my preferences for Extraversion and Intuition.

I really enjoy being structured and organized.
I can see now that this activity uses my Judging preference.

The same is true for activities that you do not enjoy or that you find difficult. Often these activities require us to use the less-preferred side of a pair.

I really enjoy ....

I can see now that this activity uses my preference(s) for...

....

....

....

I really enjoy ....

I can see now that this activity uses my preference(s) for...

....

....

....

I really enjoy ....

I can see now that this activity uses my preference(s) for...

....

....

....

· 15 ·

Think back to three activities that were hard or unsatisfying for you to complete. Did these activities use preferences that are opposite to the ones that you have picked? Here are a couple of examples to get you started:

I find it difficult to work alone for long periods of time.
I can see now that this activity requires me to use my less-preferred Introversion rather than my preferred Extraversion.

I find it difficult to attend to all the details involved in making a budget.
I can see now that this activity requires me to use my less-preferred Sensing rather than my preferred Intuition.

I find it difficult to ....

I can see now that this activity requires me to use my less-preferred

.... rather than my preferred ....

....

....

I find it difficult to ....

I can see now that this activity requires me to use my less-preferred

.... rather than my preferred ....

....

....

I find it difficult to ....

I can see now that this activity requires me to use my less-preferred

.... rather than my preferred ....

....

....

· 16 ·

As you learn more about your natural work preferences, you will continue to discover more about what activities suit or fail to suit you.

INTRODUCTION TO THE EIGHT WAYS OF WORKING

Once you understand personality type, you can find your natural way of working. There are eight natural ways of working, each combining two of the personality types. These two personality types are grouped together because they share an important characteristic: They approach the world in the same basic way. As we explore in detail each of the eight ways of working in the next chapters, we will see how the two personality types within each category are similar and also how they are different.

Your natural way of working emphasizes the part of your personality that is the most trusted, comfortable, and developed. For example, if you have a preference for Extraversion, you are most comfortable working mainly in the world around you as you speak and act. If instead you prefer Introversion, you are most comfortable working mainly in your internal world as you listen and reflect.

We all are able to carry out a wide range of work activities, and we likely will be able to see aspects of ourselves in more than one of the descriptions. However, research demonstrates that one of these eight approaches will be core or most preferred for you. This one core preference will define your characteristic approach to work. The other approaches will be used in support of, and secondary to, your preferred approach. As you develop skills and experience, you will learn to access and use all of these approaches to facilitate your success. By understanding your first and most trusted approach, you can see how the other approaches will flow and develop from what you are likely to initially do best.

Four Extraverted Ways of Working

People with extraverted ways of working are most comfortable and at their best when they are interacting with the world around them. The primary approach of such individuals is doing, talking, acting, and trying things. There are four extraverted ways of working.

RESPONDERS: ACT AND ADAPT
PERSONALITY TYPES: ESFP AND ESTP

 Responders react immediately to the environment around them by acting. They are very observant and quick to see problems and opportunities. They tend to be spontaneous and prefer responding to things that are happening right now. They like to take practical actions that do not require a lot of pondering. Responders enjoy improvising, changing, and maneuvering. They are good at fixing things or getting something done right away. They often enjoy handling emergencies or solving practical problems.

We all use this approach as we observe and respond to our immediate environment. For example, as we hammer a nail we note whether the nail is bent and adjust the direction and strength of the next blow. While to some extent everyone uses observation and action directly in this way, Responders prefer and are best at activities that focus on direct observation and action. They are in tune with and focused on the world of actions and reactions. Here is how one Responder describes her preferred way of working:

"I just want to do things and have fun right now. More than anything else, I like variety and action. I want to live for today. What's the point of life if you don't enjoy it? I want every day to be a good day."

EXPLORERS: INNOVATE AND INITIATE
PERSONALITY TYPES: ENFP AND ENTP

Explorers are constantly scanning the environment looking for associations and patterns. They naturally link ideas together and see connections. They like to focus on what *could be* rather than what *is*. They see many possibilities in everything they can sense, experience, and imagine. Explorers are enthusiastically and outwardly focused on the future and like to initiate change. They see every situation as an opportunity to try something different. They are drawn to work that requires them to anticipate the future and create new ideas.

Everyone uses this approach when they imagine a new way of doing something. While to some extent everyone sees potential in things, Explorers prefer and are drawn to activities that provide them with the opportunity to find and use patterns to create new possibilities. Here is how one Explorer describes his preferred way of working:

"I am most motivated when I can do something that no one has ever done before. I like being on the cutting edge and being the first one to think of something. I often have ideas that are new and innovative."

EXPEDITORS: DIRECT AND DECIDE
PERSONALITY TYPES: ESTJ AND ENTJ

Expeditors like to use logical analysis. They critique situations and spot flaws. They are organized and efficient, priding themselves on getting the most accomplished in the least time. Expeditors like to solve complex problems, efficiently complete tasks, and be clearly in charge. The Expeditor will quickly analyze a situation, take control, and mobilize people to get the job done. Everyone uses this approach at times to describe flaws, list pros and cons, or organize tasks. And while everyone is to some extent logical and analytical, Expeditors prefer and are best at activities that require analysis and active organization of people and resources to efficiently complete tasks. Here is how one Expeditor describes her preferred way of working:

"I like to move ahead and get things accomplished. Finishing tasks and seeing results is what motivates me to work hard. I like to manage people and oversee projects. The thing that frustrates me the most is poor planning and inefficiency."

CONTRIBUTORS: COMMUNICATE AND COOPERATE
PERSONALITY TYPES: ESFJ AND ENFJ

Contributors focus on personal relationships, values, opinions, and interactions. They actively strive to connect with others, create harmony, and cooperate. Contributors want to make sure that everyone is happy and involved. They are especially interested in organizing and coordinating events, processes, and activities that meet the needs of everyone concerned. Contributors naturally appreciate others and want to be appreciated themselves for their uniqueness and their effort.

We all use this approach when we remember a birthday, celebrate successes, engage in social or family traditions, and share losses. While everyone is focused to some extent on connecting with others, Contributors prefer and are best at activities that allow them to actively communicate and cooperate with others. Here is how one Contributor who works as a manager describes his preferred way of working:

"I strive to create a strong sense of teamwork within my staff. It is important for me to understand everyone's needs and create an environment that allows everyone to do his or her best. Within this team focus we can build strong relationships with our customers. Our job is to advocate for and meet the needs of our customers."

Four Introverted Ways of Working

People with introverted approaches are most comfortable and at their best when they can take time to think things through. They like to reflect on or interpret their experiences and plan their actions. People with introverted approaches are sometimes seen as cautious, hard to get to know, or reserved. They are often quiet and are not likely to blow their own horn. Because of this, the casual observer will not easily see the best side of people with introverted preferences and may underestimate their skills and strengths.

Because those with introverted preferences tend to use their most-trusted approach internally, you often see them doing activities that are characteristic of someone with a different approach. For example, a Responder (using an extraverted approach) and an Analyzer (with an introverted approach) both prefer to immediately react to and solve problems. To the casual observer, they seem to have the same natural approach. However, the Analyzer will actually focus more on an internal analysis of the situation while responding. The first, natural, and most-preferred approach of an Analyzer is an internal, logical analysis that focuses on understanding and analyzing the situation. The extraverted Responder, by contrast, will focus more on the external, practical aspects of the situation. For that person, analysis will, at most, be a secondary focus. It is important to recognize that these two individuals are using different natural approaches to deal with the same situation.

ASSIMILATORS: SPECIALIZE AND STABILIZE
PERSONALITY TYPES: ISFJ AND ISTJ

Assimilators like to take in detailed information and then spend time integrating that information with past experiences and knowledge. They like to gain a comprehensive understanding of the facts. Assimilators will be able to draw on this rich accumulation of facts and experiences to make decisions and take action. As they approach a situation or solve a problem, they will take time to reflect on previous experiences; they will remember and use strategies that worked well in the past. Everyone uses this approach of recalling detailed information. You are using this approach when you are able to list extensive details about your favorite type of car, music, or vacation. While everyone retains and classifies experiences to some extent, Assimilators use this approach as their primary way of understanding and dealing with the world. They are strongly focused on collecting and organizing facts and experiences. Here is how one Assimilator describes his preferred way of working while he is considering writing a historical novel:

"Before I start, I will use my experiences and the experiences of others to find out as much as I can. I love to complete research, and I will thoroughly learn historical facts and as much as I can about the process of book writing. I will then sit back and think about the project before I start. I won't go ahead haphazardly."

VISIONARIES: INTERPRET AND IMPLEMENT
PERSONALITY TYPES: INFJ AND INTJ

Visionaries like to take time to think about and find meaning in data, ideas, and experiences. They will create and revise rich mental models that help them understand and interpret their experiences. Visionaries are future oriented. They like to look at possibilities and will often make complex plans for changing systems or improving processes. Everyone uses this approach when studying and comparing theoretical models or interpreting data and ideas. While everyone seeks to understand and relate experiences to theories and mental models to some extent, Visionaries use this approach as their primary way of interpreting the world. Here is how one Visionary describes her preferred way of working:

"I like to work on my own ideas, and I go to great lengths when developing a new idea. It is important for me to plan the entire project through, from idea to implementation. My strengths are my imagination and my ability to visualize the big picture."

ANALYZERS: EXAMINE AND EVALUATE
PERSONALITY TYPES: ISTP AND INTP

Analyzers like to take time to analyze information and make logical decisions. When presented with a problem or a task, they immediately begin to logically think the situation through by collecting information, asking themselves questions, and looking for the best course of action. They like to relate principles of science, technology, or other areas of expertise to problem solving, and they like to find ways to try their ideas and test their conclusions. An Analyzer enjoys playing with things to see what will happen. Everyone uses this approach when thinking about problems or making logical decisions. While everyone seeks to internally make sense of the world using logical thinking to some extent, Analyzers use this approach as their primary way of interpreting the world. Here is how one Analyzer describes her preferred way of working:

"I really enjoyed working as an emergency medical technician with an ambulance service. Each call presented a new situation that required me to analyze the best course of action for the patient. However, after a while in the job, I realized it was too immediate. I wanted to find ways to prevent emergency situations rather than simply respond to them."

ENHANCERS: CARE AND CONNECT
PERSONALITY TYPES: ISFP AND INFP
Enhancers create personal relationships to situations. They are thoughtful and will be focused on how others feel as well as on how situations and circumstances affect others. Enhancers are careful to accommodate other people and often may put others' needs ahead of their own. They take time to assess and evaluate situations by relating them to personal and human values. Everyone uses this approach when choosing what pictures to put into a scrapbook for a friend or deciding how to customize a recipe to suit the tastes of a specific group. While everyone seeks to understand and relate experiences to values to some extent, Enhancers use this approach as their primary way of interpreting the world. Here is how one Enhancer describes his preferred way of working within a team:

"I usually point out the strengths of others and help them realize how their special skills benefit the team as a whole. I often work behind the scenes to ensure that things run smoothly. It is important that all team members get the support and encouragement they need to be the best that they can."

VALIDATING YOUR WAY OF WORKING

This section provides you with checklists to further validate your preferred way of working. Completing the checklists will also help you validate and confirm the four-letter personality type that you chose earlier in the chapter.

You can immediately narrow the process for confirming your preferred way of working by recalling whether you have a preference for Extraversion (E) or Introversion (I). Look back to the personality type you recorded on page 14 and see what you chose for your first letter. This first letter describes whether you are oriented more naturally to the world of action or to the world of reflection. Individuals with preferences for Extraversion and Introversion approach the world of work and careers in different ways. This preference is key to understanding your way of working.

If you are unsure of your preference for Extraversion or Introversion, read the introduction to extraverted ways of working on page 17 and the introduction to introverted ways of working on page 19 to help you decide. Remember that simply having a preference for Introversion does not mean that you are necessarily shy, uncomfortable when speaking in front of groups, or nonassertive in a situation of conflict. It simply means that you prefer to take time to listen and absorb, reflect on, and process information internally before you act. In a similar way, those with extraverted processes use internal reflection as a tool. However, they are more likely to act and discuss as ways of processing. The ways of working described in this book are not about what you can or cannot do. Rather, they are about what comes naturally and comfortably and what provides you with a starting point or home base from which all other things will develop.

You need to complete only one of the two checklists in the next section to reinforce your understanding of personality type and confirm your natural way of working.

Extraverted Ways of Working

Complete this checklist if you chose E (Extraversion) as the first letter in your personality type. Read through the four boxes to identify your preferred way of working. Check off all the statements that are true for you. Be careful to focus on what you *prefer* to do, not what you have learned to do or are expected by others to do. Expect that you will check preferences in more than one approach.

RESPONDERS: ACT AND ADAPT

❑ I seek opportunities to act and move around.

❑ I like to troubleshoot and improvise, focusing on practical solutions.

❑ I am observant and like to engage my senses.

❑ I like to focus on the here and now.

❑ I am not highly motivated to anticipate the future or to finish tasks at hand.

❑ Routines, predictability, and the theoretical bore me.

❑ I like to engage in hands-on experiences.

❑ I trust and understand what I can see, hear, smell, taste, or touch.

❑ I like physical challenge and immediate interactions and sensations.

❑ I react quickly and well in crisis or emergency situations.

· 24 ·

EXPLORERS: INNOVATE AND INITIATE

❏ I work with and create new ideas easily and quickly.

❏ I tend to lack follow-through and have difficulty focusing on details.

❏ I make connections and see relationships between things.

❏ I am future and possibility oriented.

❏ I anticipate, seek, and create change and help others do the same.

❏ I like to be involved in many things at once.

❏ I need changing tasks and variety to maintain my interest.

❏ I depend on bursts of creative energy, usually at the last minute.

❏ I initiate and conceptualize projects rather than complete them.

❏ I like to explore and define new ideas more than I like making decisions.

EXPEDITORS: DIRECT AND DECIDE

❏ I strive to make and live by clear rules or principles.

❏ I see situations as having clear and definite boundaries between right and wrong.

❏ I take a problem-solving, task-oriented approach to situations.

❏ I analyze situations quickly and move people to action.

❏ I am usually driven to work hard.

❏ I like to work within or create an efficient and logically structured system.

❏ I can organize and lead groups strategically.

❏ I strongly value competence, clear thinking, and logical analysis.

❏ I can, at times, be task oriented rather than people oriented.

❏ I engage in play that serves a logical purpose, such as learning a skill or exercising.

CONTRIBUTORS: COMMUNICATE AND COOPERATE

❑ I like to help others with decision making, planning, and taking action.

❑ I am warm and caring toward people and enjoy understanding others' points of view.

❑ I like to organize, coordinate, and plan activities that others will enjoy.

❑ I act to instill trust and cooperation between people.

❑ I work toward obtaining group harmony and consensus.

❑ I seek experiences that help me learn about people's values, opinions, and reactions.

❑ I like participating in social events and traditions that reward and support people.

❑ I am socially responsible and tend to frequently take on social roles.

❑ I sometimes neglect my own needs as I am busy helping others meet their needs.

❑ I like to organize, facilitate, and direct groups.

Once you have completed the checklist, go back and see which way of working had the most check marks. You will likely have check marks in more than one category. There may be two categories with a number of check marks. Take a few minutes to think about your answers and to identify which of the four descriptions seems most like you. Focus on thinking about your first and most natural approach to work. Now you are ready to choose your natural way of working.

I have a preference for Extraversion, and my natural way of working is

....

The next eight chapters explore these ways of working in depth. You will probably find it most helpful to go directly to the chapter that describes your way of working. Once you have read that chapter, go to the final two chapters of the book for ideas on how to use this information to help you find a career that works for you.

Introverted Ways of Working

Complete this checklist if you chose I (Introversion) as the first letter in your personality type. Read through the four boxes to identify your preferred way of working. Check off all the statements that are true for you. Be careful to focus on what you *prefer* to do, not what you have learned to do or are expected by others to do. Expect that you will check preferences in more than one approach.

ASSIMILATORS: SPECIALIZE AND STABILIZE

❏ I collect many useful and relevant facts.

❏ I am considered to be an expert in topics that interest me.

❏ I take a detailed project approach to tasks.

❏ I may find that an interesting and complex project will totally consume my time and attention.

❏ I loyally and conscientiously apply my personal principles or values to situations.

❏ I need to understand and agree with rules or standards before I act on them.

❏ I make decisions by considering each and every relevant fact at hand.

❏ I come across as deliberate and exacting and can work meticulously with details.

❏ I can be patient when completing routine tasks and following procedures.

❏ I can concentrate without interruptions for a long period of time.

Visionaries: Interpret and Implement

❏ I like to work with and understand abstract ideas and symbols.

❏ I create new conceptual categories and visions of what could be.

❏ I question and analyze the very nature of knowledge, truth, and understanding.

❏ I find challenge in managing the precision and multiple meanings of language.

❏ I analyze and challenge basic societal ideas and concepts.

❏ I am a determined and ingenious leader or problem solver.

❏ I like to work with difficult and complex challenges.

❏ I find theory and concepts more interesting than material facts.

❏ I like to see and understand the whole picture before I take action.

❏ I deal with the world in a decisive way.

Analyzers: Examine and Evaluate

❏ I like to use and experience the results of a logical problem-solving process.

❏ I focus on the logical principles underlying a situation rather than on the situation itself.

❏ I create links between what is and what is logically possible.

❏ I like to experience directly the results of my efforts.

❏ I want to see how my actions change the situation at hand.

❏ I primarily use logic and objectivity to interpret situations.

❏ I am most convinced by reasoning and analysis.

❏ I present a quiet, detached, and impersonal demeanor to most people.

❏ I adjust my behaviors and respond with curiosity to changing situations.

❏ I strongly resist changes that are not logical or reasonable.

ENHANCERS: CARE AND CONNECT

❑ I engage in activities that are personally meaningful.

❑ I focus on maintaining internal and external harmony in my life.

❑ I want to express my values and personal ideals in my work.

❑ I seek a higher purpose and meaning in my life.

❑ I am accepting, flexible, and accommodating unless my personal values are challenged.

❑ In cases where my values are challenged, I can become inflexible and stubborn.

❑ I have a deep sense of humanity as well as powerful emotional convictions.

❑ Casual observers will not see my important values, since they are seldom expressed.

❑ I am loyal and demonstrate strong devotion to a valued cause, person, or ideal.

❑ Although I may not show it, I can be easily hurt by feedback that is harsh or critical.

Once you have completed the checklist, go back and see which way of working had the most check marks. You will likely have check marks in more than one category. There may be two categories with a number of check marks. Take a few minutes to think about your answers and to identify which of the four descriptions seems most like you. Focus on thinking about your first and most natural approach to work. Now you are ready to choose your natural way of working.

I have a preference for Introversion, and my natural way of working is

....

The next eight chapters explore these ways of working in depth. You will probably find it most helpful to go directly to the chapter that describes your approach. Once you have read that chapter, go to the final two chapters of the book for ideas on how to use this information to help you find a career that works for you.

Still Unsure?

To identify your natural way of working, you need to focus on your most comfortable approach. If you are finding it difficult to choose between two of the ways of working, one of them is likely tapping into other parts of your personality type that you use for balance. You will find it helpful to read through the detailed descriptions of the approaches in the following chapters. You may also find it useful to observe and think about how you react in different situations and to ponder your interactions with others in terms of the preferences you have chosen. Ask people close to you how they see you in terms of these preferences.

You can also go back to the personality type descriptors listed earlier in this chapter. Review the four letters you have chosen, making sure they are the correct ones for you. You might want to complete a personality type indicator with a person qualified to administer and interpret the results; this will help you confirm both your personality type and your natural way of working.

PART TWO

Extraverted Career Paths

Introduction to the Extraverted Ways of Working

Listed below are characteristics of work activities that tend to be associated with a preference for Extraversion. If you are a Responder, an Explorer, an Expeditor, or a Contributor, you can use these descriptions as general guidelines in your quest to find meaningful work.

Tips for Those with a Preference for Extraversion
Look for work that provides you with opportunities to

- Act quickly
- Be action oriented
- Change activities regularly
- Develop and use a network of contacts
- Discuss information and ideas
- Focus on the world around you
- Have many areas of general interest
- Interact with others
- Learn as you go
- Share your thoughts and feelings
- Socialize
- Speak in front of a group
- Take breaks
- Take the initiative
- Think things through out loud
- Try new ideas
- "Wing it," approaching situations without extensive preparation
- Work at a fast pace
- Work on a variety of activities
- Work within a group

Keep these general guidelines in mind as you read your chapter, which focuses on your specific extraverted way of working.

CHAPTER THREE
Responders Act and Adapt

PERSONALITY TYPES: ESFP AND ESTP

I build log houses for a living. The work is physically demanding, but I like being active and working hard. No two houses are ever the same. We start by designing a house to suit the lot and then move right into the construction phase. It is very satisfying to see the house take shape. Each project has its own problems to solve. To me, that's part of the fun: figuring out how to maneuver around the problems to get the job done. I like being active. I don't think I would ever want to sit behind a desk or shuffle paper all day long. It's the physical work that gets me going. —A Responder

The latest research shows that about 12.8 percent of adults in the United States are Responders. The natural way of working for Responders is to be practical and active. They use observation and quick reactions to effectively solve immediate problems, read people, or create products. Responders accurately see situations for what they are and are tuned in to and aware of the facts as they exist. Approaching the world in an open-ended way, they are acutely observant, aware, and quick to jump in and act. They rapidly scan their environment and mold their behaviors smoothly and quickly in response to what they hear, touch, taste, smell, or see. Responders seek hands-on, concrete experiences, which provide them with a trusted source of knowledge that they can use in the next situation in a practical and applied way. Resourceful problem solvers, Responders excel at living in the moment.

RESPONDERS AT WORK
What Responders Do Naturally

ACT QUICKLY

Because Responders' preferred approach to the world is immediate, active, and practical, they are especially good at situations that require rapid responses. They excel in areas in which they are faced with immediate problems or have to deal with changing situations. They enjoy solving problems and dealing with crises and are attracted to exciting and fast-moving occupations.

Responders find structure, planning, and defined responsibilities confining. They do not like to be slowed down and can be restless in situations requiring routine, standard operating procedures, and administrative details. Given an opportunity, Responders may circumvent the "correct" way of doing things to maintain their ability to act quickly. They will argue the advantages of bypassing the rules, especially in emergencies. One Responder jokingly comments:

"I strongly believe the saying that it is easier to beg for forgiveness than to ask for permission. At work, asking for permission can create all kinds of roadblocks and slow me right down. I have learned to just go ahead and act—and deal with the consequences later."

Others may interpret these maverick actions as irresponsible or unpredictable. Responders' need for autonomy and control over their actions can be seen as challenging to authority.

Responders are effective troubleshooters and problem solvers, creatively using their practical bent to get the job done. Responders can become totally immersed and energized when solving a problem or involved in a crisis. They are attracted to emergency work and may become firefighters, police officers, emergency response personnel, or lifeguards.

BE ACTIVE

Responders do not like being confined to a desk. They will often find work that allows them to move around and use physical skills. One Responder working as an adult educator describes her need to get away from her desk:

"I find it tedious to sit at my desk to mark papers. When I have a lot of marking to do, I will take regular breaks and walk laps around the office area. My colleagues tease me about my pacing, but the short, active breaks are an essential coping strategy to survive sitting at my desk for a long time. When I am teaching, I set up lots of field trips and do lab work as well."

FIND PRACTICAL SOLUTIONS

Responders approach their work in a realistic manner. They are highly aware of the world around them and attend to and keep track of details in a matter-of-fact way. They are quick to accept the facts and see things as they are.

Theory, abstraction, and metaphor are, according to the Responder, overly indirect and complex ways of seeing the world. Theory may have some value when it can be directly applied, but Responder preferences are initially focused on that which is concrete. They trust what they can experience directly.

Responders will jump in and act immediately. You are not likely to find them on the sidelines or in the background. They will do whatever it takes to resourcefully get the job done. They are attracted to opportunities to be expedient, especially if the situation is exciting and of interest to them.

Responders value tangible products or results. They may express this focus in a variety of ways, such as arranging flowers, building houses, taking pictures, or growing crops. Producing these products must be interesting. Responders will be most satisfied in a changing environment that provides them with opportunities to engage in a variety of tasks.

A Responder who is a cabinetmaker describes his preferences this way:

"I find it boring to build exactly the same cabinets time and time again in a shop. I enjoy jobs that are more diverse and interesting. I like to make custom designs, adapt cabinets to odd-shaped kitchens, and find unusual applications for cabinets."

ADAPT

Responders are most engaged in environments or situations that change rapidly. Highly adaptable and flexible, they will seek and embrace change. They often find it hard to tell you their favorite work activity; they seek and enjoy a number of activities, and what they prefer most is the variety.

Responders learn from their experiences in a direct way. They often reinvent ways of doing things and are adept at trying out new things. Responders like improvising or modifying what they already know, and they are masters at creating new solutions. They may even build some excitement into their day by improvising when completing highly routine tasks. This helps them deal with the boredom they experience when dealing with the predictable.

· 38 ·

LIVE FOR THE MOMENT

Responders are grounded in and live for the moment. A combination of acute observation, an immediate response to what is sensed, and a practical approach allows them to spontaneously enjoy life as it happens. Because they like to enjoy the moment, Responders will notice and be affected by their physical work setting. They like to have a comfortable and attractive workspace.

Responders, more than people of any other type, are able to enjoy what *is*. If they dislike something, they will strive to change it immediately rather than wait for some abstract future improvement in their situation. They find immediate gratification in the world around them. One Responder describes this focus:

"I will always go for coffee when someone asks me to join them. No task is too important and no deadline too essential to prevent me from stopping for a few minutes to visit and enjoy the day."

Other types may see this behavior as verging on the irresponsible, but this ability to "seize the day" is a natural gift that others can find difficult to imitate. Do not think that Responders do not work hard. When motivated, they can accomplish a great deal quickly and can work under intense pressure. However, when they stop, they can detach and engage in play as wholeheartedly as they worked.

ENTERTAIN AND ENGAGE OTHERS

Responders' natural focus allows them to read and relate to people in an immediate and active way. They observe people carefully and see and accept them as they are. They are open-minded and tolerant of others. They can be very entertaining, are often in tune with social nuances, and are extremely sociable. Using their natural approach, they quickly develop rapport and create a fun and playful atmosphere wherever they go. Responders are often drawn to occupations where they can perform for people, and they thrive on seeing the immediate effects of their actions.

LEARN WHAT IS PRACTICAL

A focus on learning from and building on experience is a common theme among Responders. They want to learn about real things in a practical way. One Responder comments,

"I have never had a job I didn't like or didn't learn from. I learned my basic employability skills as a boy when delivering papers and working in a grocery store. Everything else I have learned has flowed from and built on those initial experiences."

· 39 ·

Many Responders find the abstract and theoretical nature of formal education especially tedious. Learning must have some result or application, or else must be fun, to grab a Responder's interest. This doesn't mean that Responders cannot or will not complete higher education. Many Responders choose careers in professional fields, such as medicine and other sciences. What it *does* mean is that Responders are often outside of their comfort zone in formal learning situations. They need to focus on and develop learning strategies, especially when presented with large amounts of abstract information. It is hard for Responders to find value in anything far removed from their day-to-day life. Studying textbooks and attending lectures can be very boring and tedious for these types.

Responders often use memorization as a learning strategy when they are faced with theory. They usually have good capacity to remember details, but this strategy may trip them up in highly complex and abstract courses. One Responder recalls her university experience this way:

"I really disliked university. One professor commented to me that I was not going to pass a highly complex course because I was trying to memorize all the details rather than learn the general ideas. Looking back, I recognize that his comments were true. Memory and observation are how I learn best. I need to engage my senses and memorize details. However, in the university setting the details presented were too many to cope with. I only survived by thinking about the work I would be able to do when I got out."

Responders prefer to learn in applied settings such as apprenticing or on-the-job training opportunities. They like to build and improve on existing skills and often excel in a specific area: Many Responders have a physical skill area in which they excel. Responders are not likely to read directions or study manuals. They more often learn by trial and error, trying something and seeing what the results are. This playful and experiential learning approach results in learning that engages them and is remembered. They are not afraid to make and learn from mistakes.

Responder Blind Spots
LONG-TERM PLANNING
Responders find long-term planning and goal setting difficult. The world around them has such a strong draw that they have to struggle to set goals beyond those they can immediately visualize and accomplish.

Responders can become caught up in responding to a situation without stopping to proactively position themselves and thus change the situation itself. They like to take risks and try new things, without careful consideration of the long-term implications. Quick fixes are not always the best. Responders may need to learn that doing what they want, and solving problems outside of the organizational structure, is not necessarily the best long-term solution for an organizational problem.

Follow-through is not a strength for Responders. Once they have dealt with an immediate problem or crisis, they tend to move on to something new. They may start several projects at once and quickly lose interest in them. The old problem no longer captures their attention or interest once it has been considered or tentatively dealt with. Responders love to "wing it" rather than prepare in advance. This can be a strength at times, and at times a disadvantage.

WORK BEFORE PLAY
The gift of living in the moment can create difficulties for Responders if they become distracted when someone is expecting them to accomplish something or meet them somewhere. Responders may also avoid or ignore important responsibilities because they are not fun or interesting. These attributes can lead to their being classified as irresponsible or unpredictable. Planning ahead, project management, and time management can be developmental areas for Responders.

EASILY BORED
Responders can easily and quickly become engaged in a task or situation. However, if their environment is not stimulating, they can also quickly become

bored and uninterested. Responders will have trouble in a predictable and routine environment, especially if they are completing repetitive tasks. The environment will not hold their attention, and they will quickly be looking for something else to do.

Although Responders dislike the routine and predictable, they are also uncomfortable with imposed change or moving totally outside of their range of experiences. They like to make variations on a theme or improvise on what *is* rather than experience something totally different and unfamiliar.

Snapshot: Responders' Natural Work Preferences

Responders are at their best when they can use their natural work preferences. By focusing on your preferences, you will be able to better assess the types of work that will be personally satisfying. The following list describes characteristics and preferences of Responders. Check off the items that are true for you.

As a Responder, I am at my best when I can

- [ ] Be active
- [ ] Do hands-on work
- [ ] Avoid structure, routine, and repetition
- [ ] Respond immediately
- [ ] Meet and interact with a variety of people
- [ ] Solve immediate problems
- [ ] Have fun and be playful
- [ ] Be spontaneous
- [ ] Interact with others
- [ ] Negotiate, collaborate, compromise, persuade, or otherwise develop rapport
- [ ] Be personally and directly involved and active
- [ ] Have varied and changing work duties
- [ ] Avoid structure, routine, and repetition
- [ ] Demonstrate practical creativity or artistry
- [ ] Work in a rapidly changing, dynamic environment
- [ ] Observe with my senses
- [ ] Tune in to facts and details
- [ ] Have freedom and the independence to act
- [ ] Stop to enjoy the moment
- [ ] Troubleshoot, adapt, and improvise
- [ ] Use a practical, realistic approach

WHAT'S KEY FOR ME?
My Ideal Work Preferences

Look back at the snapshot for the work preferences for a Responder. From the items you have checked, jot down the points that best summarize your preferences. Feel free to add points that are not on the list.

My most important work preferences are..

....

....

....

....

....

....

....

WORK THAT ATTRACTS RESPONDERS

Responders can be found in many types of work. Here are some examples that use the Responder's natural way of working.

TRADES AND TECHNICAL AREAS
Carpenter
Construction worker
Electrician
Farmer
Laboratory technologist
Machine operator
Radiological technician
Respiratory therapist

Trades and technical work often attract Responders because they are hands-on and active. Responders often enjoy working outdoors and working with equipment. If you like to work with your hands, you may want to consider trades or technical work. Trades offer on-the-job training, another advantage for the Responder. This type of learning is immediate and directly related to the day-to-day work duties. Many of these occupations also require attention to facts and details, such as making measurements, observing readings, and choosing correct parts and components. This list, matching the top choices of Responders, shows only a few of the many trades that are available. Many technologist positions are also available in a variety of fields.

EMERGENCY RESPONSE
Critical care nurse
Emergency response worker
Firefighter
Lifeguard
Police officer

Emergency response work can be a good match for Responders who are very observant and quick-acting. If you enjoy the stress and excitement of dealing with crises, a career in emergency response might be something to consider. In this type of work you will find lots of variety and change as well as opportunities to solve immediate problems.

PROVIDING SERVICES
Athletic coach
Child-care worker
Editor
Performer
Recreational attendant
Reporter
Social services worker
Teacher—adult education
Tour agent
Waitperson

Responders enjoy work that allows them to help others directly. If you enjoy collaborating or developing rapport with others, these occupations may appeal to you. There are many active and interactive opportunities in this area, from caring for children to guiding a holiday tour.

SALES, MARKETING, AND NEGOTIATING
Insurance agent
Marketing specialist
Mediator
Negotiator
Promoter
Real estate agent
Salesperson

Responders are good at "reading" others and are often skilled at sales and marketing. If you like to negotiate, compromise, and persuade others, these types of work may be for you; they will give you opportunities to offer immediate solutions to a customer's needs.

Of course, these are just a few examples. There are many other types of work that Responders will enjoy. See the next sections for work that is specifically appealing to ESFPs and ESTPs.

HOW RESPONDERS FIND BALANCE

Responders are energized by the world around them and seek to engage themselves in practical actions. This approach to life is exciting and motivating, but constantly reacting to the here and now can limit the Responder if it is the only approach used.

Responders must balance their ability to react quickly with an approach that allows them to slow down, evaluate information, and make decisions. If Responders do not develop a process for evaluating and deciding between courses of action, they can become caught up in the present. At their worst, they can appear unable to mature in the way that society expects. They may avoid responsibilities and engage in behaviors that do not seem "grown up." Although keeping a playful and childlike side is a positive attribute, if this attribute is exaggerated, the Responder may experience difficulties keeping jobs or managing relationships. Our society has many expectations that are not congruent with the natural, carefree approach of the Responder. Responders without balance may be seen as unreliable.

A well-developed decision-making approach helps Responders avoid these problems by providing a focus for their observations and actions. This decision-making focus helps them develop purpose and direction. Two approaches can be used for evaluating information: a values-based approach and a logical approach. Personality type theory calls these two approaches Feeling (F) and Thinking (T). You may want to look back to Chapter 2 to discern which approach is most comfortable for you. The words *thinking* and *feeling* have many connotations that do not really relate to how people evaluate information and make decisions. So, to avoid misconceptions, in this book Responders who prefer Feeling as a decision-making approach (ESFPs) are called Compassionate Responders, while Responders who prefer Thinking as a decision-making approach (ESTPs) are called Logical Responders.

Compassionate Responders will naturally evaluate information on the basis of personal and human values. Over time, they will also learn to adopt an analytical view of the world. They will evaluate some of their choices and actions in an objective manner and will take a closer look at the logical consequences of their actions.

Logical Responders most naturally use logical analysis to evaluate information. They will likely make their initial career decisions in a logical and analytical way. As they develop and move through life, they will also learn to evaluate and decide, using their personal values and situational needs. Over time, Logical Responders will learn to appreciate the feelings and values of themselves and others and incorporate them into their decisions. Developing rapport and understanding others will become more than an exercise in negotiation and compromise as they take a more personal look at the world around them.

Each approach has a different focus, but both allow the Responder an opportunity to make choices and move beyond the immediate world. These decision-making approaches are often used internally as ways of reflecting on and deciding between courses of action. Often, having children is a trigger for personal growth in the decision-making processes, as Responders recognize and deal with an increased level of responsibility. Over the course of their life, Responders will use and develop both ways to help them choose their actions. This natural development allows Responders to be more flexible decision makers over time.

As you go through this section, you may find it helpful to read about your most natural balancing approach first. Then, read about the other approach to balancing, to see what is in store for you as you mature and develop.

<table>
<tr>
<td>

☐ **I am most like ESFP,**
so I am a Compassionate Responder.
I will initially balance my action-oriented approach by making values-based decisions. As I mature and develop, I will also learn to balance my approach by incorporating more logical analysis into my decisions.

</td>
<td>

☐ **I am most like ESTP,**
so I am a Logical Responder.
I will initially balance my action-oriented approach by making logical decisions. As I mature and develop, I will also learn to balance my approach by incorporating the feelings and values of others and myself into my decisions.

</td>
</tr>
</table>

BALANCING RESPONDING WITH COMPASSION

The latest research shows that about 8.5 percent of adults in the United States are Compassionate Responders (ESFP). Compassionate Responders balance their approach of immediate action with an internal focus on personal values. The resulting combination leads to an awareness of people's immediate needs and a playful, considerate disposition. Compassionate Responders use their keen observation and ability to develop rapport to help, entertain, comfort, or otherwise interact with people. They learn to take time from the need to respond to the immediate situation to choose what is important and has value for them. They often rely on this personal sense of connection to identify opportunities to help others. Because Compassionate Responders have a values-based decision-making process as a balance for their Sensing, they initially express their Responding way of working differently than Logical Responders do. However, Logical Responders in midlife may also find that these values-based descriptions mirror the direction in which they are moving as they mature and develop.

What Compassionate Responders Do Naturally
HELP OTHERS

Compassionate Responders tend to be interested in people and in tune with them. Because of their keen powers of observation and their ability to sense what others are feeling, they are adept at picking up emotional cues. They are inventive helpers, finding ways to gather data and meet others' needs without getting caught up in rules and procedures. Compassionate Responders prefer to work with minimal supervision and direction; rules and structures create limits to their ability to resourcefully improvise or jury-rig a solution. However, they do enjoy working with others and are collaborative and dynamic team members.

Compassionate Responders enjoy being physically active. They are attracted to a wide range of occupations where they can provide immediate physical services for others, ranging from social work to hairdressing. They are deeply aware of others' suffering and in a crisis they will work long and hard to help.

Helping occupations allow them to use their social, values-based approach as well as their attention to detail. Compassionate Responders especially like to help others by solving practical problems. In an organization they will often be highly sociable, enjoying meeting and developing rapport with others. They are attracted to service and health-care occupations. In these settings, their personable nature can help make others feel comfortable or help them have a good time. They are also attracted to careers in education and counseling and often choose to help young children or those who have special needs or difficulties.

CONNECT WITH OTHERS

Compassionate Responders like to engage in conversations and do not hesitate to offer positive feedback and compliment others. Being generous and charming, they can easily develop rapport with and motivate others. One Responder describes her skill development in this area:

"The place where I work has a volunteer support group that I am part of. I have been able to take free training in communication and support skills. My name goes on a list, and if anyone wants to talk to someone about a problem, they can call me. I enjoy having a part to play in helping my peers."

Compassionate Responders like to share activities and experiences with others. This shared experience provides a strong connection for them and is highly valued. They thrive on social contact and are very personable. Their easy rapport and keen observation make them especially talented at sales and in entertainment work. Spending too much time socializing may be a problem for some Compassionate Responders.

Compassionate Responders tend to express themselves through their actions and will go out of their way to help others in a practical, hands-on manner. They also like others to express appreciation with tangible rewards such as gifts, touches, or the offer of a helping hand.

Finding it difficult to deal with conflicts or situations that cannot be immediately resolved by direct action, Compassionate Responders may tend to avoid or ignore such situations. They may lack the skills to deal with the abstract and may also lack the patience or interest to develop these skills. When Compassionate Responders experience difficulties in these areas, others may label them as irresponsible or unconcerned about long-term consequences. Correcting these impressions is a potential development area for the Compassionate Responder.

EXPRESS THEMSELVES

Compassionate Responders are often artistic and enjoy expressing themselves through the creation of an aesthetic product. These creative expressions can vary broadly. For example, Compassionate Responders might bake, perform a sport, or create an interesting lesson for the classroom. Their interest will be in creating something unique. Do not expect them to make the same thing the same way twice or to work on highly detailed or structured projects that require follow-through.

Compassionate Responders tend to adopt a pleasure-loving, playful approach to life. They are able to fully experience the moment with a positive, light-hearted, and optimistic attitude. Every moment and every experience is there to enjoy to the fullest. Work must provide opportunities to laugh and have fun.

The fun-loving and playful side of Responders attracts them to a variety of jobs in entertainment and promotion. As well, their practical, creative bent may lead to an interest in creating aesthetic products and services, ranging from flower arrangement to photography.

Because values are an important consideration in decision making, Compassionate Responders may mold their career planning around family needs. For example, one Compassionate Responder who is trained as a biologist loves doing fieldwork:

"I really enjoy the active, outdoor part of biology. Traveling to survey waterfowl populations, tracking mammals, and rappelling down cliffs when working with peregrine falcons are activities that I have found both fun and rewarding. Now that I am married and have a child, I am no longer doing fieldwork. It would require too much time away from being at home with my family. I need to find work that is as stimulating, yet has regular hours. This is a major challenge for me."

Snapshot: Ideal Work Environment for Compassionate Responders

By focusing on your personal preferences, you will be able to better assess the types of work that will be personally satisfying. The following list describes ideal work environments for Compassionate Responders. Check off the items that are true for you.

As a Compassionate Responder, I prefer a work environment that

- ☐ Is active and interactive
- ☐ Is collaborative
- ☐ Is flexibilile and freeing
- ☐ Is fun and playful
- ☐ Provides immediate opportunities to help others
- ☐ Emphasizes practical and concrete results or products
- ☐ Allows for social contact

Snapshot: Skills and Valued Activities for Compassionate Responders

By focusing on your personal preferences, you will be able to better assess the types of work that will be personally satisfying. The following list describes skills and activities valued by Compassionate Responders. Check off the items that are true for you.

As a Compassionate Responder, I value the following skills and activities:

- ☐ Adapting
- ☐ Attending to detail
- ☐ Collaborating
- ☐ Communicating
- ☐ Creating
- ☐ Developing rapport
- ☐ Helping
- ☐ Observing
- ☐ Practical problem solving

Work That Attracts Compassionate Responders

The following occupations tend to be of interest to Compassionate Responders. When looking for career ideas, remember to also look at the work options for Responders listed earlier in the chapter, which are attractive to both Logical and Compassionate Responders.

PRACTICAL SERVICES

Bookkeeper
Cashier
Clerical supervisor
Clerical worker
Cosmetologist
Flight attendant
Hairdresser
Library worker
Public relations specialist
Receptionist
Transportation worker
Travel agent

Many Compassionate Responders find satisfaction in work that allows them to help and assist others. If you enjoy lots of contact with people and like providing a practical service, you may want to consider a career in one of these areas. Customer service provides a practical way for Compassionate Responders to use their natural way of working. These occupations provide immediate opportunities to attend to details as well as opportunities to interact with and help others.

MEDICAL/HEALTH CARE

Dental assistant
Dental hygienist
Medical assistant
Nursing aide
Physical therapist
Physician's assistant
Primary care physician
Public health nurse

If you enjoy interacting with lots of people and are comfortable around medical or health-related procedures, you may find that a career in the medical or health area provides you with an opportunity to develop rapport with and help others. Many Compassionate Responders find it rewarding to comfort others by putting them at ease and helping them cope in frightening or uncomfortable situations.

PROVIDING COUNSELING OR SUPPORT
Counselor
Rehabilitation counselor
Religious worker
Teacher—preschool to high school

Some Compassionate Responders find counseling and teaching roles to be rewarding. They can use their helpful and practical approach to assist others. If you like helping others who are in crisis, or if you enjoy teaching and supporting others, these occupations may be satisfying. Work in these areas provides lots of opportunities to use communication skills, develop rapport, and help others.

CREATIVE WORK
Designer
Film producer
Floral designer
Musician
Photographer
Project editor
Special events producer

Many Compassionate Responders enjoy expressing their personality by creating a concrete and practical product. Photographs, films, floral arrangements, and music are all examples of how Compassionate Responders can express themselves through their work. If you have a creative side, you may choose work that will help you express yourself. Your talents may be in areas not listed here, such as glassblowing or printmaking. There are many possibilities that provide opportunities to generate income while allowing you to express yourself in a practical and creative way.

SCIENCE AND TECHNOLOGY
Aeronautical engineer
Biologist
Marine biologist
Medical technician
Veterinarian
Veterinary assistant

For the more technically oriented Compassionate Responders, there are lots of opportunities to use your practicality and observational skills. If you enjoy working with animals or using technical equipment, you may want to consider a career in science and technology. Some of these occupations allow you to work outdoors and be active, while others allow you to comfort and help people or animals.

Compassionate Responders as Leaders

Compassionate Responders bring unique strengths to the leadership role. They naturally lead and prefer to be led in a specific way.

CASUAL AND PERSONAL

Compassionate Responders are personable and casual leaders. They usually have good "people skills" and will make sure all team members are working collaboratively toward practical goals. They will not be authoritarian or like to work under someone who is authoritarian. As one Responder comments,

"I want to work with *someone, not at a level above or below them. I value working collaboratively."*

Being both observant and focused on individual needs and situations, Compassionate Responders quickly read emotions and deal with interpersonal difficulties. They focus on immediate rather than future or long-term needs. Being flexible and action-oriented, they do not worry about correct protocol. They deal with people as they are and do not put much energy into worrying about rules and conventions. Compassionate Responders use their resources effectively and do whatever needs to be done to meet their objectives.

IMMEDIATE RESPONSES

Compassionate Responders like to manage crises rather than engage in long-term planning. They immediately focus on taking direct action. Compassionate Responders will work around or avoid red tape, complex organization, and structure, and they may avoid or ignore the rules to facilitate getting the job done. Expedience is important. They want to finish the job and move on, preferably to another immediate crisis. They find the long-term and strategic planning aspects of leadership to be outside of their natural way of working. They tend to drop projects or not follow through once the immediate need has been dealt with.

Because Compassionate Responders are observant and in tune with situations, they can often spot problems earlier than others do. This quick appraisal can help them find immediate solutions. They like to work at a fast pace, with lots of variety and opportunities to react to changing situations. However, they may become engaged in a situation and move quickly, without seeking input or listening to the opinions of others. This can be an area of development and learning for them.

Snapshot: Compassionate Responders as Leaders

By focusing on your personal preferences, you will be able to better assess the types of work that will be personally satisfying. The following list describes the leadership preferences of Compassionate Responders. Check off the items that are true for you.

As a Compassionate Responder, I prefer to

- [ ] Make immediate responses
- [ ] Manage crises
- [ ] Observe
- [ ] Be personable and in tune with people
- [ ] Quickly read emotions and deal with interpersonal difficulties
- [ ] Focus on taking direct action
- [ ] Work around or avoid red tape
- [ ] Get the job done and move on
- [ ] Avoid long-term and strategic planning
- [ ] Spot problems immediately
- [ ] Work at a fast pace
- [ ] Be casual and personal
- [ ] Use my resources effectively
- [ ] Do whatever needs to be done to meet objectives

Compassionate Responders as Team Members

Compassionate Responders are good at finding common ground and motivating groups of people to work together. They are positive and high-energy team members. They are accepting of individual differences and adopt a live-and-let-live approach, accepting and valuing diversity. Having a Compassionate Responder on a team can make the work more fun, interesting, and playful.

Compassionate Responders are charming, easygoing, and personable team members. They seek cooperation and are able to help the team members link and collaborate. However, they may avoid or ignore confrontation, preferring to maintain a harmonious environment. They do not want to look into deep or complex interpersonal problems, preferring instead to deal with the immediate. They have little patience with complaining. Here is how one Compassionate Responder describes it:

"Sometimes I just feel like saying, 'Quit fighting and work with it.' People spend so much time getting caught up in discussing things that it can make me crazy."

Although this approach may be immediately useful, in the long term it can lead to an avoidance of issues. To compound the problem, sometimes Compassionate Responders take criticism personally. This combination of avoidance and personalization can create some long-term stress in relationships. Compassionate Responders may need to develop objectivity and take time to deal with causes of problems, to resolve some of their more complex issues.

Snapshot: Compassionate Responders as Team Members

By focusing on your personal preferences, you will be able to better assess the types of work that will be personally satisfying. The following list describes how Compassionate Responders like to work within a team. Check off the items that are true for you.

As a Compassionate Responder, I prefer to

- ☐ Find common ground
- ☐ Motivate groups of people to work together
- ☐ Be positive and high energy
- ☐ Value diversity
- ☐ Accept individual differences
- ☐ Make the work fun, interesting, and playful
- ☐ Be charming, easygoing and personable
- ☐ Seek cooperation
- ☐ Help team members link and collaborate

Compassionate Responders as Learners

Compassionate Responders want real-life, practical learning experiences. Classroom lectures and theoretical information bore them, especially if the information is not linked to concrete applications. Formal learning is almost always a struggle for these practical learners. Often the only thing that gets them through is the knowledge that the work they will do after the education will be practical, even if the education itself is not. Compassionate Responders like to work with and solve practical problems when learning. They seek opportunities to engage in activities such as simulations, field experience, and applied research projects.

They especially enjoy personalized activities that link learning to their specific needs and experiences. Compassionate Responders relate well to a supportive and encouraging instructor. Above all, learning must be fun and active, with lots of opportunities to interact with people and things. They like chances to try things and make mistakes. Compassionate Responders will not hesitate to play before they work and can be easily distracted from formal learning if they are not engaged. Interaction and fun are key for engaging the Compassionate Responder.

Snapshot: Compassionate Responders as Learners

By focusing on your personal preferences, you will be able to better assess the types of work that will be personally satisfying. The following list describes the learning preferences of Compassionate Responders. Check off the items that are true for you.

As a Compassionate Responder, I prefer to learn in ways that

- [ ] Are active and interactive
- [ ] Allow opportunities to try things and make mistakes
- [ ] Are hands-on
- [ ] Are fun and exciting
- [ ] Include personalized activities
- [ ] Provide support and encouragement
- [ ] Are practical and concrete rather than theoretical or abstract

---

BALANCING RESPONDING WITH LOGIC

The latest research shows that about 4.3 percent of adults in the United States are Logical Responders (ESTP). Logical Responders balance their approach of observation and action with an internal focus on logical reasoning. Thus, they are analytic as well as practical. Logical Responders like to jump into and solve problems. They are especially keen to work in high-risk and crisis situations.

They tend to be impersonal and task-oriented in their approach, communicating and solving problems in a straightforward manner. Logical Responders are also adventure-oriented. They enjoy competition and are risk takers. Because Logical Responders have this logical decision-making process as a balance for their Sensing, they initially express their Responding way of working differently than Compassionate Responders do. However, Compassionate Responders in midlife may also find that these logically based descriptions mirror the direction in which they are moving as they mature and develop.

What Logical Responders Do Naturally
DETERMINE LOGICAL CONSEQUENCES

Logical Responders use a combination of logical thinking and fast action to quickly monitor and respond to situations. They are able to quickly determine the logical causes and consequences of actions. Using logical thinking helps them balance their immediate and action-oriented focus with a grasp of the principles that underlie the situation.

They can use this logical focus to make and act on tough decisions. They tend to make accurate and effective decisions, especially when solving or dealing with practical matters. Logical Responders see problems and situations as games to play or puzzles to solve. They like challenges, can be very competitive, and will take great risks and shortcuts to "win." Logical Responders are often attracted to opportunities to promote, negotiate, and sell. Skilled trades and technically oriented occupations are also attractive to Logical Responders, as they provide opportunities to use analysis as well as to work hands-on and attend to details.

NEGOTIATE AND ACT

Logical Responders charm and disarm others by demonstrating good communication skills and a keen awareness of and ability to maneuver around power and structure. They are good at finessing the situation so that it works to their advantage. They read people well and use this ability to their advantage when negotiating. They can see human interactions as games or competitions and may focus more on winning and losing than on relationship building. They will, of course, operate from a logical sense of right and wrong, but this internal framework may differ from the norm.

Acting is more enjoyable for Logical Responders than talking, and these types are not likely to sit around discussing matters for long periods. They do not want to slow down to explain why and how their actions have solved a problem. They would rather move ahead to the next situation. They can be very restless during periods of inactivity. One Logical Responder explains his need to be active:

"When I was working as an engineer at gas plants and at pulp and paper mills, I would often jump in and help the laborers and operators. It wasn't really my job, but I like solving operating problems and getting things up and running."

REBEL AND STRETCH THE RULES

The Logical Responder combines a hands-on, practical approach with a direct and impersonal communication style. This approach can be considered unacceptable in terms of traditional feminine behavior; female Logical Responders may struggle to balance their natural preferences with societal expectations. However, both male and female Logical Responders often feel out of place in a society in which work is highly structured and routine. They may rebel against the traditional focus of steady work toward accomplishing routine goals.

Logical Responders are most satisfied in a work environment that provides rapidly changing and varied duties. They need to be able to flexibly approach problems and have the freedom to improvise and jury-rig solutions. Independence is a key characteristic for most Logical Responders; if they lack the autonomy to act, they become very frustrated.

TAKE RISKS

Logical Responders are not averse to taking risks, so they are attracted to occupations such as firefighting, police, and emergency response work. They may also pursue financial as well as physical risks, taking on work with unpredictable results, such as entrepreneurial ventures or developing land.

This active risk taking can characterize their career planning as well as their way of working on the job. One Logical Responder describes how, during her career, she has done very little planning:

"All of my career opportunities fell into place naturally. If I didn't like a job, I simply quit and immediately found another one. I would quit one job on Friday and start a new one the next Monday. It never occurred to me to stop and analyze why I didn't like the first job and why I chose the second job. I moved from opportunity to opportunity in a practical way, learning from each job along the way. I can't even imagine staying in a job for security reasons. If the interest is gone, I will get out. If a company offers an incentive for some people to leave as a cost-cutting measure, I will leave."

Snapshot: Ideal Work Environment for Logical Responders

By focusing on your personal preferences, you will be able to better assess the types of work that will be personally satisfying. The following list describes the ideal work environment for Logical Responders. Check off the items that are true for you.

As a Logical Responder, I prefer a work environment that has

- ☐ Change and variety
- ☐ Freedom to act independently
- ☐ Ability to make and act on decisions
- ☐ Freedom to stretch the rules
- ☐ Practical problems to solve
- ☐ Rapidly changing and varied duties
- ☐ Risk, challenge, and competition
- ☐ Opportunities to make quick, logical assessments
- ☐ Opportunities to work hands-on and attend to detail

Snapshot: Skills and Valued Activities for Logical Responders

By focusing on your personal preferences, you will be able to better assess the types of work that will be personally satisfying. The following list describes the skills and valued activities of Logical Responders. Check off the items that are true for you.

As a Logical Responder, I value the following skills and activities:

- ☐ Adapting
- ☐ Analyzing
- ☐ Paying attention to detail
- ☐ Negotiating
- ☐ Practical problem solving
- ☐ Promoting
- ☐ Selling

Work That Attracts Logical Responders

The following occupations tend to be of interest to Logical Responders. When looking for career ideas, remember to also look at the work options for Responders listed earlier in the chapter, which are attractive to both Logical Responders and Compassionate Responders.

SCIENCE AND TECHNOLOGY
Computer programmer
Electronics technician
Engineer
Optometrist
Park ranger
Pharmacist
Physical therapist
Pilot

Many Logical Responders are attracted to work in which they can learn about and work with science and technology. If you enjoy manipulating and understanding scientific principles in a practical way, these types of work may appeal to you. There are many opportunities emerging in the computer technologies that may be interesting to a Logical Responder with a technical focus.

RESEARCH AND ANALYSIS
Auditor
Consultant
Financial advisor
Investigator
Journalist
Land developer
Purchasing agent
Small-business manager
Stockbroker

If you have a mind for details, or if you like digging out facts, you may enjoy a career that provides you with opportunities to complete research and analysis. These occupations almost always require accurate observation and quick assessment of situations. Some of these occupations are competitive and involve risk taking and negotiation skills. So, depending on how much you relish thrills and adventure, you might prefer a relatively safe auditing career or a more exciting investigative reporting career.

COMMUNITY SERVICES
Community health worker
Correctional officer
Guard
Police detective
Probation officer

Logical Responders are attracted to jobs that allow them to work with others, often finding practical solutions to problems. If you enjoy contact with people and want to take a guiding role, these occupations may be attractive. Although not all of these occupations are risky, you can see that some of them do involve physical risk.

TRADES
Chef
Craft worker
General contractor
Laborer
Mason
Mechanic
Plumber

Trades are appealing to all Responders. For the Logical Responder, they can also provide an opportunity to solve problems. If you enjoy troubleshooting, you may find that the trades are a good way to use your logical analysis. For example, every vehicle that is brought to an auto mechanic needs to be assessed and fixed. As mentioned in the general list of occupations for all Responders, there are a number of trades to consider that may appeal to you.

Logical Responders as Leaders
Logical Responders bring unique strengths to the leadership role. They will naturally lead and prefer to be led in a specific way.

MANAGE CRISES
Logical Responders like to lead in crisis situations. They shine when finding immediate and logical solutions to problems. They are able to focus intensely

on a problem and expedite an immediate solution effectively. Logical Responders are less concerned with the impact of the solution on people than they are with its practicality. They also focus on short-term rather than long-term consequences. Others, having different ways of working, may find it hard to convince a Logical Responder leader to include long-term or personal needs in their action plans. This may create some conflict. One Logical Responder leader comments,

"Strategic planning is my biggest challenge. In the past I have avoided it as much as possible. I am impatient with the planning process. It is so much easier and more interesting to deal with the immediate needs, problems, and day-to-day activities. If given a choice, I would let the future take care of itself."

· 61 ·

WORK AROUND THE SYSTEM

Logical Responders can be very effective leaders when roadblocks are affecting their group's ability to complete tasks. They are skilled at removing, slipping under, and going around roadblocks to keep projects moving forward. These leaders shine at improvisation.

Logical Responders tend to ignore or avoid organizational structure and process and are nontraditional in their leadership approach. They are impatient with routine, structure, and stability. They prefer to work around rather than within the system, they prefer not to deal with the theoretical, the long-term, or the ambiguous.

Logical Responders use commanding behavior and a take-charge attitude to express their leadership. They usually are not cowed by or overly respectful of adhering to the proper chain of command. They will act and lead whenever it seems expedient to do so. Logical Responders do not want to work out processes for solving problems or procedures for doing things. This planning distracts from the moment and is usually inappropriate for the next changing situation. They lead with straightforward action and like independence. As one Logical Responder puts it,

"Give me some direction, and then get out of my way."

Snapshot: Logical Responders as Leaders

By focusing on your personal preferences, you will be able to better assess the types of work that will be personally satisfying. The following list describes the leadership preferences of Logical Responders. Check off the items that are true for you.

As a Logical Responder leader, I prefer to

- ☐ Manage crises
- ☐ Focus intensely on a problem
- ☐ Expedite an immediate solution effectively
- ☐ Be direct and practical
- ☐ Avoid strategic and long-term planning
- ☐ Ignore or avoid organizational structure and process
- ☐ Use a nontraditional leadership approach

- ☐ Push the boundaries of routine, structure, and stability
- ☐ Work around rather than within the system
- ☐ Use commanding behavior and a take-charge attitude
- ☐ Act and lead whenever it seems expedient to do so
- ☐ Take straightforward action
- ☐ Be independent

Logical Responders as Team Members

Logical Responders tend to be charming and get along well with others. They are highly motivated to deal with and resolve immediate conflicts. Logical Responders are masters at negotiation, persuasion, and compromise. However, if they have a difference of opinion with others, they will not hesitate to confront them. At these times they can be directly critical and blunt, which can negatively affect those who require a gentler approach.

Logical Responders are impatient with efforts to dig too deeply into ongoing causes and roots of problems. They tend to ignore or avoid efforts to analyze these matters in great detail. Like other logical types, Logical Responders may focus more on expedient actions than on considering the "people" side of problems. Their actions may upset or inconvenience others, which comes as a surprise to Logical Responders. They do not require ongoing validation the way others might. They assess themselves, rather than depend on external feedback. One Logical Responder explains,

"I don't always need to be rewarded or praised for what I do. I can see the results myself. Others' opinions don't necessarily matter as much as my own."

Snapshot: Logical Responders as Team Members

By focusing on your personal preferences, you will be able to better assess the types of work that will be personally satisfying. The following list of statements describes how Logical Responders like to work within a team. Check off the statements that are true for you.

As a Logical Responder team member, I

- ☐ Charm and get along well with others
- ☐ Do not hesitate to confront others if I disagree
- ☐ Deal with and resolve immediate conflicts
- ☐ Am a master at negotiation, persuasion, and compromise
- ☐ Can be direct and blunt at times
- ☐ Remove roadblocks and keep projects moving forward
- ☐ Am impatient with efforts to dig too deeply into ongoing causes and roots of problems
- ☐ May focus more on expedient actions than on people

Logical Responders as Learners

Logical Responders prefer learning through lots of action and hands-on activities. They enjoy competitions, challenges, and taking risks when learning. They are practical and want to get the straight facts about a topic. They become bored and disengaged when presented with abstract theory unless a logical connection can be drawn between the theory and practice. Logical Responders like learning about troubleshooting, decision making, and problem solving, especially if the models are presented in a logical and applied context. They want opportunities to immediately apply what they have learned.

Snapshot: Logical Responders as Learners

By focusing on your personal preferences, you will be able to better assess the types of work that will be personally satisfying. The following list describes the learning preferences of Logical Responders. Check off the items that are true for you.

As a Logical Responder, I

☐ Prefer hands-on activities

☐ Enjoy competitions, challenges, and taking risks

☐ Am interested in practical applications

☐ Get bored and will disengage when presented with abstract theory

☐ Want to get the straight facts about a topic

☐ Enjoy learning about and doing troubleshooting, decision making, and problem solving

☐ Am drawn to logical content, presentation, and connections

☐ Want to immediately apply what I have learned

THE RESPONDER'S GREATEST CHALLENGES

Everyone has less-preferred activities and areas for growth and improvement. Responders are no exception. Here are two major developmental areas for both Compassionate and Logical Responders, with tips on how to develop each one.

Long-Term Planning

Responders may find it difficult to see possibilities for themselves in the future. A Responder's early career path often reflects a series of opportunities that just appeared rather than a systematic effort toward a goal. The Responder may find it helpful to consider possibilities, set goals, and find ways to attain these goals rather than simply be captured by whatever comes along. Learning to set priorities and follow through with obligations can be instructive. One Responder describes her approach to planning:

"I am reactive. I might see a job in the paper and go for it. Or, if an opportunity appears, I will seize it. But I find it much more difficult to go out and look for opportunities. At times, I feel that this reactive approach gets in the way of making changes that will make my life more rewarding in the long term."

Because Responders are highly tuned in to the here and now, the concept of planning for the future is, at first, too abstract. Why make plans, they ask, when things are constantly changing? Although this adaptable focus is valuable in coping with a rapidly changing world, many satisfying careers and situations require some delayed gratification and an eye to the future. This is an especially important lesson for Responders who are raising families and have greater financial and personal responsibilities.

It may be difficult for Responders to set long-term priorities. It is unlikely that setting goals and managing time and tasks will ever be comfortable or natural for them, but most will develop some skills in this area to help them plan for the future. If you are a Responder, think of flexible goals and tentative plans. Plan to develop a skill, learn something, or gain experience in areas that will allow you more freedom in the long term. This process can be active and fun and does not have to follow the traditional process of writing goals, subgoals, and timelines.

TIPS FOR LONG-TERM PLANNING

- Take a few minutes to visualize something you would like to be able to do. Use your acute ability to focus on details to see yourself as specifically as you can. Then try to find ways to learn and move toward what you envisioned.
- Be sure to allow flexibility and freedom in your goals, or you will find them too confining.
- Think of ways to make the steps to accomplishing your goals active, fun, and interesting.
- Focus on and identify learning activities that are active and practical. Are there other, more experiential ways to meet your goals than by sitting in a traditional classroom?
- If your goal requires formal learning, find options that have on-the-job components or practicums. If there are no such options, find ways to relate theory to what you can do. Ask if you *can* complete practical projects rather than theoretical ones.
- Focus on follow-through. Break your goals into small, manageable activities and find ways to reward yourself for accomplishing them.

Focusing on the Big Picture

Responders are at their best when they are actively engaged in immediate and practical matters. This natural approach can make it hard for them to see the big picture, to interpret and integrate facts sufficiently to see patterns and possibilities. Many Responders do not see a need to focus on the big picture. It is, after all, abstract and removed from reality.

However, a future, big-picture focus allows us to imagine possibilities far beyond what we can directly experience. It is the stuff dreams are made of. Focusing on patterns and possibilities—linking and integrating information— can help Responders transfer ideas and solutions from one application to another and make decisions that will have long-term benefits.

As a Responder, you are already skilled at thinking "outside the box" to solve practical problems. You can learn to use this adaptability to help you think outside the box with ideas. Big-picture thinking can also help you understand themes that are important in your work. For example, one Responder noted, after being interviewed for a job,

"I hadn't realized how important independence is to me in my work."

Only after stopping to describe his various jobs and what he liked about them did he see the theme emerge. This realization will now be available to help him as he makes his next choices.

TIPS FOR FOCUSING ON THE BIG PICTURE

- Think of many solutions to a problem or uses for an object. Make this a game or competition with a friend. Turn off your practical side for a minute and come up with wacky and unusual ideas. This exploration into your imagination can help you learn to connect and play with possibilities.
- Think of a symbol to represent yourself. Use an animal, a piece of furniture or office equipment, or a make of car. Describe how you are like the object you are comparing yourself to. This exercise will help you move from the concrete to the abstract.
- Look for themes in your work choices. Review some of the snapshots in this chapter and, by relating them back to your experiences, try to see common links. What themes stand out, and how will they affect your next career choice? Look for both positive and negative patterns that will help you make upcoming decisions.
- Think about what you want to be remembered for when you retire from the workforce. What contribution did you make? Then evaluate how you are acting every day to make that happen.

- Allow time to reflect on and process your experiences. Ask yourself questions, such as What did I like about that? What did I not like? Why is this important to think about? How will this insight change what I do next?

Key for Me: Managing My Challenges

Is long-term planning or focusing on the big picture a challenge for you? If so, which of the strategies explored in this chapter would be helpful to try?

....

....

....

....

....

....

....

Final Tips for Responders: Doing What Comes Naturally

A Responder naturally approaches the world in an active and exploratory way. Here are a few final tips that will help you choose and develop satisfying work.

Carpe Diem

The Responder's greatest gift is the ability to "seize the day" (from the Latin injunction, *carpe diem*). Use your natural way of working to observe, react, and create whenever possible. Look at each day as an opportunity to do something meaningful. Find work that allows and encourages freedom and activity. Make sure that you find time to interact and have fun. Approach career planning by trying new things. If a type of work seems interesting, find a way to volunteer or work part-time in that field to get a feel for the day-to-day activities.

See, Hear, Taste, Smell, and Feel

Responders are acute and accurate observers of the world. If you are a Responder, you have a strong sense of the aesthetic and kinesthetic. Find ways to use your senses in a practical way. Perhaps work outdoors or with tools. Think of useful things you can make that will be attractive or things you can do that will allow you to see, hear, taste, smell, or feel the world around you. Add a personal aesthetic touch to your work environment, such as a bowl of candy, music, a picture that appeals to you, or a candle.

Seek Flexibility and Adaptability

Find opportunities to work in environments that are rapidly changing. Start up new projects or engage in many varying activities rather than few repetitive ones. Avoid workplaces that are highly structured. You may want to consider starting your own business so that you can control what you do. Work that requires immediate problem solving and adaptation will be rewarding and interesting.

Develop Rapport

Use your friendly nature and your strong ability to observe and relate to others to develop rapport. Use your positive, optimistic approach to help groups negotiate, compromise, collaborate, and cooperate. This will come naturally for the Compassionate Responder but may be more of a developmental area for the Logical Responder.

Think of the Future

Find ways to take greater control over your life by establishing and working toward a long-term goal. Visualize your future. Make your plans flexible and active, but do make some plans! Take one small, proactive step at a time.

Take Time to Reflect

Responders are active rather than contemplative. No matter what your developmental stage or situation, you may find it enlightening to take time to reflect and digest your wealth of experiences.

Now that you have learned about your work preferences, please turn to Chapter 11 to begin planning your career path.

CHAPTER FOUR

Explorers
Innovate and Initiate

PERSONALITY TYPES: ENFP AND ENTP

I work as an adult-upgrading instructor. I find it very rewarding to see adults returning to learning and succeeding at school. I really enjoy the diversity, motivation, and wealth of experiences my students bring to the classroom. —An Explorer

The latest research shows that about 11.3 percent of adults in the United States are Explorers. These individuals see the world and people as full of possibilities and potential. They like to go where no one has ever gone before, and they seek opportunities to work with people and ideas in new and unique ways. Because their approach focuses on what *could* be, they are quick to see patterns and relationships between things. Explorers tend to quickly scan their environment, absorbing and integrating information to form new ideas and connections. Inspiration and insight are the constant guides and motivating forces of the Explorer way of working.

EXPLORERS AT WORK
What Explorers Do Naturally

PLAY WITH IDEAS AND MAKE CONNECTIONS

Whatever type of work Explorers choose, it is important that they have opportunities to use their natural approach to create either new ideas or new ways of doing things. Since they enjoy the world of ideas, they often prefer to deal with things that are abstract and symbolic rather than concrete. They are more interested in possibilities than in facts and details.

Explorers do well in work that allows them to use their imagination. They can create an almost endless list of original options and possibilities for any situation. This way of working can be helpful when designing products, teaching classes, developing systems, or solving problems. For example, an Explorer working in advertising will enjoy making connections between products and marketing ideas. An Explorer who is teaching will find new ways to teach a topic to diverse groups of students.

Explorers enjoy group brainstorming and problem solving and are especially talented at taking in a wide range of ideas, opinions, and information and combining them into a solution to a problem or a way to capitalize on an opportunity.

Explorers like to adapt, improvise, and use innovative thinking. They value inspiration and score well on tests of creativity. Able to think on their feet and generate many ideas quickly, Explorers do well in work such as marketing and advertising, where new concepts, approaches, and slogans are in constant demand. Their wealth of ideas is also a strength for them in art, performing, and writing careers.

Explorers tend to have a broad range of interests and make connections between their areas of interest. They are multiskilled generalists whose expertise is in demand because of their global rather than specific focus. Whenever new ideas or new ways of combining ideas are needed, Explorers can contribute.

COMMUNICATE WITH AND INSPIRE OTHERS

It is important for Explorers to share their ideas, for they are naturally skilled communicators. They value personal expression and are assertive, outgoing, and verbally fluent. They are adept at using their verbal skills to participate in and lead groups as well as to communicate on a one-to-one level.

Work that encourages sharing and expression is satisfying for Explorers. They can use their expressive skills to teach, consult, sell, counsel, negotiate, or mediate. Whatever form of communication they choose, they tend to help others focus on the possibilities and potential in situations. Explorers naturally promote or communicate their insights. They can create and share powerful visions of what could be and are able to motivate others to see new ways of looking at things. Because Explorers like to share with others, they often act as catalysts, inspiring others to act, change, or develop in new ways.

CHANGE THINGS

Often, initial career choices for Explorers are short term and diverse. Explorers may try out any number of different types of work as they attempt to find ways to use their many ideas. Explorers seek varied opportunities to innovate and initiate. One Explorer comments,

"I can't imagine being bored. I have enough ideas to last at least three or four lifetimes. My greatest career challenge is choosing where to spend my time and energy."

Because Explorers are so tuned in to the future, they are often ahead of their time. They have a talent for seeing trends and anticipating new developments. Because others have not yet seen the need or usefulness of their futuristic ideas, Explorers often find themselves in the position of trying to sell their point of view. They can become restless and frustrated when others do not see or immediately embrace these opportunities for improvement.

Explorers can always see lots of ways to modify and improve things and thus tend to be energetic, enthusiastic, and spontaneous change agents. They are flexible and adaptable, quickly responding to or proactively creating change. They like to be first in line for future opportunities. They enjoy careers that allow them to generate and initiate new ideas and opportunities. Explorers shine in work environments that allow them the flexibility and freedom to innovate. Since they are growth oriented, they may change jobs and careers often throughout their life.

Explorers like to conceptualize ideas and use symbols and metaphors, and they often seek creative and expressive work. They may engage in a broad range of artistic, entertainment, and writing careers. Explorers may also use their creative process to improve systems or solve problems.

Since Explorers seek and initiate change, often one of their major focuses is to help others accept and move toward change. They see change as a way to facilitate growth and improvement, and they prefer situations that require them to improvise and adapt. They find opportunity in change rather than framing change as a crisis or problem. Explorers are especially likely to "buy in to" change when they see how it will improve or streamline processes. They will be resistant to anything that creates additional barriers, procedures, or red tape. Explorers will resist being told what to do in times of change, preferring to initiate or participate democratically and actively.

THRIVE ON VARIETY

Explorers prefer jobs that offer variety and the opportunity to find creative solutions to dynamic problems. They are attracted to creating new or improved products and processes. Explorers focus on what captures their attention in the moment and adapt to a variety of settings and situations. They like to work on several projects at the same time, which keeps their interest high, since they may become bored or frustrated when working at one thing too long. Explorer careers may comprise a series of projects or varied work experiences. Explorers can become very frustrated in situations where innovation is not valued. One Explorer describes his ongoing learning and development in this way:

"I want to keep blending the stuff I like together, to create new and exciting challenges."

Structured learning can be tedious and too routine for Explorers' needs. Preferring to learn from experience, they jump into new challenges beyond their current level of expertise. The concept of "just-in-time learning" applies to Explorers. They optimistically trust that they will learn and develop the needed skills and information as they do the work.

Explorers are not likely to take the time to process information in depth unless there is an immediate reason to act on it. They tend to be generalists rather than specialists and are often very skilled at integrating information from a number of sources. Because they are constantly learning as they go, they can end up in positions that are, on paper, beyond their formal credentials. This can be a barrier if formal credentials are required for advancement. Many Explorers return to learning later in life as a way to prove to others that they *know* what they can already *do*.

Explorers are interested in theories and ideas, although they are not necessarily enthusiastic about jumping through the hoops to complete formal educational requirements. Many Explorers prefer to learn by reading and discussing their ideas with others. Their enthusiasm for learning and taking in new ideas can interest Explorers in careers that allow them to carry out research and development activities. Their careers often take a number of turns and twists as Explorers find new areas to learn about and new skills to develop.

When reflecting on her personal career path, one Explorer describes how she usually changes jobs about every three years. She notes that her career planning is often insightful:

> *"I seem to know where I need to be and where I need to not be at the right time. I look back, after the fact, and see how well positioned I was for a change, but at the time I found that opportunities seemed to simply appear, and my career has flowed forward without conscious effort."*

Although not all Explorers naturally drift into ideal careers, they do tend to focus on the future and anticipate what they need to do.

Explorer Blind Spots
FOLLOWING THE RULES

Explorers can become impatient when others focus too much on procedures and routines. They prefer casual, unstructured work environments to formal, structured ones. One Explorer comments,

> *"I hate the stuffy, boardroom management meetings that are structured and not very interactive. I find it hard to sit and pay attention."*

Explorers view rules as distractions that impede the creative process and quickly become bored with routine and structure. They do not like being slowed down, and become frustrated in organizations with an overabundance of red tape and procedures. Explorers tend to not be conformists, preferring to outwit, avoid, or ignore rules and conventions. One Explorer describes his biggest frustration as trying to work within a group when solving problems:

> *"I try to approach every problem creatively, and I find myself blocked by people who are rule bound. I try to encourage 'outside-the-box' thinking whenever I can. Too often our organization becomes blocked by thinking that is linear and constrictive."*

Explorers' natural way of working is one that depends on bursts of energy and enthusiasm. They tend to work when inspired rather than have a slow, steady work pace. Working certain routine hours and days seems rigid to them. They would rather dive into a project and come up for air when they feel like it, regardless of the time of day or week. Explorers seem to thrive, more than many other types, in fast-paced and high-stress work environments.

Steady pacing and finishing work ahead of time are not characteristic of the Explorer approach. Explorers will often begin their work close to the deadline and then speed up and work long hours to complete their work on time. This work approach can be misunderstood and seen as unorthodox by many employers, who prefer less inspiration and more perspiration. Explorers may struggle in work environments in which they are expected to punch a time clock or work at a constant, steady pace. They tend to thrive in situations with tight deadlines.

As a result of their last-minute work approach, Explorers need to be able to work quickly without encountering roadblocks if they are to meet their deadlines. They will avoid rules and try to find as much independence as possible when working. They prefer work that allows them to move forward without waiting for permission or consensus. An Explorer in a highly structured and conventional environment may feel stifled. Many Explorers end up as entrepreneurs because working for themselves gives them control over their own time and allows them to implement ideas with fewer barriers. Explorers are also drawn to having their own business, as a vehicle to provide them with flexibility and variety.

DEALING WITH ALL THE DETAILS

Once engaged in starting a project, an Explorer becomes drawn in as an enthusiastic convert and advocate. Unfortunately, this easily flamed passion can also be easily doused. An Explorer can often become inspired and then tired. Conceptualizing and starting projects is much more interesting than completing projects. Explorers prefer to leave the tedious details to someone else.

Detailed planning, sequencing, and organizing of tasks in a project are usually not preferred activities of Explorers. They tend to avoid and procrastinate when required to work with routine or details. Explorers are zealous contributors when inspired but may drag their feet when required to complete the details, which, to them, are tedious. Some individuals report that they avoid completing budgets, while others avoid procedures, paperwork, and record-keeping tasks. One Explorer who runs a small business comments,

"I struggle to keep up with my paperwork. Invoicing, tax records, filing, and other administrative details are last on my list. I know they are important, but I just can't motivate myself to get at them. I would rather do almost anything else than sort through paperwork."

Explorers can lose interest and focus halfway through a project. As they turn their intuition to something else in their environment, unfinished projects can be left behind. Explorers benefit from other team members who can help them complete reality testing and attend to facts.

Explorers have the most positive team relationships when others help them sculpt and refine their vision. Without such help, their ideas and initiatives may be overly broad and unrealistic. If others can also take on the more structured and detailed tasks, a work team can be especially strong and effective.

Remember that these preferences are just guidelines and that every individual is different. A person can choose an unexpected career for his or her type and find it highly satisfying and rewarding. For example, who would think that an Explorer could like being an accountant? After all, accountants need to deal with lots of facts and details. One satisfied Explorer accountant explains that she enjoys her work immensely:

"Doing the data entry and calculations in accounting, for me, is tedious and not rewarding in itself. I have customized my business so that I consult with people, usually couples, and help them create personal financial plans. I help my customers integrate their lifestyle and values into their money management strategies. I find my work allows me to be innovative and flexible. I really enjoy showing others how to manage their money and reach their potential."

Snapshot: Explorers' Natural Work Preferences

Explorers are at their best when they can use their natural work preferences. By focusing on your preferences, you will be able to better assess the types of work that will be personally satisfying. The following list describes characteristics and preferences of Explorers. Check off the items that are true for you.

As an Explorer I am at my best when I can

- ☐ Make connections between ideas and people
- ☐ Solve problems in creative ways
- ☐ Be a catalyst, inspiring others to act
- ☐ Act independently, yet be connected to others
- ☐ Outwit, avoid, or ignore rules, structure, and conventions
- ☐ Focus on the future
- ☐ Be flexible and adaptable
- ☐ Create change
- ☐ Promote or communicate my vision
- ☐ Initiate and capitalize on new ideas and opportunities
- ☐ Start up new projects

- ☐ Work on ideas that are ahead of their time
- ☐ Engage in a variety of activities and multiple tasks
- ☐ Work when inspired
- ☐ Actively work at a fast pace when inspired
- ☐ Find freedom from unnecessary structure
- ☐ Improve processes
- ☐ Work with others in an open and exploratory environment
- ☐ Brainstorm and create many options and possibilities
- ☐ Move and act quickly without a lot of rules and limitations

·76·

WHAT'S KEY FOR ME?

My Ideal Work Preferences

Look back at the snapshot for the work preferences for an Explorer (above). Jot down in the following chart the items you checked that best summarize your preferences. Feel free to add points that are not on the list.

My most important work preferences are...
....
....
....
....
....
....
....
....

WORK THAT ATTRACTS EXPLORERS

Explorers can be found in many different types of work. Here are some examples that use the Explorer's natural way of working.

ARTS AND ENTERTAINMENT
Actor
Artist
Entertainer
Photographer

Explorers are drawn to work that provides opportunities to perform or create artistic products. If you enjoy being the center of attention or creating products, you may be attracted to a career in the arts. There are many options for performance, depending on your specific skills in drama, music, dance, or other expressive areas. Also, depending on your talents and interests, a wide range of artistic opportunities are available, from blowing glass to throwing pottery. For some Explorers, these artistic pursuits are hobbies. For others, they become the main source of income.

COMMUNICATIONS
Attorney
Editor

Journalist
Newscaster
Reporter
Social scientist
Speech pathologist

If you are verbally fluent or if you enjoy expressing yourself in words, you may want to consider a career that focuses on communication. Whether you choose to study human communications, write, help others communicate, or argue a viewpoint, a wide range of careers beckon in the communications field.

MARKETING

Advertising director
Marketer
Public relations
Publicist

Marketing is closely related to communications. Explorers are often skilled at persuasion and negotiation. If you enjoy marketing products or influencing the opinions of others, you may find a career in marketing is for you. You can use your wealth of ideas to create innovative advertising or promotional strategies.

PLANNING AND CREATING

Conference planner
Consultant
Entrepreneur
Inventor
Research assistant
Strategic planner

Explorers like to "vision" and plan for the future and often work as consultants or entrepreneurs. If your ideas tend to be ahead of their time and your thinking is somewhat outside the box, you may want to find a career that will allow you to plan and create cutting-edge systems and processes.

Of course, these are just some examples. There are many other types of work that Explorers will enjoy. See the next sections for work that is specifically appealing to ENFPs and ENTPs.

How Explorers Find Balance

Explorers are energized by the world around them. They are constantly taking in new information and actively seeking patterns and possibilities. This approach to life is exciting and motivating, but it can also be exhausting. Young Explorers often feel overwhelmed by all of the possible career options available to them and can spend a number of years exploring their options. They may, at times, envy those who seem to be more focused. Being able to see a multitude of options can be a barrier to action.

Explorers must balance their ability to see many possibilities with an approach that allows them to evaluate information and make decisions. There are two approaches to evaluating information: a values-based approach and a logical approach. Personality type theory calls these two approaches Feeling (F) and Thinking (T). You may want to look back to Chapter 2 to discern which approach is most comfortable for you. The words *feeling* and *thinking* have many connotations that do not really relate to how people evaluate information and make decisions. So, to avoid misconceptions, in this book Explorers who prefer Feeling as a decision-making approach (ENFPs) are called Compassionate Explorers, while Explorers who prefer Thinking as a decision-making approach (ENTPs) are called Logical Explorers. Compassionate Explorers most naturally evaluate information on the basis of personal and human values. Logical Explorers most naturally use logical analysis to evaluate information.

Each approach has a different focus, but both allow Explorers to stop, consider, and evaluate their ideas. As individuals consider and evaluate their options, they can focus and further define their efforts. These decision-making approaches are often used internally as Explorers reflect on and decide between courses of action. Over the course of their life, Explorers will use and develop both approaches to help them pick and choose from their wealth of ideas. This natural development allows Explorers to become more flexible decision makers over time.

One Compassionate Explorer describes how she is learning to use her logic more in her decision making:

"I first learned to make a business case and use logic to negotiate resources for projects at work. It took me longer to learn to negotiate for myself. In the past I valued and focused on helping others and maintaining harmony. I often considered others' needs before my own. It has been a big step for me to learn to negotiate for what I need personally. I can now convince myself, logically, to take care of myself first."

This Compassionate Explorer has realized the importance of her personal needs and has learned to use logic and analysis to meet them. She will always have a natural preference for making personal and subjective decisions. However, as she has developed, she has seen the need for integrating a logical component into her decisions.

As you read this section, you may find it helpful to read your most natural balancing approach first. Then read about the other approach to balancing to see what is in store for you as you mature and develop.

☐ **I am most like ENFP,** so I am a Compassionate Explorer. I will initially balance my Exploring by making values-based decisions. As I mature and develop, I will also learn to balance my Exploring by incorporating more logical analysis into decisions.

☐ **I am most like ENTP,** so I am a Logical Explorer. I will initially balance my Exploring by making logical decisions. As I mature and develop, I will also learn to balance my Exploring by incorporating values of others and myself into decisions.

BALANCING EXPLORING WITH COMPASSION

The latest research shows that about 8.1 percent of adults in the United States are Compassionate Explorers (ENFP). Compassionate Explorers balance their approach of innovation and initiation with an internal focus on values. They rely on their personal sense of responsibility and integrity to help them identify opportunities to help others and develop human potential. They will challenge and work to change accepted beliefs and practices if they feel these are not aligned with their internal sense of fundamental human values. They are often attracted to work that provides a positive atmosphere, opportunities to help others, a platform to express themselves, and chances to use their wealth of ideas. Because Compassionate Explorers have a values-based decision-making process as a balance for their Intuition, they initially express their Exploring way of working differently than Logical Explorers do. However, Logical Explorers in midlife may also find that these values-based descriptions mirror the direction in which they are moving as they mature and develop.

What Compassionate Explorers Do Naturally
ADVOCATE AND ENCOURAGE

Compassionate Explorers strive to improve people's situations, energetically and enthusiastically encouraging and persuading others. They advocate for the individual within organizations, initiating programs, processes, and projects that help individuals learn and grow. They value and encourage diversity, enjoy working with a wide variety of people, and often coach others to use empathy when interpreting situations or dealing with others.

Authenticity and openness are strongly valued and admired by Compassionate Explorers. They often develop communication skills in training, counseling, facilitating, motivating, negotiating, recruiting, and resolving conflicts. Compassionate Explorers focus on relationships and growth and enjoy developing skills that enhance these areas.

CREATIVELY EXPRESS THEMSELVES

Many Compassionate Explorers possess a creative and expressive side. They are concerned with what makes us human and unique. Compassionate Explorers are drawn to the fine arts and often work as musicians, composers, and writers. They also enjoy teaching art, drama, and music.

SEE POSSIBILITIES AND POTENTIAL FOR PEOPLE

Optimism is a key characteristic of this type. Compassionate Explorers see and explore personal and career growth possibilities for themselves and others. They like to find and champion ways to help others grow and develop. Because they process information through a lens of values and personal priorities, they are very perceptive to the needs, situations, and motivations of others.

Compassionate Explorers are often found in occupations related to counseling, teaching, religion, and the arts. One Compassionate Explorer, who works with teens, describes his greatest reward as seeing kids become hopeful, rather than scared, as a result of his interventions.

ESTABLISH RAPPORT

Compassionate Explorers are sociable and friendly, suited well to work that enables them to connect and establish rapport with others. One Compassionate Explorer describes her most preferred work activity as doing presentations:

"I am energized by interacting with the group and enjoy sharing information and meeting new people. I am constantly learning from and about others."

Compassionate Explorers prefer environments that are participative and supportive. Unlike their Logical Explorer counterparts, they see situations in shades of gray rather than black and white. They may find it difficult to work in environments that are overly judgmental, logical, critical, or analytical, where they may feel that they are undervalued or personally criticized.

SENSE ATMOSPHERE AND MORALE

Compassionate Explorers are particularly sensitive to issues of working relationships, organizational climate, and morale. Because they prefer a work environment that is harmonious and supportive, they are especially unhappy in environments that do not validate, appreciate, or celebrate individuals for their unique and valuable contributions. They often work best when they have a mentor or support system within their work environment. A Compassionate Explorer may leave an organization rather than put up with interpersonal conflicts or values clashes. One Compassionate Explorer describes the effect of people on her career:

"As I look back, I can see that people I work with are more important to me than the jobs. I stayed at jobs that didn't really suit me because I enjoyed the people and felt cared for and validated. I would leave jobs I liked rather than work in a negative environment."

Snapshot: Ideal Work Environment for Compassionate Explorers

By focusing on your personal preferences, you will be able to better assess the types of work that will be personally satisfying. The following list describes ideal work environments for Compassionate Explorers. Check off the items that are true for you.

As a Compassionate Explorer, I prefer a work environment that is

- ☐ Appreciative
- ☐ Creative
- ☐ Focused on helping others
- ☐ Meaningful; serving a higher purpose
- ☐ Cooperative and harmonious
- ☐ People oriented
- ☐ Supportive
- ☐ Warm and understanding

Snapshot: Skills and Valued Activities for Compassionate Explorers

By focusing on your personal preferences, you will be able to better assess the types of work that will be personally satisfying. The following list describes skills and activities valued by Compassionate Explorers. Check off the items that are true for you.

As a Compassionate Explorer, I value the following skills and activities:

☐ Adapting   ☐ Motivating

☐ Communicating   ☐ Negotiating

☐ Counseling   ☐ Recruiting

☐ Creating   ☐ Resolving conflicts

☐ Facilitating   ☐ Training

Work That Attracts Compassionate Explorers

The following occupations are typically of interest to Compassionate Explorers. When looking for career ideas, remember also to look at the work options listed for Explorers earlier in the chapter, which are attractive to both Logical Explorers and Compassionate Explorers.

ARTISTIC/CREATIVE
Cartoonist
Composer
Fine artist
Interior designer
Musician
Writer

Compassionate Explorers create interesting products that amuse, enlighten, or otherwise appeal to others. If you like to express yourself in this way, you may be well suited for an artistic career. Web page design and computer-assisted design are relatively new fields that young Compassionate Explorers are drawn to. Some Compassionate Explorer artists enjoy teaching their craft as well as creating products.

SUPPORTING/TEACHING
Educational and vocational counselor
Educational consultant
Human resources personnel
Junior college teacher
Ombudsman
Preschool teacher
Psychologist
Rehabilitation counselor
Religious worker
School counselor
Social worker
Special education teacher
Teacher of art, drama, or music
Trainer/workshop provider
Youth counselor

Many Compassionate Explorers choose occupations in which they can advocate for, teach, support, and counsel others. If you see great potential and possibilities in people and you enjoy supporting and encouraging others, these types of careers may be for you.

HEALTH AND WELLNESS
Dental hygienist
Health and wellness teacher
Health-care worker
Nutritionist
Occupational therapist
Speech pathologist

Many Compassionate Explorers work in the health-care field. They often take preventive or educational roles as they assist their clients.

Compassionate Explorers as Leaders
Compassionate Explorers bring unique strengths to the leadership role. They will naturally lead and prefer to be led in a specific way.

EMPOWER AND COACH

Compassionate Explorers see empowerment as a key leadership function. They strive to help others develop their potential. They are not likely to give specific directions or to command others to do specific tasks, preferring instead to listen to and use others' ideas or give general guidelines and information. Compassionate Explorers view leadership as coaching, mentoring, or guiding rather than as directing or controlling. They see autonomy as an expression of trust and confidence in their abilities.

Compassionate Explorers enthusiastically champion initiatives that provide possibilities and improve processes for people. Their organizational focus is on the people. They believe that people will naturally grow, develop, and work to their potential if they are given the opportunity. Compassionate Explorers want to develop systems and processes that empower, motivate, and allow people to contribute.

GIVE A PERSONAL TOUCH

Compassionate Explorers want leadership to be personal and caring. For them, building relationships and rapport are essential leadership activities. They strive to be caring, compassionate, genuine, and ethical. For Compassionate Explorers, leadership is a personal activity that entails getting involved with and coming to personally know, understand, and inspire people. They have a natural talent for seeing, acknowledging, and using individual strengths. Compassionate Explorers help people find niches, develop strengths, and compensate for weaknesses. One Compassionate Explorer describes her greatest leadership challenge as learning to cut back on hand-holding some of her people:

"When I first became a leader, I was constantly involving and encouraging everyone. I have now learned that some of my staff see my personal involvement as interference rather than encouragement."

Explorers using compassion in a leadership role may actually get lost in and distracted by learning people's stories and needs. They can lose sight of the task or performance at hand. They want to understand personal events and situations and feel that knowledge will contribute to their ability to help people perform more effectively. Compassionate Explorer leaders seek to please others and are motivated by positive feedback, mentorship, encouragement, and inspiration. Their performance at work can be directly and strongly affected by interpersonal conflict. Those who have different ways of working may see Compassionate Explorers as overly involved and emotional.

PARTICIPATIVE AND DEMOCRATIC

Explorers using compassion prefer an environment in which leadership is democratic and participative. They will likely seek feedback on and support for their progress. They want everyone to have a voice in the decision-making process. Compassionate Explorer leaders tend to give information rather than direction, expecting that others will act on the information given. They usually trust intuition and values more than facts or logic when making decisions. One Compassionate Explorer demonstrates her dependence on intuition and values in hiring decisions with the following statement:

"I look for the values underlying the candidate's commitment. But then, everything is values, isn't it?"

Snapshot: Compassionate Explorers as Leaders

By focusing on your personal preferences, you will be able to better assess the types of work that will be personally satisfying. The following list describes the leadership preferences of Compassionate Explorers. Check off the items that are true for you.

As a Compassionate Explorer leader, I prefer to

☐ Empower and coach

☐ Help others develop their potential

☐ Give general guidelines and information

☐ Enthusiastically champion initiatives

☐ Focus on the people within the organization

☐ Give leadership a personal touch

☐ Build relationships and rapport

☐ Get involved and personally know, understand, and inspire people

☐ See, acknowledge, and use individual strengths

☐ Be participative and democratic

Compassionate Explorers as Team Members

Compassionate Explorers add value to a team by carrying out their preferred activities, innovating and initiating projects that benefit people. They excel at getting projects started. Enamored of the team concept, they thrive in situations that use individuals' strengths and abilities to move toward a goal. They are sensitive to group dynamics and often highlight and then integrate the ideas and input of group members. Compassionate Explorers are enthusiastic team contributors and supporters. They seek to please others and can be overly sensitive to feedback that is objective and task focused.

Compassionate Explorers have a strong orientation toward promoting diversity and individualism. They value each individual's unique contributions and can often rally team members to use their strengths collectively. On a team they often take the roles of appreciating, encouraging, and inspiring others.

One Compassionate Explorer describes his greatest developmental task as a shift from sympathy to empathy:

"I have learned to listen to and understand other people's problems without getting sucked into them. I used to feel personally drained and distraught from hearing about others' emotional pain, until I learned to step back and regain some objectivity."

Snapshot: Compassionate Explorers as Team Members

By focusing on your personal preferences, you will be able to better assess the types of work that will be personally satisfying. The following list describes how Compassionate Explorers like to work within a team. Check off the items that are true for you.

As a Compassionate Explorer team member, I

- ☐ Like to initiate projects that benefit people
- ☐ Excel at getting projects started
- ☐ Thrive in situations that use individual strengths
- ☐ Am sensitive to group dynamics
- ☐ Highlight and then integrate ideas and input
- ☐ Seek to please others
- ☐ Can be overly sensitive to feedback that is objective and task focused
- ☐ Promote diversity and individualism
- ☐ Appreciate, encourage, and inspire others

Compassionate Explorers as Learners

Compassionate Explorers like to be personally involved and supported in their learning. They are always interested in applied theories and models that encourage individual growth. Compassionate Explorers dislike the structure and routine nature of formal education and prefer to have a mentor or coach. They enjoy interaction and group activities, finding that they learn from the other participants as well as the facilitator. When inspired, Compassionate Explorers are enthusiastic and motivated learners. They appreciate feedback that is personalized and positive but can be negatively affected by critical feedback or impersonal evaluating or teaching approaches. They function best when the facilitator is interested in and concerned about the learner as a unique person. Compassionate Explorers have broad interests and may read or learn about a wide range of topics. They enjoy integrating what they have learned to help people and using their learning in multiple applications or across disciplines.

Snapshot: Compassionate Explorers as Learners

By focusing on your personal preferences, you will be able to better assess the types of work that will be personally satisfying. The following list describes the learning preferences of Compassionate Explorers. Check off the items that are true for you.

As a Compassionate Explorer learner, I

- ☐ Am enthusiastic and motivated
- ☐ Multitask
- ☐ Like group work
- ☐ Read extensively and have wide interests
- ☐ Prefer to have a mentor or coach
- ☐ Like to learn about and generate new ideas
- ☐ Dislike structure and routine
- ☐ Am sensitive to critical feedback
- ☐ Need connections, support, and praise

BALANCING EXPLORING WITH LOGIC

The latest research shows that about 3.2 percent of adults in the United States are Logical Explorers (ENTP). Logical Explorers balance their approach of innovation and initiation with an internal focus on logic and analysis. They like to create a complex system of patterns and models through which they interpret and integrate new information. This internal system of thinking lets them quickly adapt to new ideas. Thus, Logical Explorers are fluid, creative thinkers who are constantly building and adjusting their mental models. These models often promote effectiveness and improvement of processes. Because Logical Explorers have this logical decision-making process as a balance for their Intuition, they initially express their Exploring way of working differently than Compassionate Explorers do. However, Compassionate Explorers in mid-life may also find that these logic-based descriptions mirror the direction in which they are moving as they mature and develop.

What Logical Explorers Do Naturally
PLAY WITH THEORIES AND MODELS
Logical Explorers tend to use their intuition and logical thinking to explore theoretical possibilities and find creative solutions to problems. They are often found in occupations related to science, management, technology, and the arts. In these areas they tend to be innovative and imaginative creators of change. They are especially interested in designing and improving systems and processes. They create models that incorporate a logical and efficient flow of processes. One Logical Explorer describes his strong appetite for cleaning up organizational messes:

"I thrive on making order out of chaos. I like to put systems and processes in place that make the organization sing."

SOLVE PROBLEMS
Logical Explorers effectively analyze situations and problems. They tend to be excellent problem solvers, especially if they can work on complex and abstract problems that require new and innovative solutions. Because of their preferences for solving problems and initiating change, you can find Logical Explorers in management and leadership roles. They often become engineers, computer systems analysts, consultants, inventors, lawyers, planners, developers, politicians, and troubleshooters. They enjoy the challenge and learning involved in science, research, teaching, and investigation roles. Technology is an area of interest because of the rapid change and development in that field.

Logical Explorers like to work within the "big picture" and want to implement their visions across traditional departments and functions. They set up new systems and models, sometimes gambling their work security on the results of their vision. As a consequence, at their best, they can be powerful leaders and visionaries, creating complex and multifaceted projects. One Logical Explorer notes,

"I need freedom to determine the scope of my project. I inevitably expand the scope rather than restrict it. However, one of my challenges is to limit my projects rather than try to impact everything at once."

CONVINCE OTHERS

Logical Explorers enjoy roles that allow them to negotiate. They are also very persuasive and do well in investing careers, public relations, sales, and marketing. They will seek environments in which independent problem solving is encouraged. One Logical Explorer describes his favorite work activity as leading a small group of four to eight people discussing a situation, problem, or issue:

"I love to debate issues and brainstorm solutions. I feel that my strength is bringing together and integrating the input of the group members."

Logical Explorers often develop precise speech and debating ability. This allows them to explain and defend their visions and to convince others of the correctness of their solutions.

VALUE INDEPENDENCE AND COMPETENCE

Logical Explorers enjoy working with others who are independent and competent. They are more likely than Compassionate Explorers to become managers and leaders. Relating well to others, direct and unpretentious, Logical Explorers are quick to learn the importance of incorporating a values-based component into their interpersonal communications. One Logical Explorer comments,

"I like to throw light on the problem, not heat."

He goes on to relate how he has learned to listen to and appreciate the perspectives of others and uses this information to help make his decisions. Logical Explorers see the importance of values and situational factors and incorporate these aspects as a part of their systemic approach.

Logical Explorers focus on competition, strategies, knowledge, and competency, and they will develop skills that enhance these areas. They expect and value expertise and competence both from themselves and from those around them. Their success is determined by their ability to solve problems, so any skills that facilitate successful problem solving are valued and developed.

Autonomy is a key motivator for Logical Explorers. They will strongly resist being told what to do and how to do it. They want to independently align their efforts to a greater vision, personally carving out a meaningful piece that will impact their organization as a whole.

· 91 ·

SEEK CHALLENGE

Logical Explorers enjoy working in environments that reward competition, drive, and performance. They enjoy challenges and new experiences. Others may perceive them as confrontational because they like to challenge and be challenged. Sometimes they take risks, either physical or psychological, as a way to add challenge to their work. They enjoy improvising and maneuvering. For the Logical Explorer, risk taking extends to the world of ideas as well as the physical realm.

Snapshot: Ideal Work Environment for Logical Explorers

By focusing on your personal preferences, you will be able to better assess the types of work that will be personally satisfying. The following list describes the ideal work environment for Logical Explorers. Check off the items that are true for you.

As a Logical Explorer, I prefer a work environment that

☐ Is abstract and conceptual

☐ Is calm and rational

☐ Provides challenge

☐ Is project oriented

☐ Is focused on solving problems

☐ Employs strategic planning

☐ Uses logical thinking skills

Snapshot: Skills and Valued Activities for Logical Explorers

By focusing on your personal preferences, you will be able to better assess the types of work that will be personally satisfying. The following list describes the skills and valued activities of Logical Explorers. Check off the items that are true for you.

As a Logical Explorer, I value the following skills and activities:

- ☐ Adapting
- ☐ Communicating
- ☐ Creating
- ☐ Debating
- ☐ Designing
- ☐ Inventing
- ☐ Logical analysis
- ☐ Persuading
- ☐ Precision of speech
- ☐ Problem solving
- ☐ Systems thinking

Work That Attracts Logical Explorers

The following occupations are of interest to Logical Explorers. When looking for career ideas, remember also to look at the work options listed for Explorers earlier in the chapter, which are attractive to both Logical Explorers and Compassionate Explorers.

SCIENCE PROFESSIONALS
Biologist
Chemical engineer
Engineer
Mechanical engineer
Physician
Psychiatrist
Researcher or investigator

Logical Explorers often work as professionals in areas that require depth of information and an analytical approach. If you have an interest in completing an academic program and you enjoy solving complex problems, these careers may be of interest to you.

TRADES AND TECHNOLOGY

Computer programmer
Computer specialist
Computer systems analyst
Construction worker
Developer
Electrician

Trades and technology occupations often use the same logical, problem-solving approach as the careers listed in the previous section. Although you can take university courses in computer science, occupations in the technical and trades area can often be entered with shorter technical training or on-the-job experience. If you are a good troubleshooter and you like lots of variety, you may find a career in trades and technology satisfying.

LEADERSHIP

Consultant
Executive
Manager
Political analyst
Politician

Many Logical Explorers want to create and share visions. Within organizations they often take on positions of leadership. If you like strategic planning and are interested in managing people and projects, leadership might be a good career direction.

PROVIDING SERVICES

Attorney
Corrections and probation officer
Investment counselor
Planner
Public relations specialist
Salesperson

Logical Explorers work in a wide range of services that require independent thinking and problem solving. These occupations allow Logical Explorers to use their negotiation and communication skills in a variety of contexts.

Logical Explorers as Leaders

Logical Explorers bring unique strengths to the leadership role. They will naturally lead and prefer to be led in a specific way.

VISIONARY

Logical Explorers are visionaries; creating and sharing their vision is a key part of their leadership role. They can become totally immersed in projects that will actualize their vision, approaching them with great energy and excitement. They assume that others will be inspired to work independently toward projects or goals with the same end in mind.

INDEPENDENT

Logical Explorer visions are often based on a need to analyze and solve problems or to improve processes or systems. Logical Explorers can become frustrated when trying to lead in environments that are either too directive or lacking in vision. They want control over their piece of a project. Logical Explorers seek independence as a way to efficiently complete tasks. One Logical Explorer explained how she leads and likes to be led with the following analogy:

"I need a general reference point or goal and then autonomy to get there. If we need to go to the moon, I can get there. Just tell me that's where you want to go, and leave me to my own devices. But I can't function efficiently if you just say you want me to go somewhere."

Logical Explorers value others who are quick to see, share, and develop ideas. They want followers who can, on their own, efficiently and competently complete pieces of work that tie into the overall vision, goal, or project. A source of great satisfaction for someone with this leadership approach is getting his or her people to a place where they can see problems as opportunities. Some followers like this hands-off leadership approach, but others, with different approaches to working, feel that more concrete direction or instruction from a leader would be helpful.

ANALYTICAL AND TO THE POINT

Logical Explorers take in and organize information from many sources. As leaders they communicate using logical, analytical language and are precise and to the point. They are not likely to look to others for feedback, instead using their internal logic and analysis to guide their progress. They may not take the time to explain all the details of their visions, rather giving an outline and a few major components. Some followers may not receive enough information to understand the rationale behind actions and decisions and may have trouble "buying in."

Logical Explorer leaders do not like to repeat themselves and fail to see the need for being overly encouraging or giving positive feedback. They prefer to deal with problems using logic rather than emotion or empathy. To some other types, this approach can seem critical, indifferent, or uninvolved.

Logical Explorers tend to be skeptical and questioning. They trust and use logical analysis as they strive for knowledge and insight. They like to work with abstract and complex problems and opportunities, finding or creating innovative solutions and actions. They also highly value competence in themselves and others. They judge others on their competency, knowledge, and ability to generate innovative ideas.

FLEXIBLE

Logical Explorers are constantly taking in new information and shifting their mental models to fit the data. They consider, discuss, and play with alternative solutions that may seem in direct opposition to each other. While Logical Explorers are simply speculating about possibilities, those whom they lead may find it difficult to understand and align with the ever-changing perspectives. Logical Explorers like to reframe problems as opportunities. As a result, at times, those working under them may be unsure and confused about which direction to take.

Snapshot: Logical Explorers as Leaders

By focusing on your personal preferences, you will be able to better assess the types of work that will be personally satisfying. The following list describes the leadership preferences of Logical Explorers. Check off the items that are true for you.

As a Logical Explorer leader, I prefer to

- ☐ Create and share my vision
- ☐ Assume others will be inspired to work
- ☐ Seek independence and control
- ☐ Work with others who are quick to see, share, and develop ideas
- ☐ Analyze
- ☐ Communicate precisely and to the point
- ☐ Use my internal logic and analysis to guide my progress

- ☐ Deal with problems using logic rather than emotion or empathy
- ☐ Strive for knowledge and insight
- ☐ Solve abstract and complex problems
- ☐ Find or create innovative solutions and actions
- ☐ Judge others on their competency and knowledge
- ☐ Play with alternative solutions
- ☐ Reframe problems as opportunities

Logical Explorers as Team Members

Logical Explorers contribute to a team when they are able to design strategies to solve problems or capitalize on opportunities. They value team contributions, as long as the team is focused and working toward a goal or completion of a project. They like to get things moving and will often initiate action. They are likely to be tolerant of diversity, although they may be intolerant of those who are not competent or not meeting the expected standards. Team members who are rule bound or slow to change can frustrate them.

Logical Explorers can be good at motivating others, but they also can become impatient with spending what they think is unnecessary time explaining their rationale to others. At times their communications can be overly task oriented rather than people focused.

Snapshot: Logical Explorers as Team Members

By focusing on your personal preferences, you will be able to better assess the types of work that will be personally satisfying. The following list describes how Logical Explorers like to work within a team. Check off the items that are true for you.

As a Logical Explorer team member, I

☐ Contribute strategies to solve problems or capitalize on opportunities

☐ Value team contributions, as long as the team is focused and working toward a goal

☐ Like to get things moving

☐ Often initiate action

☐ Am tolerant of diversity

☐ Am intolerant of those who are incompetent

☐ Get frustrated by team members who are rule-bound or slow to change

☐ Am good at motivating others

☐ Become impatient with spending unnecessary time explaining my rationale

Logical Explorers as Learners

Logical Explorers engage both their interest in new ideas and their focus on the logical when learning. They love to debate and analyze ideas and naturally critique and evaluate information. Instructors who are not experts will quickly be dismissed as the Logical Explorer questions and challenges their knowledge. Incompetence will not be tolerated in someone in a teaching role, and the Logical Explorer will quickly disengage from the learning process.

Logical Explorers enjoy experimenting with and learning about theories and models. They may not attend to the facts or details, but they easily capture ideas and relationships between ideas. They enjoy playing with words as ways to capture ideas, and they often debate the fine meanings and implications of words and concepts. Since competency is key to this way of working, Logical Explorers are always seeking ways to learn more and expand their knowledge base.

> ### Snapshot: Logical Explorers as Learners
>
> *By focusing on your personal preferences, you will be able to better assess the types of work that will be personally satisfying. The following list describes the learning preferences of Logical Explorers. Check off the items that are true for you.*
>
> As a Logical Explorer learner, I
>
> ☐ Am an adaptable generalist
> ☐ Like to be stimulated by ideas
> ☐ May avoid routine learning tasks
> ☐ Can debate all sides of an issue
> ☐ Need complexity to stay interested
>
> ☐ May have trouble following through
> ☐ Am assertive and questioning
> ☐ Am independent
> ☐ Need an expert and competent teacher

THE EXPLORER'S GREATEST CHALLENGES

Everyone has less-preferred activities and areas for growth and improvement. Explorers are no exception. Here are three major developmental areas for both Compassionate Explorers and Logical Explorers, with tips on how to develop each one.

Managing Time and Tasks: Focusing on Facts and Details

Theories and possibilities are much more exciting to Explorers than reality. As a result, Explorers dislike work that requires them to attend to reality and to specific facts and details. They can have difficulty carrying out routine and sequential tasks, from which they are readily distracted. They procrastinate or avoid completing these types of activities. They can also easily find themselves disorganized with details, having trouble finding resources and pieces of paper they need, since organizing and filing information is not their strength. This lack of reality testing and disorganization can be a serious drawback. The results can be disorganized filing systems, missing paperwork, and a stressful last-minute frenzy to complete tasks.

One Explorer human resources manager was notorious for being too busy and disorganized to answer e-mail or voice messages. Employees began grumbling that she was unapproachable. She became distressed because she wanted to meet her employees' needs. The human resources manager finally surrendered her scheduling to an associate. Together they map out her fixed time commitments, and then requests are prioritized and, when possible, delegated.

Explorers can also get into trouble by taking on more than they can practically handle. They are drawn to new projects and can easily envision the successful results. Finding attention to details tedious, Explorers may not map out details before committing to tasks and projects. In their enthusiasm, they commit to the project only to find, after the fact, that accomplishing it entails more time and energy than they have available.

Explorers often experience stress in their last-minute rush to attend to the details. In the bigger picture, this lack of reality testing and attending to details can create situations where Explorers greatly underestimate the time and energy necessary for their projects or miss such significant practical information that their projects need to be refocused or redesigned. They may end up frustrated, overcommitted, and overwhelmed.

Explorers can lose credibility and have difficulty marketing their ideas to others when they lack the details to back up their proposals and ideas. Their ideas can be seen as impractical, or pie in the sky, by those with other ways of working. One Explorer describes his development in the following way:

"I used to 'wing it' more often when presenting my ideas. I have learned to do my homework and carry out more research and investigation. I now bring the numbers and details with me to meetings to back up my ideas."

Being a Compassionate Explorer, he also is learning to present his ideas with more logic and less passion.

TIPS FOR MANAGING TIME AND TASKS

- Compensate by having someone else manage details rather than trying to manage them yourself. Ask assistants, partners, or colleagues to take organizing or detail roles in your projects. Many Explorers learn to hire people who are good with details as an essential coping strategy.
- Delegate and prioritize your tasks and commitments. Remember that saying yes to something automatically results in saying no to something else.
- Teach yourself to estimate time more accurately. Perhaps estimate how long a small project will take you. Then be observant. Note what details you missed and see how far off your estimate was. Try again with your next project, revising your estimating process using what you have learned.

- Recognize when you are procrastinating. Learn to pay attention to details before they pile up and create a last-minute rush to a deadline.
- Keep your goals and dreams in mind as you plod through the details. Relate the mundane tasks to the "big picture."
- Devise your own system to manage time and organize materials. Traditional time-management strategies seem to be written by those with Sensing and Judging preferences and are often too inflexible and structured for Explorers. However, do incorporate some of the basics such as making lists, setting deadlines, and rewarding yourself for completing your task.
- Accept that you do prefer to complete tasks in a last-minute rush, and make sure to plan extra time at the end of a project to accommodate your way of working. As much as possible, let yourself play when you can and work when you are inspired.

Developing Patience: Reflecting and Listening

Explorers may get into trouble when they share their many ideas without reflecting on and evaluating them. Others may misinterpret their stream of consciousness, verbalizations, and quick idea-generation as premature or disorganized thoughts. Also, because they play verbally with opposing viewpoints and "what if" scenarios, they can seem highly changeable and unpredictable. Their input can seem critical as well as ungrounded in the current realities.

This problem can be exaggerated if Explorers become impatient when they are unable to move toward their vision. Often they want to make sweeping changes of a broad scope but find that the effort is great and the speed of progress slow. They are especially frustrated with procedures, bureaucracy, and red tape that, in their mind, serve no useful purpose.

A Compassionate Explorer shared that one of her biggest lessons as a teacher was to learn to let silence happen in her classroom:

"My initial teaching approach was to ask a question, wait a few seconds, and, if there was no response, fill the silence with an answer or another question. After I learned about my preferences, I realized that I might not be allowing time for processing and reflection of the concepts. Now I ask a question and wait for an answer, which usually comes several seconds after I would have gone ahead. My classroom is much richer because of the greater level of interaction."

Explorers can feel stifled in organizations that do not change quickly. They may see the standard operating procedures as blocks to their progress. Explorers do not have a need to conserve and preserve the old ways and realities. This, coupled with the fact that their ideas are often ahead of their time, makes the change process too tedious for their liking. One Logical Explorer explains that he finds great comfort in the concept of critical mass:

"I know now that when enough people are on board with an idea, then it can start to move forward. Years ago, I would get extremely frustrated when it took almost a year to move an idea forward. Now I put my creative energy into slowly building support and acceptance of ideas on a long-term basis. I have learned to position my ideas carefully and work at a speed that the organization will accommodate."

Other Explorers may become dissatisfied or leave organizations that are slow to act. They may start their own businesses or work in more change-oriented cultures.

TIPS FOR DEVELOPING PATIENCE
- Listen to others. This will help ground your ideas in the current realities and also allow you to understand other viewpoints.
- Especially listen to the viewpoints of those who like to conserve and work with the current realities. This will help you recognize the degree of investment there is in the old ways. It can also help you find links and continuity between the old and the new. You can then use these links to help others accept change and move forward.
- Think about your audience before you speak. Remember that some types prefer straight talk and can get lost and frustrated if they must interpret metaphors and symbolic language.
- Try silence. Allow pauses in conversations. Others may need time to process your new and innovative ideas.
- Remember that your ideas are on the cutting edge. Accept that it will take time for others to get on board.

Paying Attention to the Here and Now
Explorers are dynamic, future-oriented change agents. When working in their inspired mode, they can become so caught up in a project that they neglect their physical needs for a healthy diet, exercise, and time off. They can become exhausted and unhealthy. As well, their trusted ability to generate ideas can, at its worst, create so many options that Explorers become overwhelmed and

unfocused. Explorers need to learn when ideas are impractical and when their mind or body needs a break.

If Explorers fail to find strategies to regenerate, they can lose their energy and enthusiasm. Even so, they find it hard to stop thinking about their projects. One Explorer describes her challenge this way:

"I'll go have a steam bath, wanting to relax, but I inevitably end up thinking about something else. My mind automatically seems to move into the future. I find that getting involved in performing in a play can really get me grounded in the here and now because I need to focus."

This is perhaps the hardest development step for Explorers: to learn to pay attention to their immediate environment and become more practical. They must recognize that inspiration needs to be balanced with an understanding and appreciation of their physical needs and limitations.

If Explorers do not develop this practical focus, they may find themselves out of balance, constantly seeking new ideas, people, and possibilities in an irresponsible, disorganized manner. Explorers need to learn to consider and incorporate details into their visions rather than either ignoring or being overwhelmed by them. Some Explorers learn to depend on partners or colleagues to help them in this regard, wheras others develop skills in this area directly.

Many Explorers in midlife also begin to consciously learn to pay more attention to and appreciate the physical world. Their focus on future rewards and accomplishments begins to blend with a more practical and present focus. They learn to enjoy spending time alone and to set aside time both to take care of themselves and to experience their environment. A Logical Explorer describes how, in his forties, he has begun to pay attention to the physical world:

"I am taking time to paint and draw as a way to teach myself how to spend time in the here and now. When trying to capture an image, I am forced to slow down and really look at things. At first I was impatient with the activity. Many of my initial drawings went right into the garbage. However, over time I have found myself to be much more grounded and observant. I can create quite accurate and detailed images now."

There are no specific timelines and deadlines for moving through development. Some individuals find that they naturally are interested in evolving over time. Others find that they need to make a concentrated effort to assess and develop their less-preferred approaches. No matter what their developmental stage or situation, Explorers may find it enlightening to take time alone to focus on their senses and pay attention to the details in their immediate environment without making links or inferences.

TIPS FOR PAYING ATTENTION TO THE HERE AND NOW

- Attend to the physical basics: healthy diet, sleeping, and regular exercise. The earlier Explorers notice that their physical limits are being stretched, the less likely they are to experience physical exhaustion and associated illnesses.
- Explorers may also find it helpful, although challenging, to learn to stop and "smell the roses," to take time to literally enjoy the environment and sensory experiences.
- Exercises such as journaling and meditation can help Explorers learn to reflect and attend to their inner world and help them see how their work is affecting their body.
- Pursuing creative leisure activities, such as writing, performing, and creating artwork, can be a satisfying change from the Explorer's work commitments.

Is managing time and tasks, developing patience, or attending to the here and now a challenge for you? If so, which of the strategies explored in this chapter would be helpful to try? ....

....

....

....

....

....

....

....

KEY FOR ME: MANAGING MY CHALLENGES

FINAL TIPS FOR EXPLORERS: DOING WHAT COMES NATURALLY

An Explorer naturally approaches the world of work in an open and exploratory way. Here are a few final tips that will help you choose and develop satisfying work.

Embrace Change

Explorers naturally embrace career development. They are change oriented and can easily visualize new ideas and options. Find books, inventories, and tests that help you learn about yourself. Career-planning materials that provide general guidelines, integration of information, and theoretical interpretations will be more helpful than quick surveys or prescriptive tools. Seek out people to talk to and things to do that allow you to discuss and try out new ideas.

To satisfy needs for personal growth and variety, look for ways to change your positions and duties. This can be within an organization, moving between organizations, or in a self-employment environment. Work options should allow opportunities for personal development, ideally in multiple areas. It is not unusual for an Explorer's career path to have a wide variety of projects and responsibilities. Look for opportunities to change, learn, and develop within your environment.

Be Flexible

Explorers are by nature interested and successful in a wide range of work environments and will value opportunities to innovate and initiate. Focus on a career path rather than a specific choice of work. Your quick grasp of ideas and possibilities allows you to find links and connections between separate fields of endeavors. You will tend to do your best career research when you focus on how various jobs and tasks can interrelate and overlap. A focus on transferable skills and interests can help you see a wider range of possibilities.

Consider Becoming Your Own Boss

Explorers are well suited to entrepreneurship because of their vision and adaptability. Explore self-employment as a possibility. Many Explorers choose self-employment in their own business, contract work, or consulting as ways to minimize or avoid the structure, politics, and policies that can slow them down in more formal working relationships.

Explorers can easily identify many business opportunities. They often enjoy an extensive network of contacts and like to share ideas. They are enthusiastic marketers when they are passionate about their endeavors. However, as entrepreneurs, they do face the challenges of creating a workable structure and dealing with details while working within their creative and flexible preferences.

Track Your Accomplishments

You may not always have the formal education or certification to back up your competencies. It may be important for you to track your progress and skill development through a portfolio or set of annotated references. You may need to find creative ways to show people what you can do.

Get the Facts

Explorers need to make sure they get the facts. Overcommitment can be a serious problem since Explorers can easily see possibilities but may not focus on the practical facts and details. They will often say yes to just about anything they can envision but may not fully recognize the scope of what they have committed to, since they have not stopped to map out the details and test reality. Decide whether time and task management are problem areas for you. If they are, develop strategies in these areas.

Learn to Reflect and Relax

It is helpful for Explorers to find ways to reflect. Use a journal or another means to record your thoughts and feelings. Explorers can neglect these internal sources of information, especially in the early stages of their career development. Find ways to develop your reflection, listening, and patience. As well, learn to live in the present and take time to enjoy what *is,* rather than what might be.

Now that you have learned about your work preferences, please turn to Chapter 11 to begin planning your career path.

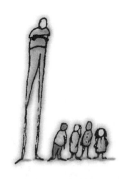

CHAPTER FIVE

Expeditors
Direct and Decide

PERSONALITY TYPES: ESTJ AND ENTJ

As a financial counselor, I enjoy helping others organize their financial affairs, make decisions, and take action that will lead to an improved financial situation. I enjoy working with budgets and finding ways to help people manage their money more effectively—An Expeditor

The latest research shows that 10.5 percent of adults in the United States are Expeditors. Expeditors approach the world primarily through logical analysis and decision making. They like to evaluate information and are at their best when they are directing or organizing people, events, or ideas. They are stimulated to establish cause-and-effect relationships and connections between things. Using logical decision making as a guide, Expeditors quickly analyze situations, decide on the best course of action, and take immediate steps based on their conclusions. They are often focused on implementing or improving things. Expeditors are task oriented and work in a highly efficient manner. They like to take charge and mobilize others.

EXPEDITORS AT WORK
What Expeditors Do Naturally

USE LOGIC AND ANALYSIS

Because Expeditors prefer to approach the world through the use of logical thinking, they are often skilled in analysis and can quickly point out flaws and inconsistencies. They are able to approach problems calmly and objectively, with a clear focus, and make decisions quickly.

Expeditors can be quite skeptical and are not likely to be fooled easily. They want to see clear and logical evidence before they will accept anything. Reason, rather than opinion or passion, best convinces them. Expeditors are likely to ask questions and challenge others' opinions and conclusions. They find debate and argument helpful ways to process information.

Occupations that require quick thinking and decision making are of interest to Expeditors. They prefer work that allows them to analyze and evaluate. You will find Expeditors in scientific occupations such as engineering, research, computer operations, and systems analysis. One Expeditor physician describes his logical analysis and quick decision making as his greatest strengths in emergencies:

"I walk into the emergency room and automatically begin to consider and discard possible explanations for the symptoms until I come up with a diagnosis. My mind automatically shifts into algorithm mode, quickly hypothesizing possible causes until I can make a diagnosis. Rapidly and efficiently, I then mobilize all the staff to deal immediately with the problem."

DECIDE AND ACT

Expeditors are often found in leadership and management roles. They do not hesitate to tell people what they should be doing and are clear and frank in the direction they provide. Because they are so decisive and action oriented, they find inefficiency frustrating. They will make sure to set things into action and move projects forward. Expeditors are able to make and stand by tough decisions, keeping the end goal in mind. They will find and use the resources they need to get the job done. Having an Expeditor in charge will ensure that the job is completed on time and meets high standards. One Expeditor comments,

"I think that most people are indecisive and want someone to be the quarterback. I like to take the quarterback role and act quickly and efficiently."

RESPONSIBLE, STRUCTURED, AND PRINCIPLED

Expeditors prefer to work within well-defined rules and principles. One Expeditor comments,

"What is most important to me is to work within an organization that provides structure and clear expectations. Once I know exactly what is expected of me, I want to have the autonomy and authority to go ahead and get my work done."

Expeditors immediately and easily link their rules and principles to their current situations and apply them responsibly. They are strongly driven by a sense of right and wrong and often see things as either black or white. They can apply principles without becoming distracted by the subjective aspects of a situation. For some Expeditors, principles are a major factor in their career satisfaction. As one Expeditor puts it,

"The one key thing for me in a job is moral grounding. I could not work at something that violates my principles. For example, I wouldn't want to defend the guilty."

Expeditors value working in environments that provide structure. They are often most satisfied in traditional organizations that provide a hierarchical approach to advancement. Since they are often high achievers, they will tend to move up the advancement ladder in these types of organizations and assume leadership positions.

Expeditors frequently have their own businesses. They usually start their businesses fairly formally, rather than casually, creating the structure and processes they prefer. They are often found in the consulting occupations, especially in the area of management consulting.

GET RESULTS

Expeditors naturally prefer to keep order and complete tasks, which results in well-developed time- and task-management strategies. They are good at planning, delegating, and completing projects. They strive to make sure deadlines are set and met. They often have their time tightly booked and are highly productive.

Their need for action, their decisive approach, and their logical task analysis all provide Expeditors with the tools to quickly produce results. Expeditors will do what they need to do to get the job done. They are conscientious and can be counted on to follow through and complete tasks by their deadlines.

Others can interpret Expeditors' task orientation and emphasis on processes and procedures as a disregard for the people who are affected by the systems. Their objectivity in actions and communications can create an impression that they are cold and insensitive. However, although they may lose sight of the human elements as they focus on getting the job done, Expeditors are not indifferent to the people in a system; in fact, they will try to best serve people by creating or using efficient systems. One Expeditor leader describes this dilemma:

"When doing project work, I take charge and move the team efficiently toward its goals. I know the staff values my decisive nature. However, sometimes in meetings, when I approach interpersonal issues with the same no-nonsense approach, the staff is frustrated. I find it hard to understand what they want me to do in these circumstances."

Stereotypically, this analytical decision maker has been seen as a male, usually the male in power or authority. Female Expeditors may encounter resistance when they use a take-charge approach. This can be a struggle as they strive to express their natural way of working in a society that traditionally has seen only men in positions of control and authority. One female Expeditor describes her dilemma:

"I have always been very assertive and will always express my opinions strongly. I like to take charge. More than once this trait has gotten me into trouble. I have been labeled intimidating and controlling by my co-workers. I certainly don't intend to be controlling; I am simply trying to get the job done."

UPHOLD HIGH STANDARDS

Expeditors set and maintain high standards in their work and strive to ensure that those standards are met. They value competence and accountability, taking on responsibility and expecting others to do the same. Expeditors are always looking for ways to improve themselves and the processes and people around them. They see knowledge and learning as tools to help them be even more expedient in their work. This task-focused, results-oriented, hard-working, competency-driven approach is especially suited for leading and directing. As leaders, Expeditors expect high standards from others as well as themselves. As one Expeditor leader explains,

"I like to be given room to do things my way, and I want others to take the same ownership. However, before I can give others autonomy, I need to make sure that I can trust their skills, knowledge, abilities, and ethics."

Expeditor Blind Spots

VALIDATING AND APPRECIATING

Because they approach the world primarily through analysis, Expeditors tend to question, examine, criticize, and take a stand on issues. They especially enjoy debate and a full and frank discussion of ideas. Their communications tend to be task-oriented, direct, and to the point. While this method of communication is efficient, others may find it condescending or overly critical. Expeditors can be surprised to learn that their clear, calm feedback is often interpreted as cold, harsh, overly sarcastic, or verbally abrasive. They are at times even unaware of the reaction to their feedback until someone specifically mentions that it is a problem.

WORK BEFORE PLAY

Expeditors can be counted on to get the work done, effectively and promptly. To do this, they will work very hard and do whatever needs to be done. It is sometimes difficult for them to learn to relax. Even their play must be organized and, in some cases, goal driven. Many Expeditors find that they cannot relax until the work is all done, and they may miss opportunities to enjoy the moment. As well, their sense of responsibility and accountability leads them to assume many obligations. Expeditors may feel it is their responsibility to take charge, fix things, and find the answers. They can overload themselves with work and become stressed. One Expeditor comments,

"My biggest challenge is to learn to relax and go with the flow. Having kids has been a major learning experience for me. It is almost impossible to predict what will happen next. All my planning gets thrown right out the window. I find it very hard to let go of being in control of what is going on around me."

DECIDING TOO FAST

Their decisive approach to the world and focus on logical analysis leads Expeditors to make quick decisions. Once decisions are made, Expeditors are strongly driven to accomplish tasks to implement them and move toward the goal. They often become impatient when collecting additional data and reaching consensus with others; they may see such exploratory activities as unproductive, thinking that they are spinning their wheels and wasting their time. However, efficiency is not always equivalent to effectiveness. The Expeditor may head, much too quickly, in the wrong direction. Slowing down to thoroughly evaluate the situation can ensure that the Expeditor is making the best decision on how to wisely spend time and energy.

The same dilemma can occur when Expeditors are sharing their goals with others. They tend to tell others what to do, rather than taking the time to explain and engage others in their projects. Although this seems to be the most efficient short-term way to complete the project, in the long run, others may block or not support the efforts because they have not bought into the project.

Snapshot: Expeditors' Natural Work Preferences

Expeditors are at their best when they can use their natural work preferences. By focusing on your own preferences, you will be able to better assess the types of work that will be personally satisfying. The following list describes characteristics and preferences of Expeditors. Check off the items that are true for you.

As an Expeditor, I am at my best when I can

- ☐ Use logical analysis
- ☐ Solve problems
- ☐ Make decisions
- ☐ Act on my decisions quickly
- ☐ Direct, control, organize, and plan
- ☐ Work within or create structures and efficient processes
- ☐ Manage projects
- ☐ Work with competent, independent, and task-oriented co-workers
- ☐ Critique, discuss, or debate issues
- ☐ Set and meet deadlines
- ☐ Complete work efficiently

- ☐ Determine or apply rules and principles to situations
- ☐ Leave emotional and personal issues outside the work setting
- ☐ Ignore subjective factors
- ☐ Make black-and-white judgments
- ☐ Plan, delegate, and schedule tasks
- ☐ Provide direction to and evaluate others
- ☐ Accomplish results
- ☐ Complete work that meets high standards of quality
- ☐ Improve myself and others
- ☐ Work in a structured environment

WHAT'S KEY FOR ME?

My Ideal Work Preferences

Look back at the snapshot for the work preferences for an Expeditor. From the items you have checked, jot down the points that best summarize your preferences. Feel free to add points that are not on the list.

My most important work preferences are ....

....

....

....

....

....

....

....

....

WORK THAT ATTRACTS EXPEDITORS

Expeditors can be found in many different types of work. Here are some examples that use the Expeditor's natural way of working.

PROFESSIONAL AREAS

Accountant

Attorney

Dentist

Engineer

Judge

Nurse

Physician

School principal

Social worker

Teacher—technical

Expeditors like to take charge and often find it helpful to earn credentials. If you are attracted to academics, you may want to pursue a professional career. Such a career can provide the Expeditor with independence and decision-making authority. Each of these professions requires a different combination of skills, interests, and values. If you are interested in becoming a professional, you will need to evaluate which specific occupations are good matches for you.

DATA MANAGEMENT AND ANALYSIS

Analyst
Auditor
Banker
Computer analyst
Computer specialist
Credit investigator
Telecommunications worker

Many Expeditors work in data management and analysis. If you especially enjoy making logical analyses and managing details, these careers may suit you. Almost all industries and businesses have work that requires analysis of data and processes.

LEADERSHIP/MANAGING PEOPLE

Administrator—wide range of organizations
Corrections officer
Manager—wide range of organizations
Probation officer

Expeditors often move into leadership positions. If you like to take charge, such an occupation will provide you with opportunities to manage and organize people and projects. Leadership positions often initially flow out of experience in a specific field. Once you have developed leadership skills, you can apply your experience to leadership roles in different types of companies.

Of course, these are just some examples. There are many other types of work that Expeditors will enjoy. See the next sections for work that is specifically appealing to ESTJs and ENTJs.

HOW EXPEDITORS FIND BALANCE

Expeditors use analysis and decisiveness as their preferred approach to situations. They are most comfortable when they are making and acting on logical decisions based on their previous experiences. However, to be effective, they need to balance their decisive nature with an effective way of taking in new information.

There are two approaches Expeditors can use to take in information: attending to practical details and seeing possible patterns. Personality type theory calls these two approaches Sensing (S) and Intuition (N). You may want to look back to Chapter 2 to discern which approach is most comfortable for you. The words *sensing* and *intuition* have many connotations that do not really relate to how people take in information, so, to avoid misconceptions, in this book Expeditors who prefer Sensing as a way to take in information (ESTJs) are called Practical Expeditors, while Expeditors who prefer Intuition as a way to take in information (ENTJs) are called Insightful Expeditors. Practical Expeditors balance their tendency to act and decide with a focus on the current facts, details, and practical applications. They tend to initially work toward immediate results rather than systemic changes. Insightful Expeditors most naturally take in information as patterns and possibilities. They balance their logical decisiveness with input in the form of ideas and possibilities.

Each approach has a different focus, but both provide the Expeditor with additional information for decision making. These approaches are mostly used internally as Expeditors input information into their logical analysis. Over the course of their life, Expeditors will use and develop both approaches to take in information as they refine their decision making. This allows them to become more flexible and attend to different types of information over time. Both approaches help Expeditors generate new ideas, understand additional facts and details, and focus their career path. This balance, between evaluating ideas and identifying new facts and patterns, is a key development step for Expeditors.

As you go through this section, you may find it helpful to read your most natural balancing approach first. Then read about the other approach to balancing to see what is in store for you as you mature and develop.

☐ **I am most like ESTJ,**
so I am a Practical Expeditor.
I will initially balance my decisive
nature by focusing on facts and
details. As I mature and develop,
I will also learn to balance my
approach by focusing on patterns
and possibilities.

☐ **I am most like ENTJ,**
so I am an Insightful Expeditor.
I will initially balance my decisive
nature with a focus on ideas and
possibilities. As I mature and
develop, I will also learn to balance
my approach by focusing on facts
and details.

BALANCING EXPEDITING WITH PRACTICALITY

The latest research shows that about 8.7 percent of adults in the United States are Practical Expeditors (ESTJ). Practical Expeditors use concrete facts and immediate goals as inputs for their decisions and analysis. They prefer to solve immediate and tangible problems using a matter-of-fact, results-oriented approach. Adept at tracking, managing, and attending to facts and details, they are especially good at administering programs, processes, procedures, and projects. Although Practical Expeditors will find ways to make inefficient processes more efficient, they are more likely to maintain and implement things than to change them. They enjoy the smooth operation of standard procedures.

Because Practical Expeditors have a practical, detail-oriented focus as a balance to their decisive nature, they initially express their Expediting way of working differently than Insightful Expeditors do. However, Insightful Expeditors in midlife may find that these detail-oriented descriptions mirror the direction in which they are moving as they mature and develop.

What Practical Expeditors Do Naturally
ADMINISTRATE AND IMPLEMENT

Practical Expeditors like working toward concrete or practical results and define their goals and priorities realistically, clearly, and specifically. They can then work steadily toward meeting their goals by completing specific tasks. This approach allows them to be highly organized and efficient in their efforts. Practical Expeditors are usually skilled at obtaining and coordinating, in a timely fashion, all the resources necessary to complete a task or project. They often seek and enjoy administrative roles as ways to use their organized and detailed approach. They want the freedom and autonomy to act and take control of the task within their responsibility area. When given this opportunity and work environment, they can make things happen. As one Practical Expeditor explains,

"I enjoy doing the administrative tasks. I get a sense of satisfaction when things are on track and moving according to plan."

Practical Expeditors can be found in a wide range of activities that require management, implementation, or evaluation. Observation, attention to detail, and accuracy are common attributes of Practical Expeditors. They often engage in occupations that require organization of detailed data. Work in areas such as auditing, accounting, and data management is attractive to them. One Practical Expeditor describes her work as a contract manager:

"I enjoy managing many projects. It's rewarding to oversee people and to see results from the projects that succeed."

Practical Expeditors tend to see things as clearly black or white and are not comfortable with ambiguity or situational variances in decisions or actions. They like to follow and create clear rules and procedures that help get the job at hand done efficiently. Practical Expeditors hold to clear standards and live by them strictly. They are loyal, responsible, and often strongly tied to their community and the organizations they belong to.

PRESERVE THE STATUS QUO

Practical Expeditors like to work within and maintain a structured environment with clearly defined expectations. Past experiences provide a strong reference point for their current analysis and decision making. They respect and advocate tried-and-true methods, seeing stability in established routines and procedures. Standard operating procedures make sense to Practical Expeditors, and they will have very little patience for those who do not follow the rules. Redesigning and redefining are often seen as a waste of time and energy that could be better spent working the plan. Practical Expeditors prefer stability and predictability to change and uncertainty. They avoid taking risks when possible, preferring to work in organizations that are stable and in roles that are predictable. One Practical Expeditor has this to say about structure:

"I like structure and schedules to the point that I am lost without them. If they are not there, I will set them up."

Practical Expeditors work well when they are given clearly defined, tangible results to achieve. They collect information and reason, using a systematic, step-by-step manner. Their focus is on making the best of the existing systems and structures rather than questioning, redefining, or changing what already exists. Practical Expeditors want to use resources effectively and get the job done. They enjoy roles where they can directly and specifically help others by providing them with information or helping them complete forms, procedures, or routine and structured tasks.

As they develop, Practical Expeditors will begin to look at the patterns and possibilities along with the facts and details. They will learn to work more strategically toward longer-term goals. They will balance the here and now and their tangible accomplishments with a focus on more global results.

· 118 ·

GET THE JOB DONE
Practical Expeditors are very punctual and responsible and expect the same of others. They have a strong work ethic and will do whatever it takes to get the job done.

Follow-through and attention to detail are important to Practical Expeditors. Timelines, schedules, and meeting deadlines are of utmost importance to this type of leader, which may put pressure on both themselves and others. They expect others to be efficient and task-oriented and can be impatient with less steady work approaches.

Practical Expeditors dislike wasted time and unfocused effort. They see established traditions and rituals as useful social conventions and seldom engage in small talk or social niceties outside of these events. They focus their time on getting the job done. Practical Expeditors see the importance of combining efforts with others when working toward a goal. They are usually highly dependable and accountable.

Practical Expeditors set high standards for themselves and for others. They can sometimes take on too many responsibilities and may become overcommitted. Their high self-expectations can be stressful. One Practical Expeditor explains,

"I am usually very good at managing details. However, sometimes I get too busy. I find it very challenging to keep up with the details for the thousand and one things that need to be done. I am constantly trying to tie up all the loose ends."

Snapshot: Ideal Work Environment for Practical Expeditors

By focusing on your personal preferences, you will be able to better assess the types of work that will be personally satisfying. The following list describes ideal work environments for Practical Expeditors. Check off the items that are true for you.

As a Practical Expeditor, I prefer to

☐ Attend to and organize details

☐ Clearly define expectations, tasks, and results

☐ Establish standard operating procedures

☐ Attend to immediate and tangible tasks, products, and results

☐ Maintain the status quo

☐ Organize and manage tasks and people

☐ Experience practical interactions with others

☐ Work in a predictable and stable environment

Snapshot: Skills and Valued Activities for Practical Expeditors

By focusing on your personal preferences, you will be able to better assess the types of work that will be personally satisfying. The following list describes skills and activities valued by Practical Expeditors. Check off the items that are true for you.

As a Practical Expeditor, I value the following skills and activities:

☐ Administration of people, data, or projects

☐ Analysis

☐ Attention to detail

☐ Decision making

☐ Evaluation

☐ Observation

☐ Organizing

☐ Practical problem solving

☐ Reasoning

☐ Time and task management

Work That Attracts Practical Expeditors
The following occupations tend to be of interest to Practical Expeditors. When looking for career ideas, remember to also look at the work options for Expeditors listed earlier in the chapter which are attractive to both Practical Expeditors and Insightful Expeditors.

TRADES

Construction worker
Cook
Crafts worker
Farmer
General contractor
Steelworker

Practical Expeditors often enjoy work where they can produce a tangible product. If you enjoy being physically active and working toward a concrete goal, a career in the trades may be for you. Many of these occupations also allow you to work outside.

SERVICE PROVIDERS

Community health worker
Financial advisor
Funeral director
Government employee
Legal assistant
Medical professional or technician
Pharmacist
Public relations specialist
School-bus driver
Teacher—trade

Practical Expeditors are often organized and efficient service providers. If you enjoy contact with the public and organizing and coordinating day-to-day events or activities, you may want to consider these occupations.

LAW ENFORCEMENT AND SECURITY

Detective

Guard

Investigator

Law enforcement officer

Military officer

Park ranger

Security guard or consultant

Good at maintaining rules, Practical Expeditors often are drawn to careers in law enforcement and security. If you especially like structure and clearly defined roles, these careers may be suitable for you. Some of these occupations also provide opportunities to analyze and solve problems.

SALES

Insurance agent

Purchasing agent

Real estate agent

Salesperson

Some Practical Expeditors like to use their organizational abilities to sell or purchase goods. If you are handy at tracking practical details and you have an entrepreneurial side, you may find a career in sales suitable. Some of these occupations work on a commission basis. The Practical Expeditor, with lots of personal initiative and follow-through, will often be able to do well.

MANAGEMENT

Office manager

Project manager

Public official

Supervisor

No matter what career field you choose, you may find yourself attracted to management and administrative roles. These roles provide a wide range of opportunities to use your decisive nature and natural strength for organizing and dealing with multiple details.

Practical Expeditors as Leaders

Practical Expeditors bring unique strengths to the leadership role. They naturally lead and prefer to be led in a specific way.

TASK ORIENTED

Practical Expeditors are highly organized and task-oriented leaders. They have clearly developed plans, roles, and responsibilities for those they lead, and they expect that others will perform them as defined. When in charge, Practical Expeditors give clear, precise, and detailed instructions. Their efficiency is a major strength. If a Practical Expeditor is in charge of the project, you can count on its getting done well and on time.

CLEAR EXPECTATIONS AND FEEDBACK

When leading, Practical Expeditors are likely to have very clear standards and expectations. To a Practical Expeditor, clarity and specificity are the best ways to help others work effectively and independently.

Practical Expeditors are quick to point out any deviations or inaccuracies in the work of others; they can be critical if others do not fulfill their responsibilities or complete their share of the workload. They especially have difficulty understanding and will confront those who are nonconformists or who do not follow the rules or standard operating procedures. Poor planning on the part of others is another source of irritation for these leaders.

TRADITIONAL

Practical Expeditors see the usefulness of stability and belonging in an organization, and seek to maintain traditions and rituals. They are loyal and are strong contributors in an organization. They are most content to implement and follow rules and procedures rather than question or change them, especially if the rules and procedures are logical and useful. They value the traditional, hierarchical organizational system and see a practical usefulness in a clearly defined chain of command. They believe that leadership should be based on experience, respect, and authority. Practical Expeditors will not work well under a leader whom they perceive as not having these attributes.

Snapshot: Practical Expeditors as Leaders

By focusing on your personal preferences, you will be able to better assess the types of work that will be personally satisfying. The following list describes the leadership preferences of Practical Expeditors. Check off the items that are true for you.

As a Practical Expeditor, I prefer to

☐ Focus on the task at hand

☐ Be highly organized

☐ Have clearly developed plans, roles, and responsibilities

☐ Give clear, precise, and detailed instructions

☐ Provide clear standards, expectations, and feedback

☐ Point out any deviations or inaccuracies

☐ Confront those who do not follow the rules or standard operating procedures

☐ Maintain traditions and rituals

☐ Be loyal and a strong contributor to the organization

☐ Follow rules and procedures

☐ See practical usefulness in a clearly defined chain of command

Practical Expeditors as Team Members

Practical Expeditors like to belong to teams and are very loyal and cooperative team members. They gain a great sense of satisfaction when a group works toward and achieves a goal that requires shared contributions.

Work teams need to be functional and efficient, or Practical Expeditors may feel they are wasting their time. They work best with competent and efficient people with clearly defined levels of supervision. Practical Expeditors prefer to keep relationships on a professional level at work. They will not hesitate to share their opinions and adopt a take-charge approach when working on a team, especially if the team seems to be working too slowly or inefficiently.

Snapshot: Practical Expeditors as Team Members

By focusing on your personal preferences, you will be able to better assess the types of work that will be personally satisfying. The following list describes how Practical Expeditors like to work within a team. Check off the items that are true for you.

As a Practical Expeditor, I prefer to

☐ Work toward goals that require shared contributions

☐ Be loyal and cooperative

☐ Work on teams that are functional and efficient

☐ Work with competent and efficient people

☐ Have clearly defined levels of supervision

☐ Keep relationships on a professional level at work

☐ Share my opinions

☐ Take charge, especially if the team is working inefficiently

Practical Expeditors as Learners

As Practical Expeditors experience the world, they are constantly striving to control, organize, and accomplish tasks. They greatly value learning for the additional information and competencies it can provide. When learning, Practical Expeditors focus on obtaining facts and details. Memorization and logical analysis are learning strengths for them. At times, they may have difficulty seeing the big picture, and they will struggle if information is too ambiguous or theoretical. They can quickly become bored with theory that has no practical application.

Practical Expeditors want the facts presented in a logical, sequential, and practical framework. When information is not presented in this way, Practical Expeditors will need to reorganize it to make sense. Making order from disorder seems like a waste of time to them, and they will begin to doubt the competency of the writer or teacher who is not logical, sequential, and practical. They do well in structured learning environments with clear expectations.

Both types of Expeditors are quick to question ideas and facts. Practical Expeditors are especially interested in the accuracy and precision of the data given and will check to make sure the sources of the data are reliable. They enjoy debating and competing while learning and appreciate opportunities to discuss with others what they are learning.

Snapshot: Practical Expeditors as Learners

By focusing on your personal preferences, you will be able to better assess the types of work that will be personally satisfying. The following list describes the learning preferences of Practical Expeditors. Check off the items that are true for you.

As a Practical Expeditor, I prefer to learn in ways that

☐ Allow me to take control, organize, and accomplish tasks

☐ Help me attain new information and competencies

☐ Offer useful facts and details

☐ Lend themselves to memorization and logical analysis

☐ Make connections between theory and practical application

☐ Present facts in a logical, sequential, and practical framework

☐ Provide structure, order, and clear expectations

☐ Offer accurate and precise data

☐ Support debating and competing

☐ Provide opportunities to discuss what I am learning

BALANCING EXPEDITING WITH INSIGHT

The latest research shows that about 1.8 percent of adults in the United States are Insightful Expeditors (ENTJ).

Insightful Expeditors incorporate their internal vision of patterns and possibilities into their decision making. They like to build on and improve structures and systems, taking an objective, visionary, long-term, and strategic approach. This combination of preferences is especially useful for long-range goal setting and planning.

When working toward their vision, Insightful Expeditors are able to blend and attend to both short-term and long-term goals. Once they have developed a vision, they will energetically take the initiative to make sure it is realized, quickly creating and implementing a workable plan. Insightful Expeditors want to be in charge of the work being done and will direct others to complete the plan. Their career themes tend to focus on ways to logically organize, change, and develop systems, people, and processes.

Because Insightful Expeditors have a visionary, long-term focus as a balance to their decisive nature, they initially express their Expediting way of working differently than Practical Expeditors do. However, Practical Expeditors in midlife may find that these vision-based descriptions mirror the direction in which they are moving as they mature and develop.

What Insightful Expeditors Do Naturally
WORK WITH CHALLENGE AND COMPLEXITY

Insightful Expeditors like their work to be challenging and complex. They enjoy taking on multifaceted projects and are able to simultaneously manage myriad complex aspects efficiently. They can see the bigger picture and are especially engaged when they are managing a number of people working toward a strategic goal.

Insightful Expeditors look for ways to advance within organizations and especially enjoy being in positions of control. They are independent. They do not like being under the control of others and will question authority. If they must work for someone, that person must be competent and knowledgeable to gain the respect of the Insightful Expeditor. One Insightful Expeditor comments,

"I don't like being told what to do or how to do it."

Insightful Expeditors strive to develop their knowledge and competencies. They tend to see connections quickly and are impatient with others who do not. They are intensely focused on learning, and especially on integrating and synthesizing information.

IMPROVE SYSTEMS AND PROCESSES

Insightful Expeditors are focused on patterns rather than facts and details. Because of this, they like to be in charge of and improve systems and processes, and the improvements they seek will make the systems more efficient and organized. Processes and procedures will be valued and followed if they are logical and efficient; however, Insightful Expeditors will not hesitate to change any processes or procedures that lack these characteristics. They are not likely to take away the structures in place, but they will streamline or redesign them. They like to fine-tune what already exists.

Creating and working toward long-term visions is the domain of Insightful Expeditors. They are much more focused on improving and developing systems, models, and processes than are their Practical counterparts. They love the challenge of critiquing and evaluating in the global sense, finding ways to change old methods and develop new methods to do work effectively. One Insightful Expeditor describes the frustration inherent in getting others to look ahead:

"One of my biggest work challenges is getting people to see the long-range consequences of their actions. I can see so clearly where their current actions are taking them. Sometimes I feel like I have to wave my arms and yell, 'Hey, there's a cliff ahead. . . . Can you see it?'"

LEAD

Insightful Expeditors are often found in leadership positions, taking charge and being decisive and effective managers. They tend to be intolerant of incompetence and wasted effort and believe that everything can be improved. To accomplish this, they are constantly cutting waste and inefficiency and searching for ways to improve systems. They like to take control and delegate to others. They naturally lead and expect others to follow. Others may perceive them as overly critical or task oriented because of their intense project focus.

Expeditors take charge using clear, assertive, and direct communications. They are willing to make the tough decisions and stand by them. As one Insightful Expeditor puts it,

"You can count on me to communicate openly. If I see something that isn't right, I will call attention to it. It's important to put everything on the table and deal with it directly."

You will most often find Insightful Expeditors in leadership positions where they can have input into long-term, strategic planning. They prefer working within organizations that provide them with opportunities for advancement and increased leadership responsibility.

Opportunities to use logical analysis to solve problems will also attract Insightful Expeditors, especially when given freedom to make and act on decisions. As well, they prefer to work with other competent and goal-driven individuals, especially in a structured environment where achievement and independence are valued.

Snapshot: Ideal Work Environment for Insightful Expeditors

By focusing on your personal preferences, you will be able to better assess the types of work that will be personally satisfying. The following list describes the ideal work environment for Insightful Expeditors. Check off the items that are true for you.

As an Insightful Expeditor, I prefer a work environment that has

- [ ] Variety and complexity of tasks
- [ ] Opportunities for directing and organizing
- [ ] Opportunities for leadership and advancement
- [ ] Long-term planning and decision making
- [ ] Multifaceted problems to solve
- [ ] Opportunities to put vision into action

Snapshot: Skills and Valued Activities for Insightful Expeditors

By focusing on your personal preferences, you will be able to better assess the types of work that will be personally satisfying. The following list describes the skills and valued activities of Insightful Expeditors. Check off the items that are true for you.

As an Insightful Expeditor, I value the following skills and activities:

- [ ] Debating
- [ ] Decision making
- [ ] Designing
- [ ] Problem solving
- [ ] Logical analysis
- [ ] Long-range planning
- [ ] Persuading
- [ ] Using precise speech
- [ ] Expediting resources to meet long-range goals
- [ ] Achieving results
- [ ] Systems planning

Work That Attracts Insightful Expeditors

The following occupations tend to be of interest to Insightful Expeditors. When looking for career ideas, remember to also look at the work options for Expeditors listed earlier in the chapter, which are attractive to both Practical Expeditors and Insightful Expeditors.

PROFESSIONAL AREAS

Architect
Biologist
Chemist
Consultant—general, or in education, business, or management
Economics analyst
Electronics expert
Psychiatrist
Psychologist
Researcher
Scientist
Social scientist
Teacher—science, social science, university, English

As mentioned earlier, professional positions are often a choice for Expeditors. The Insightful Expeditor is especially drawn to the abstract and theoretical nature of a formal university education. If you enjoy academics, you may find these professions appealing.

ARTS AND DESIGN

Actor
Designer
Fine artist
Photographer

If you have an artistic flair, you may be suited to a career in arts and design, which will allow you to express your creativity. These occupations will provide you with opportunities to use your wealth of ideas. This is a very broad field; think about your specific skills and the media you enjoy working with.

BUSINESS

Corporate trainer
Executive
Financial planner
Franchise owner
Human resources positions
Marketing professional
Mortgage broker
Stockbroker
Sales manager

Often Expeditors are attracted to careers in business. As mentioned before, Expeditors are often found in a variety of management and administrative positions. These careers may be of interest to you if you have an entrepreneurial or leadership focus. The human resources and corporate training positions may suit you if you have a specific interest in organization development.

Insightful Expeditors as Leaders

Insightful Expeditors bring unique strengths to the leadership role. They naturally lead and prefer to be led in a specific way.

NATURAL LEADERS

As you have already seen, Insightful Expeditors are strongly drawn to leadership roles. Because they are task and goal oriented, they may be impatient with processes that seek consensus and agreement, preferring instead to lead through directing and controlling. Being highly independent themselves, they will organize the work into parts and then expect others to work independently and competently toward completion of the tasks. They are frustrated by incompetence and dependency, assuming that everyone is automatically task and deadline focused. Efficient and decisive, they will be sure to get the job done.

CHANGE AGENTS

Insightful Expeditors tend to be change agents who work well using the structure and resources provided within an organization. They are unlikely to thrive on risk taking. Their emphasis on results and accountability make them especially well-suited to move an organization forward, using and adapting the structures and systems that are already in existence. They will actualize their visions.

Snapshot: Insightful Expeditors as Leaders

By focusing on your personal preferences, you will be able to better assess the types of work that will be personally satisfying. The following list describes the leadership preferences of Insightful Expeditors. Check off the items that are true for you.

As an Insightful Expeditor leader, I prefer to

- ☐ Direct and control
- ☐ Work independently
- ☐ Organize the work into parts
- ☐ Let others work independently
- ☐ Work with competent people
- ☐ Assume that everyone is task and deadline focused

- ☐ Focus on tasks and goals
- ☐ Act as a change agent
- ☐ Emphasize results and accountability
- ☐ Move an organization forward
- ☐ Use and adapt structures and systems already in existence

Insightful Expeditors as Team Members

Insightful Expeditors contribute most to a team when they are able to analyze, organize, and solve problems. They value team contributions, as long as the team is focused and working toward a goal or completion of a project. They like to get things moving and will often initiate action. They are likely to be tolerant of diversity, although they may be intolerant of those who are not competent or not meeting their expected standards. Task completion is seen as the ultimate goal. Teamwork and collaboration are a means to the end and are not of value in themselves, unless they add efficiency to the process.

Insightful Expeditors can be good at motivating others, but they can also become impatient with spending what they think is unnecessary time explaining their rationale to others. Explaining things slows down the action and makes it harder to meet deadlines. So, at times, their communications can be overly task oriented rather than people focused. They are likely to take control of a team and direct rather than encourage or motivate others. It is more important to them to be deemed competent than to be popular. One Insightful Expeditor explains,

"I would rather be respected than liked."

Snapshot: Insightful Expeditors as Team Members

By focusing on your personal preferences, you will be able to better assess the types of work that will be personally satisfying. The following list describes how Insightful Expeditors like to work within a team. Check off the items that are true for you.

As an Insightful Expeditor team member, I

- ☐ Contribute most when analyzing, organizing, and solving problems
- ☐ Need the team to be focused and working toward a goal
- ☐ Like to get things moving
- ☐ Will often initiate action
- ☐ Am tolerant of diversity
- ☐ Am intolerant of incompetence
- ☐ See task completion as the ultimate goal
- ☐ Am good at motivating others
- ☐ Can become impatient explaining my rationale
- ☐ Am likely to take control of a team and direct
- ☐ Value being respected and deemed competent

Insightful Expeditors as Learners

Insightful Expeditors like to learn about theory and concepts. They enjoy learning and using precise words and ideas. They also enjoy complexity and are stimulated by the world of ideas and possibilities. They often argue semantics and seek opportunities for discussion and stimulating debate. Insightful Expeditors strongly value knowledge and competence and are usually motivated to stay current in their areas of expertise.

Insightful Expeditors need to understand the logical framework behind theories and ideas; information will be matched against the framework as they integrate facts with theory. They will be quick to question the information and will check the credibility of its source. Insightful Expeditors see staying current as an important expression of their competence. They want to ensure that the ideas they are learning are well validated and that their instructors are competent. Here is how one Logical Expeditor describes his learning preferences:

"I don't like to accept someone else's authority. I like to do direct research and draw my own conclusions. I always critically analyze what I see and hear."

Insightful Expeditors enjoy learning environments with clear expectations. However, once the expectations are made clear, they will want to control the learning situation as much as possible. They are organized and will set their own short- and long-term learning goals. They can be competitive learners and want to know exactly what they need to do to excel. In a classroom setting, they may focus on getting the highest marks.

Snapshot: Insightful Expeditors as Learners

By focusing on your personal preferences, you will be able to better assess the types of work that will be personally satisfying. The following list describes the learning preferences of Insightful Expeditors. Check off the items that are true for you.

As an Insightful Expeditor learner, I

- ☐ Like to learn about theory and concepts
- ☐ Enjoy learning and using precise words and ideas
- ☐ Am stimulated by complexity and the world of ideas and possibilities
- ☐ Like to argue semantics
- ☐ Seek opportunities for discussion and stimulating debate
- ☐ Can be a competitive learner
- ☐ Am quick to question the information

- ☐ Need to understand the logical framework behind the theories and ideas
- ☐ Will check the credibility of the information sources
- ☐ Ensure that instructors are competent
- ☐ Want clear expectations
- ☐ Want to control the learning situation as much as possible
- ☐ Am organized
- ☐ Set my own short- and long-term learning goals

THE EXPEDITOR'S GREATEST CHALLENGES

Everyone has less-preferred activities and areas for growth and improvement. Expeditors are no exception. Here are three major developmental areas for both Practical Expeditors and Insightful Expeditors, with tips on how to develop each one.

Empathizing and Collaborating

Because Expeditors are time and task focused, they may see the development of working relationships as blocks to effective task completion. Co-workers with different preferences may find this task-oriented focus overly impersonal. They may feel undervalued by interactions with Expeditors.

This communication style has an especially strong effect when the Expeditor is in a position of control over another person. The Expeditor may make good, logical decisions that are supported by a strong business case, and the course of action may be expedient and effective. However, it may adversely affect many individuals within the organization. An Expeditor may not focus at all on the personal side, and instead will see just the overall logical good of the decision. One Expeditor manager described how he dealt with this specific issue:

"I have learned to take the time to incorporate the more personal and situational factors, such as impact on specific people, into my decision-making framework. I add them in as additional variables to consider. I still have to remind myself that others will place a greater weight on these variables than I naturally would."

TIPS FOR EMPATHIZING AND COLLABORATING

- Take time to stop and understand the motivations and situations of others.
- Seek feedback on your communication style.
- Practice listening without judgment.
- Offer understanding rather than solutions when others share problems. Often people can find their own solutions. They may simply want to share their feelings and situation.
- Find opportunities to give positive feedback.
- Remember that some people find debate, arguments, and competition tiring and uncomfortable.

Keeping Options Open

Because Expeditors are eager to start on and complete tasks, they may jump to their decision without considering all the possible courses of action. A self-assured, decisive nature makes it difficult to access the skills of flexibility and adaptability.

To avoid inefficiency, Expeditors may choose to take action—any action—rather than be stuck in inactivity. This can be a problem when they are in career transition. They may be so focused on finding work immediately that they fail to take the time to assess themselves and their situation thoroughly. Making a quick career decision can start them down a path that may not be the best in the long term. This can especially be a problem for Practical Expeditors, who are more focused on immediate results than Insightful Expeditors are.

TIPS FOR KEEPING OPTIONS OPEN

- Take time to generate and consider more options than the obvious ones.
- Seek and consider additional input from others.
- Remember that efficiency does not always lead to effectiveness. Acting quickly may get the job done, but a more thorough, careful approach will get it done right.
- Wait a while before deciding.
- Plan to be spontaneous. (This concept may seem to be an oxymoron to other types.)

Using a Values-Based Decision-Making Approach

Expeditors at their best are logical and analytical. Their least-developed side is their sensitivity to and acceptance of a values-based approach. Expeditors may have difficulty accepting an emotional response or using Feeling judgment, since it may make them feel out of control and overly involved. The Feeling is seen as a block to or distraction from the thinking process and thus may be suspect. Because the Feeling approach is subjective and illogical, it is not easily classified or interpreted into the Expeditor's strongly trusted logical framework. Being strong minded and dominant can block the gifts of openness and vulnerability that come from the Feeling side. Expeditors can also fall out of touch with their personal values and needs, ignoring that which they cannot logically explain.

· 135 ·

Because Expeditors are strongly dependent on their logical decision-making abilities, they may consider the values-based decision-making process to be inadequate, unpredictable, and unreliable. Thus, they may not be able to tap into their emotional responses and subjective needs as easily as some other people can.

Expeditors may have difficulty interpreting nuances of emotions that are expressed by others. One Expeditor wanted to check her ability to read emotions in others:

"Throughout the day, upon meeting a person, within the first few minutes, I would say, 'You must be feeling . . . ' I then stated how I thought he or she was feeling, based on my quick assessment. At the end of the day I found I had misinterpreted people's feelings almost all of the time. I learned that I need to stop and check my perceptions."

This Expeditor noticed that she had gained considerable information about how the people really were feeling, which she would have completely missed in the past. Even their own personal responses can take Expeditors by surprise. When they become emotional, they can often feel out of control or off balance. These responses are very difficult for Expeditors, since they pride themselves and expend considerable energy on being in control.

Not focusing on values and the personal side of matters can also affect Expeditors' ability to offer positive feedback, which they may perceive as contrived. Overly positive reactions seem insincere to them, and Expeditors will comment that they are not quite sure how to offer positive feedback that is genuine. It goes against their natural need to critique and to offer clear, concise suggestions for improvement. Expeditors may miss critical feedback that is buried within positive feedback, thinking that the initial positive feedback indicates no need for adjustments. This is frustrating for the person giving feedback, who sought to first appreciate and then offer suggestions. These misinterpretations and misunderstandings in feedback are common issues between individuals with Thinking and Feeling decision-making preferences.

Expeditors do, of course, have emotions and values as much as any other type. They are often most comfortable expressing their values in actions. For example, they may be reliable providers for or teachers of their children, or they may take up coaching or other community work.

· 136 ·

TIPS FOR USING A VALUES-BASED DECISION-MAKING APPROACH

- Test your thoughts about emotions. Ask people how they are feeling, and then listen carefully. Compare what you hear with your internal sense of what emotions you thought they were expressing.
- Assess the effects of your decisions on others. Especially consider what others will like or dislike, and how they will feel.
- Look for values and personal factors that underlie the decisions of others. Consider how a values-based decision is another rational way of looking at the world. The decisions make sense when the values are understood.
- Weigh options in a decision using personal subjective beliefs and values, as well as logical pros and cons.

KEY FOR ME: MANAGING MY CHALLENGES

Is empathizing and collaborating, keeping options open, or using a values-based decision-making approach a challenge for you? If so, which of the strategies explored in this chapter would be helpful to try?

....

....

....

....

....

....

FINAL TIPS FOR EXPEDITORS: DOING WHAT COMES NATURALLY

An Expeditor naturally approaches the world in an analytical and directive way. Here are a few final tips that will help you choose and develop satisfying work.

Analyze and Decide

Expeditors demonstrate a natural strength in logical analysis and decision making. Find opportunities to use this strength. Many types of work require analysis and interpretation of data, either at the fact or the pattern level. Analysts, decision makers, and evaluators are needed in a wide range of industries.

It is important to recognize your need for closure. Often Expeditors take any work offered, simply to be working toward and accomplishing goals. This, coupled with a strong sense of responsibility, may lead them into jobs that are less than ideal. Keep your options open, at least for a short while, as you move through transitions.

Use Your Organizational Skills

Expeditors are highly effective at accomplishing whatever they set their minds to. This task-oriented strength helps them as they move through the career planning or job search process. Expeditors looking for work are good at using lists, making contacts, and following through. These characteristics give them an advantage over less-organized career seekers.

Find Your Comfort Zone

There are no right or wrong careers for any way of working. However, people tend to be more satisfied doing work in which they can use their natural approach. Expeditors' strength is in their ability to plan, organize, and accomplish. Make sure that the work you take on provides you with opportunities to engage in these activities. Leadership or administrative responsibilities are also key areas of comfort and satisfaction for Expeditors.

Add a Feeling Side to Your Decision-Making Approach

Accessing and appreciating a subjective and personal side to decision making will be a developmental growth area. This side, when integrated into your strong, logical framework, will allow you to make well-rounded decisions. Learn to focus more on the personal and emotional components of your life. Integrate personal values and situational variables into your logical mode of thinking.

Many Expeditors in midlife begin to consciously get in touch with their emotions and personal values. Reflective exercises such as keeping a journal can help you to stop, value, and appreciate this "softer" side. Some Expeditors explore and become more interested in finding greater personal meaning in their life. An increased interest in the spiritual and intangible may become a focus as they explore their values and personal needs.

Let Go Sometimes

An Expeditor cannot always be in control. Things happen that are outside of an individual's ability to control or even influence. A learning challenge for Expeditors is to relinquish their strong sense of responsibility during these times. No matter what their developmental stage or situation, Expeditors may find it enlightening to take time alone to focus on their senses and pay attention to the details in their immediate environment without analyzing them. As they mature, Expeditors will benefit from learning to let go of some decision making, control, and sense of responsibility and enjoy unexpected moments.

Now that you have learned about your work preferences, please turn to Chapter 11 to begin planning your career path.

CHAPTER SIX

Contributors
Communicate and Cooperate

PERSONALITY TYPES: ESFJ AND ENFJ

I bring a love of people and learning to my work as an elementary school teacher. It's important for me to know that I can make a difference in the lives of the children I work with. Every day when I walk into the classroom I am aware that what I do can affect a child for the rest of his or her life. I consider my job to be both a powerful honor and a weighty responsibility.
—A Contributor

The latest research shows that about 14.8 percent of the adults in the United States are Contributors. These individuals approach the world in a personal and involved way. They are focused on communicating, helping, and working with people, and they want to express and share their values and feelings. Interested in understanding and supporting others, they are open and warm. Contributors like to give and receive positive feedback and are strong team players. They enjoy organizing and coordinating people, events, and projects that provide opportunities for interaction and collaboration. Communication and cooperation are key to the Contributor's natural way of working.

CONTRIBUTORS AT WORK
What Contributors Do Naturally

DEVELOP RAPPORT
Contributors enjoy a wide range of activities that allow them to interact with others. They value and like to participate in conversations. For Contributors, discussions and conversations are essential sources of information for collecting, understanding, and sorting out other people's opinions and feelings. They use this information to help people work together more effectively and to meet others' needs. Contributors are personable and tactful communicators who value cooperation and collaboration. They are quick to empathize with others.

Contributors are attracted to opportunities to work in human services. These areas allow them to communicate with and help others. Contributors are also drawn to and do well in sales and customer service. They thrive in environments in which they can interact often and be directly involved with people.

Establishing and maintaining relationships is the natural focus of Contributors. They are naturally caring and concerned and want to please others. Contributors work to uphold personal, community, and societal values. They strongly identify with and value their social roles and enjoy providing services to people. They relish caring for and taking responsibility for others. A Contributor describes his philosophy of customer service:

"I like to build relationships with customers. I am here to listen to their needs and provide solutions that work. In my experience, too many service providers are too busy selling products to actually take the time to find out what the customer really wants."

EXPRESS THEMSELVES AND THEIR VALUES
Contributors approach the world in an active, decisive, and personal manner. They make decisions by assessing and evaluating the effects on people or the values inherent in each option. This approach is as systematic and predictable as a logical one, although it may seem random and emotional. For example, a Contributor may choose to stop and help a hurt puppy, even if it will make him or her late for an appointment. This decision is based on the value of being kind to animals and respecting all life. We can predict that this person will act in a similar way in another situation that involves the same value.

Contributors are warm and friendly and often express their emotions openly. They may express positive emotions more than negative ones, wanting to maintain social harmony. They enjoy encouraging others and are quick to offer applause and positive feedback. This type of encouragement is motivating for them to receive as well, and they thrive in environments in which others appreciate them with words and actions.

This warmth and expressiveness can present difficulties for the male Contributor. Our society has not traditionally viewed males as emotionally expressive or nurturing. Because of this, male Contributors must balance their need to meet others' expectations and their need to express themselves. This may be a challenge for them when they are defining their way of relating to others.

CREATE HARMONY

Contributors naturally create and maintain harmony within groups. They thrive on communicating and cooperating with people, and they will often support, serve, or advocate for others. They identify with and are focused on helping others reach their goals. Contributors are usually positive and optimistic. They will actively work within groups to make sure that all group members are included and accepted.

No matter what career field the Contributor chooses, it is important that the working environment be a supportive and harmonious one in which people are valued, recognized, and encouraged for their efforts. For Contributors, the atmosphere and morale around them greatly affects their ability to work effectively. They want to be able to express themselves openly as well as get and receive positive feedback. Contributors find office politics and hidden agendas frustrating and devastating to their morale. One Contributor explains,

"The people I am working with are as important as what I am working at, or maybe even more important. I find it almost impossible to survive in a workplace where there is conflict, lack of trust, or backstabbing."

COORDINATE PEOPLE TO COMPLETE PROJECTS

Contributors enjoy working in environments that allow them to decide and act quickly. Because they are decisive and task oriented, they like to plan, organize, and coordinate people and activities. They are persistent and conscientious in following through. They like order and are most comfortable when things are decided or settled. They can become impatient if others are not meeting deadlines and expectations, although they prefer to understand and help others rather than criticize them.

Contributors like to engage in and belong to a wide variety of social groups. They are natural leaders and like to organize events and activities that will benefit and involve people. Contributors are reliable and responsible workers who will get the job done with the maximum amount of cooperation and collaboration. Here is how one Contributor describes her role on a team:

"I can keep everybody happy and get everyone in the group moving in the same direction. I put a lot of energy into mediating conflicts and exploring issues to make sure everyone is on the same page."

CONTRIBUTE TO SOCIETY

Contributors often define themselves by the work they do and the roles they play. They tend to judge both others and themselves by how well they are meeting society's expectations to be "good" at their role, whether the role is parent, community member, worker, or spouse. Contributors often are active in community service. One Contributor explains her involvement in a community environmental group:

"I have a strong commitment to the environment. I donate my time to projects that improve my city. Sometimes I feel guilty if I don't wash out and recycle every can or if I use a disposable cup. I can be pretty demanding of myself."

Contributors want to live their ideals and are devoted and loyal. They focus on and foster social relationships. This can lead them to become overcommitted. They may feel that if they do not take care of things, attend an event, take on that extra responsibility, or remember a birthday, they are letting people down. This tendency to put others' needs ahead of their own can overwhelm and create stress for Contributors. In addition, they may be unwilling to express their dissatisfaction with the very situation they created, not wanting to hurt anyone's feelings.

Contributor Blind Spots
PERSONALIZING FEEDBACK
Contributors need and value positive feedback. They define themselves, more than other types, through their performance of their roles, and they rely on

others to help them see how well they are doing. It can be difficult for Contributors to accept negative feedback, seeing it as general disapproval. They work hard and strive to do well in all their roles, and they are deeply affected when they feel that others are disapproving or unhappy with their performance.

Indifference or lack of any feedback can be seen as negative rather than neutral. One Contributor described his need for feedback:

"I like to get what I call 'love letters'—some type of written confirmation and appreciation recognizing my efforts and achievements. Giving and receiving affirmations is key to my work satisfaction. Sometimes I see this part of my personality as overly needy or egotistical. It has taken me some time to accept this need for external affirmation as part of who I am."

NOT MEETING THEIR OWN NEEDS

Contributors can become so busy and involved in meeting everyone else's needs that they ignore their own. They enjoy being needed and helping others. However, this helping can get out of balance, and Contributors can become overinvolved and overcommitted. They may find themselves in conflict, trying to balance multiple roles and responsibilities. They want to be model workers, spouses, parents, and community members. At the end of the day, there may be little time left to dedicate to their personal needs.

One Contributor describes how overwhelmed she felt returning to the workplace when her two children were old enough to stay home alone for brief periods:

"Initially I was exhausted. I was still carrying out all the home roles that I had done before I went back to work, as well as taking on an additional work role. My home role included housework, meal preparation, homework support, and chauffeuring my boys to many structured activities such as hockey and Scouts. I was also involved in fundraising and other volunteer activities. I wanted to do all my roles well and felt responsible for each and every one."

Even now, several years later, if one of her children is having a social or school problem, she feels that maybe she should be doing more to help him. This sense of multiple obligation and responsibility is not unusual for a Contributor.

Snapshot: Contributors' Natural Work Preferences

Contributors are at their best when they can use their natural work preferences. By focusing on your preferences, you will be able to better assess the types of work that will be personally satisfying. The following list describes characteristics and preferences of Contributors. Check off the items that are true for you.

As a Contributor, I am at my best when I can

- ☐ Communicate and interact
- ☐ Develop rapport
- ☐ Build relationships
- ☐ Express my emotions and values openly
- ☐ Serve, support, facilitate, or mentor others
- ☐ Be valued for my efforts
- ☐ Offer positive feedback and encouragement
- ☐ Receive positive feedback and encouragement
- ☐ Work to benefit society

- ☐ Plan and organize tasks
- ☐ Coordinate groups
- ☐ Help others work more effectively together
- ☐ Take responsibility for helping others
- ☐ Be involved in nurturing groups or teams
- ☐ Work in areas that align with my personal values
- ☐ Demonstrate my responsibility and reliability
- ☐ Follow through and get the job done

WHAT'S KEY FOR ME?

My Ideal Work Preferences

Look back at the snapshot for the work preferences for a Contributor (above). From the items you have checked, jot down the points that best summarize your preferences. Feel free to add points that are not on the list.

My most important work preferences are..

....

....

....

....

....

....

....

....

WORK THAT ATTRACTS CONTRIBUTORS

Contributors can be found in many different types of work. Here are some examples that use the Contributor's natural way of working.

SUPPORTING/TEACHING
    Child-care worker
    Child-welfare worker
    Counselor—career, alcohol and drug abuse, employee assistance
    Religious or spiritual worker
    Social services worker
    Speech pathologist
    Teacher—middle school, high school, language, preschool, special
       education, adults

Contributors are strongly drawn to teaching and counseling positions and work with both adults and children. They find it rewarding to see others learn and grow. If you value helping others in a group setting, or if you like one-on-one counseling or teaching, some of these careers might be for you.

HEALTH AND WELLNESS
Dental hygienist
Dietitian
Family physician
Health education practitioner
Home economist
Nurse
Optometrist
Pharmacist
Physical therapist
Recreational director

Contributors like to help others in the physical realm as well as the mental and spiritual. They often focus on learning and prevention, helping others learn to take care of themselves. Many Contributors like to teach others how to make good decisions. If you are focused on health and wellness, you may find these types of careers rewarding.

BUSINESS
Administrator
Human resources worker
Manager
Public relations specialist
Sales associate
Supervisor

If you have a flair for organizing people and resources to get the job done, you may be attracted to a leadership role. Contributors take on a wide variety of administrative and supervisory positions. They also enjoy roles in sales and public relations. These careers may appeal to you if you are especially outgoing and customer oriented.

Of course, these are just a few examples. There are many other types of work that Contributors will enjoy. See the next sections for work that is specifically appealing to ESFJs and ENFJs.

How Contributors Find Balance

Contributors use a personal, subjective decision-making approach to situations. They are most comfortable when they are making and acting on values-based decisions using their subjective impressions. However, to be effective, they need to balance their decisive nature with an effective way of taking in new information.

There are two approaches Contributors can use to take in information: attending to practical details and seeing possible patterns. Personality type theory calls these two approaches Sensing (S) and Intuition (N). You may want to look back to Chapter 2 to discern which approach is most comfortable for you. The words *sensing* and *intuition* have many connotations that do not really relate to how people take in information, so, to avoid misconceptions, in this book Contributors who prefer Sensing as a way to take in information (ESFJs) are called Practical Contributors, while Contributors who prefer Intuition as a way to take in information (ENFJs) are called Insightful Contributors.

Practical Contributors will balance their tendency to act and decide with a focus on the current facts, details, and practical applications. They often are attracted to opportunities to express their values and work with others in an immediate and concrete way. Insightful Contributors most naturally take in information as patterns and possibilities. They balance their decisiveness with input in the form of ideas and possibilities. Their early career themes tend to focus on ways to organize, change, and develop systems, people, and processes that will have long-term effects.

Each approach has a different focus, but both provide the Contributor with additional information for decision making. These approaches are mostly used internally as Contributors factor information into their decisions. Over the course of their life, Contributors will use and develop both approaches to take in information as they refine their decision making. This allows them to become more flexible and attend to different types of information over time. Both approaches help Contributors generate new ideas, understand additional facts and details, and focus their career path. This balance, between evaluating ideas and identifying new facts and patterns, is a key development step for Contributors.

As you go through this section, you may find it helpful to read about your most natural balancing approach first. Then read about the other approach to balancing to see what is in store for you as you mature and develop.

☐ **I am most like ESFJ,** so I am a Practical Contributor. I will initially balance my decisive nature by focusing on facts and details. As I mature and develop, I will also learn to balance my approach by focusing on patterns and possibilities.

☐ **I am most like ENFJ,** so I am an Insightful Contributor. I will initially balance my decisive nature with a focus on ideas and possibilities. As I mature and develop, I will also learn to balance my approach by focusing on facts and details.

BALANCING CONTRIBUTING WITH PRACTICALITY

The latest research shows that about 12.3 percent of adults in the United States are Practical Contributors (ESFJ). Practical Contributors focus on the here and now, seeing and evaluating situations accurately and providing for the immediate needs of others. They are especially interested in being of service to others in a direct and practical way. They quickly and easily relate and connect to others. They pay attention to details and will remember people's day-to-day situations: Practical Contributors will ask you how your sick child is doing, remember your birthday, and make sure the meal they prepare is appropriate for your allergies and diet. They will be quick to notice when you cut your hair, buy new clothes, or lose some weight. Practical Contributors offer these personal and practical touches often and easily.

Because Practical Contributors have a practical, detail-oriented focus as a balance to their decisive nature, they initially express their Contributing way of working differently than Insightful Contributors do. However, Insightful Contributors in midlife may find that these detail-oriented descriptions mirror the direction in which they are moving as they mature and develop.

What Practical Contributors Do Naturally

CELEBRATE PEOPLE

Practical Contributors see the value in and understand the world through established social norms, rituals, and traditions. Because of this focus, their decisions are based more on acceptable behaviors and social obligations than on their immediate emotional responses to situations. Upholding these rules and traditions is important for Practical Contributors. They especially like to see and celebrate others' successes.

One Practical Contributor working as a manager described his experience as he recently completed an intensive certificate program at work:

"I completed the learning while also maintaining my regular work duties. This intensive learning required eighteen months of significant effort on my part. At the end of it all, a certificate arrived one day in the mail. No ceremony or public recognition was made. I found the nonevent rather disheartening. I wanted to be given some sort of recognition for my hard work. So, when one of my employees completed the same program, I had the certificate sent to me so that I could present it to the employee at a meeting of his peers. This celebration of people through recognition and validation is very important to me."

Loyalty and duty are also important to Practical Contributors. They will work very hard for an organization and will feel especially betrayed if the organization does not treat its people well. In an unclear or ambiguous situation, the lack of predictability will be uncomfortable for them. Rapid organizational change or impersonal management can also create stress for Practical Contributors.

Practical Contributors will notice and be affected by their physical work setting. They like to have a comfortable and attractive workspace. They appreciate physical gestures of appreciation such as thank-you cards or small gifts that they can display.

SERVE THE COMMUNITY

Practical Contributors tend to take on many roles in their community, and they are often actively involved in a number of community organizations. They enjoy making immediate and useful contributions; and they often do volunteer work and assume responsibilities within organizations. One Practical Contributor explains:

"I like community work. I do feel an obligation to contribute, but I also get lots of satisfaction from being involved. I enjoy the social contact and the affirmation I get from others. It feels really good to make a contribution to something that is important to me."

Their strong community focus often attracts Practical Contributors to work in health care, education, and service careers. They are naturally drawn to work that allows them to help others in a short-term, immediate, and practical way. They like to energetically take concrete and practical actions to benefit others.

Because Practical Contributors are friendly, warm, and both in tune with and able to describe the needs of others, they can be good at sales. They are especially good at selling practical products. They have the facts at their fingertips and are very helpful and willing to please their customers. They also enjoy working in customer service. Practical Contributors need and value opportunities to talk and interact with others at work.

Often, Practical Contributors are drawn to careers that are traditionally acceptable or that have been demonstrated by a role model. Sometimes tradition and personal experiences can get in the way of their expressing their personal preferences. Or traditions and personal experiences may be key components of their personal preferences. Practical Contributors must learn to sort out societal expectations from personal preferences as they create their career path.

BE INVOLVED WITH OTHERS

Practical Contributors are usually very busy, scheduling time to meet many obligations and accomplish many practical things in a typical week. They are responsible, dependable, and conscientious workers. They enjoy organizing things to run smoothly. Routines, structure, and schedules feel comfortable to Practical Contributors.

Ironically, by expending considerable energy keeping in touch and modeling the appropriate and accepted societal values, Practical Contributors can actually *lose* touch with their own personal values. They tend to naturally network and let what they hear from others define the norms of the time. They are adept at fitting into and supporting these norms. However, the more they focus on adopting and maintaining general societal norms, the less they are able to turn inward to understand and accept their personal needs. This is especially true if their personal needs and values are different from those of the accepted mainstream.

Learning to separate societal ideals from personal experiences and values is a strong lesson for Practical Contributors. This lesson helps them accept themselves for who they are rather than for who they should be. It also gives them the freedom to accept others and take more personal risks.

WORK THE PLAN

Practical Contributors prefer to use a steady, step-by-step approach in their work. Structure and procedures make it easier for them to complete tasks efficiently. They like to work with accurate details and prefer to complete practical tasks rather than abstract ones. They are good at observing and anticipating people's needs.

Practical Contributors prefer a stable and predictable work environment over one that is rapidly changing or highly unpredictable. They value and will follow rules and procedures. Practical Contributors are most comfortable when expectations, directions, and tasks are clearly defined and concrete deadlines are laid out. In these situations, they will meet and exceed expectations demanded of them. They work well when they are able to set up practical routines and schedules. Ambiguous situations and unclear chains of command are frustrating because they can get in the way of getting the job done. One Practical Contributor describes his pet peeve as playing politics:

"I don't like to have to convince others in my organization to buy my solutions. Spending time selling ideas rather than doing things seems to me to be a waste of valuable time."

Practical Contributors are task oriented and decisive. Because of these characteristics, they prefer to work in organizations that allow them to complete projects efficiently. They like to work on teams with other conscientious and reliable people, working in harmony to complete tasks. Practical Contributors often look to careers in administration, supervision, or coaching as ways to use these preferences. They enjoy the organization and results orientation that these positions require.

Snapshot: Ideal Work Environment for Practical Contributors

By focusing on your personal preferences, you will be able to better assess the types of work that will be personally satisfying. The following list describes ideal work environments for Practical Contributors. Check off the items that are true for you.

As a Practical Contributor, I prefer a work environment that offers

- ☐ A friendly and appreciative atmosphere
- ☐ People contact
- ☐ Positive feedback
- ☐ Personalized management
- ☐ Teamwork and collaboration
- ☐ Opportunities to help others in a practical way
- ☐ Stability, structure, and predictability

Snapshot: Skills and Valued Activities for Practical Contributors

By focusing on your personal preferences, you will be able to better assess the types of work that will be personally satisfying. The following list describes skills and activities valued by Practical Contributors. Check off the items that are true for you.

As a Practical Contributor, I value the following skills and activities:

- ☐ Communication skills
- ☐ Collaboration
- ☐ Organization
- ☐ Attention to facts and details
- ☐ Time and task management

Work That Attracts Practical Contributors

The following occupations tend to be of interest to Practical Contributors. When looking for career ideas, remember to also look at the work options for Contributors listed earlier in the chapter, which are attractive to both Practical Contributors and Insightful Contributors.

OFFICE SERVICES

Bank employee
Bookkeeper
Cashier
Clerical worker
Legal assistant
Medical secretary
Office machine operator
Office manager
Receptionist
Secretary

Many Practical Contributors like the structure and organization of an office environment. If you enjoy working with customers or following the direction of others, you may find that you are suited for an office services position. Look for supportive environments that provide opportunities to organize tasks and coordinate with co-workers.

HEALTH AND WELLNESS/TEACHING

Athletic coach
Community health worker
Dental assistant
Dentist
Licensed practical nurse
Lifeguard
Massage therapist
Medical assistant
Medical technician
Optician

Pediatric medicine
Pharmacist technician
Radiology technologist
Respiratory therapist
Teacher—elementary, reading
Teacher's aide

Practical Contributors are drawn to occupations that are focused on mind and body wellness. Many of these positions require extensive interaction with others. In some cases, the interaction is carried out as individuals are undergoing medical procedures that can be intimidating or uncomfortable. If you especially enjoy comforting others and helping them in a variety of situations, these types of careers might be for you.

TRADES AND PERSONAL SERVICES
Caterer
Construction worker
Cosmetologist
Hairdresser

Many Practical Contributors help people by becoming skilled in a trade area. They often choose a trade that requires interaction with others. If you enjoy practical helping, a career in one of these areas could be just the one for you. Occupations such as catering and hairdressing require a creative personal touch. If you have a creative flair, think about which personal services you might enjoy providing.

COMMUNICATIONS
Editor
Graphic designer
Media worker

Communicating through words or images can be attractive to Practical Contributors. Occupations in this field require considerable attention to detail. If you are skilled with words or images, you may enjoy working in the communication field.

SUPERVISORY OR LAW ENFORCEMENT ROLES
Corrections officer
Guard
Police detective
Site supervisor

Enforcing rules or supervising others can be attractive to Practical Contributors. If you like structure and adhering to procedures, these occupations might be a good match for you.

OTHER SERVICES
Flight attendant
Funeral home director
Insurance agent
Real estate agent
Restaurant worker
School-bus driver
Veterinarian

Practical Contributors are attracted to a wide range of opportunities to work with the public. If you enjoy providing customer service, you may want to consider an occupation in this area.

Practical Contributors as Leaders
Practical Contributors bring unique strengths to the leadership role. They naturally lead, and prefer to be led, in a specific way.

RESPECT AUTHORITY
Practical Contributors tend to value and model the traditionally accepted hierarchical organizational structure. They respect authority and want others to respect it as well. Practical Contributor leaders define and delegate tasks, taking time to match people to tasks in a personal way. They are focused on schedules and deadlines and provide clear and specific instructions. Practical Contributors lead by example. They do not expect anyone else to do what they are not willing to do themselves.

CREATE AND MAINTAIN HARMONY

Harmony is important to Practical Contributor leaders. They strive to make sure everyone is fitting in and working well together. Their efforts are based on assumptions regarding what will help people in general and will reflect organizational traditions and rituals, such as reward programs and celebrations.

BE SUPPORTIVE

Practical Contributors lead in a personal and supportive way. They share information and stay in touch with the progress of projects. Practical Contributor leaders pay close attention to the needs of the individuals they work with. However, in a situation requiring them to produce quick results, they may make general decisions as to peoples' needs based on conventional standards rather than on specific data from the individuals involved. These leaders may need to look beyond the socially acceptable standards by listening to and understanding individual needs that are different from the norm. This may be especially true in the area of gender issues, where Practical Contributors tend to operate and make decisions based on traditional male and female roles rather than attending to the specifics of the situation. However, a Practical Contributor who has accepted nontraditional roles will be a strong and vocal advocate.

GET THE JOB DONE

Practical Contributors are steady, responsible, and reliable leaders who can be counted on to follow through with deadlines and responsibly get the job done. They assume that others will take a task-oriented approach as well and are surprised and disappointed if they do not. Others who are not contributing as expected are judged quite harshly, since not living up to expectations is unacceptable for Practical Contributors. These leaders may personally compensate for and complete the work not done, putting immense strain and stress on themselves rather than delay a deadline.

Practical Contributors take feedback about the performance of one of their staff very personally. At times, they can even see someone else's behavior as a reflection of their leadership ability. Learning to step back and assess others objectively is sometimes a challenge for this type of leader.

Snapshot: Practical Contributors as Leaders

By focusing on your personal preferences, you will be able to better assess the types of work that will be personally satisfying. The following list describes the leadership preferences of Practical Contributors. Check off the items that are true for you.

As a Practical Contributor leader, I prefer to

- ☐ Respect authority
- ☐ Define and delegate tasks
- ☐ Lead by example
- ☐ Match people to tasks in a personal way
- ☐ Focus on schedules and deadlines
- ☐ Provide clear and specific instructions
- ☐ Create and maintain harmony
- ☐ Be personal and supportive
- ☐ Share information
- ☐ Stay in touch with the progress of projects
- ☐ Pay attention to the needs of the individuals I work with
- ☐ Be responsible and reliable
- ☐ Follow through with deadlines and responsibly get the job done

Practical Contributors as Team Members

On a team, Practical Contributors want to be sure that everyone is involved and feeling good. They are naturally affirming and supportive of others. Using their well-developed communication skills, they tend to help the group find and maintain harmony and consensus. They enjoy cooperative interactions and value a positive, well-functioning team. Practical Contributors provide a positive and organized focus that helps get the job done.

They can provide balance to teams, having both a task-oriented approach for getting the work done and a values-based approach for providing a positive environment that rewards members for their effort. These two characteristics can help them smooth out team conflicts and move the team toward its goals. However, Practical Contributors may find the process of conflict resolution painful, especially if others on the team have strong and differing opinions. They may try to smooth things over too quickly or avoid conflicts rather than deal with the discord.

Practical Contributors can become frustrated when others fail to meet their expectations. They may benefit from learning to understand and accept others' personal values and ways of working. For example, some workers are motivated to do their best work as the deadline approaches, or to work in bursts of creative energy. Other workers are focused in the present and stay motivated by frequent breaks and opportunities to stop and enjoy the moment. These workers are not out to defy or devalue the traditional work ethic; they are simply approaching the task in the way that works best for them. Accepting these personal differences can help Practical Contributors work effectively with different types of people.

· 160 ·

Snapshot: Practical Contributors as Team Members

By focusing on your personal preferences, you will be able to better assess the types of work that will be personally satisfying. The following list describes how Practical Contributors like to work within a team. Check off the items that are true for you.

As a Practical Contributor team member, I

- [ ] Ensure that everyone is involved and feeling good
- [ ] Help the group find and maintain harmony and consensus
- [ ] Enjoy cooperative interactions
- [ ] Move the team toward its goal
- [ ] Am a positive force for getting the job done
- [ ] Like to help smooth out team conflicts
- [ ] Value a positive, well-functioning team

Practical Contributors as Learners

Practical Contributors tend to do well in a classroom setting—as long as the information is useful. Practical applications, personal stories, and real-world examples help them understand the material. They are good at time and task management and like to work under deadlines. They learn well in structured and routine settings.

It is important to give Practical Contributors clear direction and expectations in a learning situation. Support, encouragement, and a positive atmosphere are also important for Practical Contributors. They want someone to monitor their progress. Memorization and attention to detail are strengths of Practical Contributor learners. They are usually hardworking and persistent.

Snapshot: Practical Contributors as Learners

By focusing on your personal preferences, you will be able to better assess the types of work that will be personally satisfying. The following list describes the learning preferences of Practical Contributors. Check off the items that are true for you.

As a Practical Contributor learner, I

- ☐ Like useful information and practical applications
- ☐ Appreciate personal stories and real-world examples
- ☐ Am good at time and task management
- ☐ Work well under deadlines
- ☐ Like structured and routine settings
- ☐ Am hardworking and persistent
- ☐ Need clear direction and expectations
- ☐ Am at my best in a positive atmosphere that provides support and encouragement
- ☐ Want someone to monitor my progress
- ☐ Am good at memorization and attention to detail

BALANCING CONTRIBUTING WITH INSIGHT

The latest research shows that about 2.5 percent of adults in the United States are Insightful Contributors (ENFJ). Insightful Contributors balance and enhance their Contributor focus by imagining possibilities for others. They see potential for growth and development and often act as mentors. This focus takes them away from deciding immediately and allows them to explore options and opportunities for themselves and others. Insightful Contributors are often strong advocates and teachers.

Because Insightful Contributors have a visionary, long-term focus as a balance to their decisive nature, they initially express their Contributing way of working differently than Practical Contributors do. However, Practical Contributors in midlife may find that these vision-based descriptions mirror the direction in which they are moving as they mature and develop.

What Insightful Contributors Do Naturally

SUPPORT GROWTH AND DEVELOPMENT

Insightful Contributors are naturally drawn to work that allows them to help others in a long-term, growth-oriented way. They use their warmth and vision to help others see possibilities and make personal decisions that will improve or enrich their lives. They can often be found teaching, counseling, and working in religious and spiritual areas.

Insightful Contributors are especially well suited to guiding others. Their abilities to develop rapport, see potential in others, and keep tasks on track are a powerful combination of attributes that they can use to help others develop their potential. Insightful Contributors coach and mentor others in a positive, encouraging, and task-focused manner. One Insightful Contributor describes her approach:

"I like to support people and make sure I give them lots of guidance initially. Then I tend to back off and give them room to make their own decisions."

GENERATE POSSIBILITIES

Many Insightful Contributors have a creative bent and like to work with ideas and possibilities. This can be expressed in a variety of ways. Some express themselves as writers, artists, entertainers, or designers. Others like to create options and possibilities for others as they counsel and mentor. Some Insightful Contributors use their creativity in the classroom as teachers. One teacher describes her favorite activities at work:

"I like creating projects and new ideas to hook kids on learning. I change my lessons and activities regularly, always searching for ways to meet the needs of all the students in my classes."

BUILD RELATIONSHIPS

Building working relationships is a strong theme for Insightful Contributors. They tend to be empathic and tolerant and have a good appreciation for and understanding of others' viewpoints and individual differences. Insightful Contributors often have highly developed communication skills and maintain close relationships. They can be very negatively affected in the workplace by unpleasant working relationships. Atmosphere and morale are important considerations for an Insightful Contributor's job satisfaction.

· 162 ·

Insightful Contributors seek and embrace change. They are always on the lookout for opportunities to help people manage and thrive in times of uncertainty. Insightful Contributors may be somewhat restless no matter what they are doing, since they are continually imagining new options and possibilities. To an Insightful Contributor, change is a good thing, because with it come development and growth—key processes that help people realize and achieve their potential.

ORGANIZE PEOPLE AND PROJECTS

Insightful Contributors are usually actively engaged in many projects and communicate with many people. Being able to plan and organize is important to them. Their nature pulls them toward making and following through with decisions. They tend to be somewhat more flexible and less structured in their planning than Practical Contributors, because of their focus on the big picture. As one Insightful Contributor explains,

"I like to have my activities organized and scheduled, although I can jump in and organize things on the spot without planning in advance if I have to. Fortunately, I have a well-developed network of contacts I can tap into to get things done."

Finding rules and procedures limiting and confining, Insightful Contributors prefer to work in organizations or situations in which general guidelines are offered, rather than specific rules or procedures. They are more comfortable working with ambiguity and making personal judgments than they are working in an overly formal, rule-driven situation. They like to work in changing and complex situations, which they tend to approach with a plan in mind. They function best when they can arrange tasks in an orderly and productive way.

Insightful Contributors are often creative and effective problem solvers. One of their strengths is an ability to organize projects and mobilize people to complete their tasks. This works well as long as people are respected and allowed to complete their work in a positive and nurturing environment. The potential of the people is often their first and foremost focus, no matter what specific environment they are in. They can lose track of the task at hand if the project is creating conflict, stress, or strain for the people involved. When this occurs, they will tend to deal with the emotions and interpersonal conflicts first.

DO IT ALL

Insightful Contributors may find many projects and possibilities interesting, and new ideas stimulate them. However, if they are not careful they may find themselves overcommitted and overwhelmed with projects. They are idealistic and can sometimes create unrealistic expectations of themselves and others. These attributes, as well as the general desire of all Contributors to be responsible and meet others' needs, can create great role stress and overload.

Learning to balance their Insightful Contributor way of working with a more practical approach will help them in this regard. One Insightful Contributor comments on her personal development in this area:

"I am just now, in my fifties, learning to focus on the fact that I have needs and that these needs are important, too. I have been so busy meeting everyone else's needs and helping everyone else grow that I haven't taken the time to stop and understand what I need myself."

Snapshot: Ideal Work Environment for Insightful Contributors

By focusing on your personal preferences, you will be able to better assess the types of work that will be personally satisfying. The following list describes the ideal work environment for Insightful Contributors. Check off the items that are true for you.

As an Insightful Contributor, I prefer a work environment that offers

- ☐ Support and appreciation
- ☐ Opportunities to help people develop
- ☐ Opportunities to organize and manage people
- ☐ Multiple projects and possibilities
- ☐ Opportunities to generate ideas
- ☐ A focus on possibilities and potential

> ### Snapshot: Skills and Valued Activities for Insightful Contributors
>
> *By focusing on your personal preferences, you will be able to better assess the types of work that will be personally satisfying. The following list describes the skills and valued activities of Insightful Contributors. Check off the items that are true for you.*
>
> As an Insightful Contributor, I value the following skills and activities:
>
> ☐ Communication   ☐ Generating ideas
>
> ☐ Organization   ☐ Creativity
>
> ☐ Time and task management   ☐ Counseling

Work That Attracts Insightful Contributors

The following occupations tend to be of interest to Insightful Contributors. When looking for career ideas, remember to also look at the work options listed for Contributors earlier in the chapter, which are attractive to both Practical Contributors and Insightful Contributors.

ARTS AND DESIGN

    Actor
    Artist
    Composer
    Designer
    Entertainer
    Musician

Many Insightful Contributors enjoy occupations that provide opportunities to create ideas or perform for others. If you have an artistic bent, you may want to consider a career in arts and design. Opportunities in this area are numerous. You will need to consider how you want to express yourself and find a market for your work. Some Insightful Contributors choose to express their creativity as a hobby rather than as a career.

MARKETING AND COMMUNICATIONS
  Advertising
  Communications director
  Interpreter
  Journalist
  Librarian
  Sales manager
  Writer

Insightful Contributors often have a flair for expressing themselves using language. They are attracted to occupations that allow them to communicate words and ideas. If you are excited by marketing ideas or enhancing communications, these careers might suit you.

COUNSELING AND TEACHING
  Consultant—general, management
  Counselor—runaway youth, suicide and crisis, school
  Home economist
  Nursing consultant
  Nursing educator
  Occupational therapist
  Social scientist
  Psychiatrist
  Psychologist
  Teacher—health, art, drama, music, English, university, junior
    college

Both Practical Contributors and Insightful Contributors are drawn to careers that provide opportunities to help others. If you enjoy teaching groups or working to help others on a one-on-one basis, you might enjoy these types of careers. This kind of work will allow you to develop rapport and have meaningful interactions with others.

Insightful Contributors as Leaders
Insightful Contributors bring unique strengths to the leadership role. They naturally lead and prefer to be led in a specific way.

MENTOR

Insightful Contributors enjoy leading others. They bring a strong combination of vision, strategic planning, task orientation, and people skills to a leadership role. They often see their role as a mentor or coach, guiding others to become the best they can be. Their leadership approach is personal and cooperative. They expect others to contribute and participate in planning and decision making. Insightful Contributors are strong advocates of employee development. One of the driving forces of Insightful Contributors is a need to help others develop their full potential.

DEVELOP POTENTIAL

Being change and growth oriented, Insightful Contributors look for ways to develop potential. Being decisive and task-oriented, they also look for ways to accomplish tasks and meet goals. This combination of task and people orientations can provide an effective leadership combination, since overemphasis on one or the other can create conflicts and misunderstandings within groups. A careful balance of these two, sometimes opposing, focuses is an important challenge for this type of leader.

ADVOCATE

Insightful Contributors listen to others and are sensitive to and aware of the atmosphere and climate within their organizations. They strongly advocate for organizations to value the people who work within them. Insightful Contributors strive to make organizational systems more flexible and able to accommodate the needs of the workers.

ACHIEVE GOALS

Like other decisive types, Insightful Contributors are task oriented and enjoy organizing and coordinating resources toward a goal. More than the other decisive types, however, they will take time to make sure that the means justify the end in terms of employee motivation and morale. Insightful Contributors use cooperation and collaboration to achieve goals. They resist the use of other strategies such as wielding position power, criticizing unfairly, or threatening consequences. They are turned off by and uninterested in playing organizational politics or engaging in power struggles. These activities can result in considerable stress for the Insightful Contributor.

· 168 ·

Snapshot: Insightful Contributors as Leaders

By focusing on your personal preferences, you will be able to better assess the types of work that will be personally satisfying. The following list describes the leadership preferences of Insightful Contributors. Check off the items that are true for you.

As an Insightful Contributor leader, I prefer to

- ☐ Be personal and cooperative
- ☐ Advocate employee development
- ☐ Help others develop their full potential
- ☐ Be sensitive to and aware of the atmosphere and climate
- ☐ Accomplish tasks
- ☐ Organize and coordinate resources toward a goal
- ☐ Pay attention to employee motivation and morale
- ☐ Use cooperation and collaboration to achieve goals

Insightful Contributors as Team Members

Insightful Contributors are positive and enthusiastic team members. They tend to help the team move forward by organizing and mentoring others. They can also be a creative source for new ideas, especially ideas to develop people or systems. Insightful Contributors help their team by providing a balance between generating ideas and taking action.

On a team, positive interactions, collaboration, and harmony are important to Insightful Contributors. They actively support other team members with words and actions. Insightful Contributors are especially talented in seeing potential in others, and they encourage others to develop their potential and achieve their best. In a group they make sure that everyone has an opportunity to contribute and use his or her skills. They value and expect similar support themselves.

Insightful Contributors will explore and want to understand any interpersonal conflicts that are occurring in the group. They see this as a helpful, team-building approach, since they work best in a harmonious environment where personal values and needs are expressed. However, this focus on interpersonal relationships and creating harmony can seem like a waste of time to people who prefer other ways of working.

Snapshot: Insightful Contributors as Team Members

By focusing on your personal preferences, you will be able to better assess the types of work that will be personally satisfying. The following list describes how Insightful Contributors like to work within a team. Check off the items that are true for you.

As an Insightful Contributor team member, I

- ☐ Am positive and enthusiastic
- ☐ Help the team move forward
- ☐ Like to organize and mentor people
- ☐ Am a creative source for new ideas
- ☐ Like to develop people and systems
- ☐ Value positive interactions, collaboration, and harmony
- ☐ Actively support other team members

Insightful Contributors as Learners

Insightful Contributors enjoy the social aspects of formal learning. They seek opportunities to discuss ideas and connect with a broad range of people. They like to learn about theory, especially in the humanities and social sciences.

Insightful Contributors are especially sensitive to how the instructors present information. They will tune out instructors who do not share their values or affirm their opinions. Insightful Contributors will learn from their classmates as well as from their instructors.

One Insightful Contributor who facilitates adult education groups comments,

"I learn as much as my participants do when I facilitate a session. My learning is about people—how they approach things and what is important to them. This learning is one of the most important reasons I continue to do this type of work."

Insightful Contributors like organization and are good at managing time and tasks. They dislike learning environments that are disorganized or too unstructured. They are usually hardworking and persistent learners.

Snapshot: Insightful Contributors as Learners

By focusing on your personal preferences, you will be able to better assess the types of work that will be personally satisfying. The following list describes the learning preferences of Insightful Contributors. Check off the items that are true for you.

As an Insightful Contributor learner, I

☐ Enjoy the social aspects of formal learning

☐ Seek opportunities to discuss ideas

☐ Like theory

☐ Like organization

☐ Connect with a broad range of people

☐ Learn from my classmates as well as from instructors

☐ Am sensitive to how instructors present information

☐ Tune out instructors who do not share my values or affirm my opinions

☐ Excel at managing time and tasks

☐ Dislike learning environments that are disorganized or too unstructured

☐ Am hardworking and persistent

THE CONTRIBUTOR'S GREATEST CHALLENGES

Everyone has less-preferred activities and areas for growth and improvement. Contributors are no exception. Here are two major developmental areas for both Practical Contributors and Insightful Contributors, with tips on how to develop each one.

Making Logical Decisions

A major strength of Contributors is their ability to make decisions that take into account individual needs and situations. However, it is helpful to also consider the logical consequences of a decision. Contributors can learn to expand their decision-making strength by incorporating logical analysis. Contributors are action oriented and like to come to closure. This can create some difficulties for them, especially if they make a quick, values-based decision in the heat of the moment. Logic and analysis can help Contributors avoid decisions they may later regret. One Contributor describes his experiences:

"I once made a rather impulsive decision to quit a job that was based on an interpersonal conflict. All I really accomplished was to hurt myself. If I could do it again, I would approach the situation in a different way."

This balance is important, especially if the decisions are being made at emotional times or about emotional matters. Subjective decisions may focus only on a short-term consequence or a particular value. However, these decisions can have significant emotional and practical consequences in both the short and long term.

TIPS FOR MAKING LOGICAL DECISIONS
- When making a decision, stop to weigh the pros and cons of options. List them, and look at each with an objective eye.
- Follow each option through to its logical conclusion. Focus on the specific implications of your decisions in the short and long term.
- Make sure your options are reasonable as well as appealing.
- Imagine trying to explain and justify your decision to someone who is very logical. What questions would he or she ask? How would you answer?
- Defer a decision if you are emotional or upset. Take time to think logically about what you are feeling.

Not Taking Things Personally

Contributors may miss out on opportunities for growth and improvement because they find it hard to listen to and incorporate critical feedback. This is, in part, related to the way they like to give and receive feedback themselves. Contributors are particularly affected by how feedback is presented. Being naturally affirming and supportive, they usually give negative feedback gently and with great care for a person's feelings. They often mention a positive attribute first and then add a suggestion for improvement. They are careful not to make global statements that might hurt a person's feelings or self-esteem.

Contributors want to receive feedback in the same way they like to give it. However, not everyone shares Contributors' approach to feedback. Many people prefer a direct and no-nonsense sharing of areas for improvement, including a full and frank critical analysis. When Contributors receive this type of feedback, they feel hurt and personally attacked. They are more likely to react sensitively to feedback when they are under stress or unsure of themselves. They may feel that the person giving the feedback does not like them or respect them. One Contributor explains,

"I know I have a tendency to take things personally. I always put 110 percent into my work, and even a tepid evaluation can make me feel undervalued. I always do the best I can with what I have, and I need others to appreciate that."

At their worst, Contributors may feel criticized by a suggestion or comment that is not even intended as feedback. For example, imagine that someone walks into an office and says, "I really like the way the furniture in the room is arranged now." An overly sensitive Contributor might think that the person is indirectly criticizing the way the furniture was *before*. This, of course, is an overly dramatic example, but it does capture the subjective and personal way in which a Contributor can interpret feedback from others.

TIPS FOR NOT TAKING THINGS PERSONALLY
- Consistently remind yourself to separate critical feedback of behaviors and performance from an attack on you as a person.
- Make your new mantra "All good people make mistakes."
- When you start to feel criticized, remember that not all people affirm and support as a way of communicating; there are other ways of relating, so try to accept feedback in the way it is given.
- Minimize your chances of misunderstanding by clarifying what you hear. Ask the person providing feedback to specify what he or she means and to give examples.
- Ask for additional positive feedback. Acknowledge the negative feedback, and then ask if there was anything that worked or was done well. You may be pleasantly surprised by the positive feedback that the person did not bother to mention.
- If you find yourself taking things more personally than usual, you may be in a particularly stressful or uncomfortable situation or time. Try to isolate the source of your stress and lower your stress level, or back away from the situation and assess what is different about it.

KEY FOR ME: MANAGING MY CHALLENGES

Is making logical decisions or not taking things personally a challenge for you? If so, which of the strategies explored in this chapter would be helpful to try? ....

....

....

....

....

....

....

FINAL TIPS FOR CONTRIBUTORS: DOING WHAT COMES NATURALLY

A Contributor naturally approaches the world in a personal and involved way. Here are a few final tips that will help you choose and develop satisfying work.

Celebrate People

Use your natural aptitudes to validate, affirm, and support others. Find ways to acknowledge your success and the successes of others. Surround yourself with others who are positive and nurturing. You will be able to use your natural way of working when you are engaged in working with others in an environment that affirms and supports people.

Collaborate

Find opportunities to work with others in a collaborative way. Use the role of community volunteer, family member, mentor, teacher, leader, or learner to help you develop working relationships. Sharing and contributing are your natural approach, so, when possible, avoid environments that are overly competitive, political, or impersonal.

Plan and Organize

Managing tasks and time are strengths for you. Find ways to use your organizational abilities. Planning, coordinating, organizing, and arranging are all areas where you will likely excel. You may find yourself most engaged if you work on projects that require you to organize people. A Contributor's natural approach is a powerful blend of focus on tasks and people: You can get a task done while bringing out the best in the people involved.

Add a Touch of Logic and Analysis

Lead with your heart, but learn to support your decisions with your head. Adding a focus on analysis will ensure that your decisions take you where you want to go. Consider your own needs especially, and logically assess whether you are too busy helping others to take good care of yourself.

Take a Step Back

Take critical feedback with a grain of salt. Acknowledge it. Think about it. Perhaps change some behaviors if you need to. But do not take critical feedback as a personal insult or as criticism of you as a person.

Learn to Reflect and Relax

Contributors are active rather than contemplative. No matter what your developmental stage or situation, if you are a Contributor you may find it enlightening to take time to reflect on and digest your wealth of experiences. Relaxation can be difficult for you because Contributors are both task and people focused. You like to get your work done and will strive to meet others' needs before you play. Perhaps it is necessary for you to plan in some playtime.

Now that you have learned about your work preferences, please turn to Chapter 11 to begin planning your career path.

PART THREE

Introverted Career Paths

Introduction to the Introverted Ways of Working

Listed below are characteristics of work activities that tend to be associated with a preference for Introversion. If you are an Assimilator, a Visionary, an Analyzer, or an Enhancer, you can use these descriptions as general guidelines in your quest to find meaningful work.

Tips for Those with a Preference for Introversion
Look for work that provides you with opportunities to

- Avoid frequent interruptions
- Be calm and quiet
- Be careful
- Concentrate on one task
- Get information ahead of time
- Enjoy one-on-one or small group interactions
- Have a private workspace
- Have specialized knowledge
- Have time alone
- Have time to formulate your words
- Learn something in depth
- Look at something thoroughly
- Observe
- Reflect
- Think before acting
- Use caution
- Use time to prepare

Keep these general guidelines in mind as you read your chapter, which focuses on your specific introverted way of working.

CHAPTER SEVEN

Assimilators Specialize and Stabilize

PERSONALITY TYPES: ISFJ AND ISTJ

All the work I have done is related to helping others fix their problems. I started out as a nursing orderly and then worked as an emergency medical technician. I liked the immediate results and immediate gratification of the emergency work. For the last twenty years I have worked as a police officer. One of my favorite parts of my job now is the investigative work. I enjoy leading a team that puts the pieces together and solves the crime.
—An Assimilator

The latest research shows that about 25.4 percent of adults in the United States are Assimilators. Assimilators approach the world in a decisive way. They are interested in organizing people and resources to get the job done. At first glance they may seem like Practical Contributors if they are ISFJs, or Practical Expeditors if they are ISTJs. However, what you do not see at a casual glance is the Assimilator's internal preference for collecting and organizing data and relating them to past experiences. This internal focus is the guiding force of both ISFJs and ISTJs. As they work toward goals, Assimilators are constantly guided by and focused on a sense of what worked in the past. This internal focus of practicality and attention to experience is their natural way of working.

Assimilators' practical and detailed approach is immediate and automatic. It both provides a way to interpret new information and allows Assimilators to smoothly adjust their actions as they examine situations. Assimilators may not necessarily reveal their complex internal storehouse of past experience or explain the data and examples they draw on to make their decisions. Appearing calm, quiet, and serious, they are content to use their knowledge as an internal guide that allows them to understand and interpret their current situation. Because of this internal focus, we are sometimes surprised by Assimilators' actions, since we are not privy to all the data that directs their behavior.

ASSIMILATORS AT WORK
What Assimilators Do Naturally

ACCUMULATE INFORMATION
Assimilators are naturally tuned in to the world around them as they take in and remember facts and details. They are strongly grounded in and focused on their experiences as a way of understanding and explaining the world. They often become subject area experts in their field. Assimilators are able to recall specific details such as numbers, names, and dates. They want to know as much as possible about the important things in their world. Here is how one Assimilator describes his focus on details as he explains his strategy for learning:

"I was good at formal learning. I took copious notes, copying everything that the instructor wrote on the blackboard and adding more. I worked hard, memorized lots of facts, and was mentally alert. I especially liked lectures. They seem to be an efficient way to communicate a large amount of information in a short amount of time."

Of all ways of working, the Assimilators, as a group, appear the most diverse. That is because each Assimilator collects different data and experiences and sees the world in his or her own unique, highly specialized way. Assimilators tend to accumulate only the information that they feel is relevant to their situation. Thus, they may have a wealth of specialized information in one subject area and know very little about something else. This interesting attribute can be puzzling to the casual observer, who can be surprised to find what specific pieces of information are captured or ignored by the Assimilator, depending on what is important to him or her.

One Assimilator describes her work experience as an ongoing specialization:

"I have been working in the area of aboriginal affairs for several years. I have been involved in managing and coordinating a number of projects including research, fund-raising, promoting diversity, training, counseling, and directing. I have managed staff, written policy, implemented procedures, negotiated, and trained others. Key to all of this work has been my ongoing interest in and accumulation of information about aboriginal people."

This Assimilator demonstrates how her past experiences and work opportunities provide a rich storehouse of practical information she can use, no matter what specific job or role she is involved in within her area of expertise. Having a strong theme or expertise is common for an Assimilator. If this is your preferred way of working, you may want to ask yourself, "What is my area of expertise? What common thread of experiences have I been building?" One Assimilator summarizes his career focus this way:

"My life has taken me down many paths. I have enjoyed some of them more than others. I can pick what path to take, and I use my experience to pick the right path."

ATTEND TO AND ORGANIZE THE DETAILS

Not only do Assimilators remember the details, but they are able to organize and track multiple facts and projects without losing detail. They often appear very exacting and precise as they ensure that all data are dealt with accurately and efficiently. One Assimilator comments,

"I enjoy moving to a new office, since I can use the opportunity to check if there is anything that needs organizing."

Assimilators want to consider every fact and detail before choosing a course of action. They need to understand and organize all the information at hand. As they are assessing a situation, they will be searching for relevant data from past experiences. They can, at times, seem to others somewhat too careful, exacting, and methodical. You will never go wrong having an Assimilator review contracts, budgets, and other important papers for you. He or she will find any discrepancies or missing details. Just do not ask him or her to take a quick look for you, as Assimilators want to be meticulous in their assessment.

TRUST WHAT THEY KNOW TO BE TRUE

Assimilators have a strong sense of priorities that has developed from years of taking in and making sense of the information around them. They trust what they know to be true from their experiences. Assimilators carefully and diligently organize and build their knowledge on an ongoing basis. Experienced Assimilators will be able to tell you, in their area of expertise, what will work and what will likely not work. They are able to draw on and share many practical examples. Assimilators like to stick with what is tried and true. Because of this preference, they can be perceived as somewhat inflexible, but highly dependable and conscientious. One Assimilator summarizes his practical focus:

"I don't like to reinvent the wheel. I prefer to use the wheel to get to where I am going."

Because Assimilators retain and trust experiences, they take time to look inward and compare the present situation to past experiences before choosing a course of action. They pay attention to and weigh all the relevant facts and information before deciding. They decide carefully, but once they decide, they hold firm to their chosen course. At that point, they can be very difficult to dissuade. Assimilators can become extremely loyal to a person or an organization. Once their loyalty is established, they may find it difficult to change jobs even if the work is not meeting their personal needs. Assimilators, when engaged, become determined, dedicated, and committed workers. They will keep their word, honor their commitments, and follow things through to their conclusion.

FOLLOW PROCEDURE

Assimilators approach tasks systematically. They like to follow a sequential, approach, carefully and thoroughly completing each step. Assimilators see the value of standard operating procedures, rules, and regulations and are careful to follow them. They often take on the responsibility of ensuring that others are following these standards as well. Many Assimilators take the role of administrators and supervisors, with a strong orientation toward following the rules.

Assimilators do not like to take shortcuts and can become impatient with those who do. They know that the standard procedures have been tried and tested and, because of that, need to be followed. They can be very exacting and detailed in this regard and come across as highly responsible, serious, and predictable. They like to stabilize and maintain systems and are most content when things are running smoothly and according to plan.

Assimilators are highly conscientious and are most comfortable in environments that allow them to complete well-defined and well-structured tasks. They like to have a plan in place before they start and are uncomfortable "making it up" as they go along. For this reason, Assimilators may hesitate to start something if they cannot visualize and specifically define the final result. They need to sit back and think a project through, rather than start haphazardly.

Assimilators' ideal work environment is one that provides stability and order. They dislike disorder and work best when given clear directions and expectations. They are able to work well in situations that require them to adhere to well-defined rules, procedures, and regulations. They understand and like to work in organizations with clearly defined levels of authority. Established routines and organizational traditions provide a sense of long-term security and stability for Assimilators. They enjoy preserving and working within a predictable environment.

GET THE JOB DONE

Assimilators are task focused and reliable. They can be counted on to follow through and get the job done. Extremely hardworking, they will labor at a steady pace to meet all deadlines. They will meticulously attend to even the most minute details and will, at times, have highly specific standards and expectations that others find difficult to meet. Assimilators demonstrate extremely high levels of accountability and feel obligated to meet and take on responsibilities.

They may take on too many responsibilities and have difficulty meeting their own standards. This can be very stressful for them, since they want to complete every task carefully and thoroughly. It is important for Assimilators to carefully assess the impact of additional responsibilities before they agree to take them on. However, even when they know an additional responsibility may be stressful, they often are dutiful and loyal and will take on the responsibility anyway. Learning to say no and limit themselves to what they can manage practically is a challenge for Assimilators.

Assimilators may take on responsibility for an entire project, rather than for only their role in it. Their sense of responsibility may lead them to assume the roles of others who are not getting their jobs done, and they often end up doing more than their share of the work. They can end up working long hours under considerable stress to ensure that timelines and obligations are met. This can create great stress and discomfort for Assimilators, who may not say anything to others until they become overwhelmed and extremely frustrated with the situation.

BE PRACTICAL

Assimilators are highly practical. They want to see or hear the facts presented simply and clearly. They are often skilled at organizing resources and people toward completing a goal. This practical ability to organize resources is combined with high levels of responsibility and task orientation. Assimilators will ensure that the job gets done, marshaling resources and organizing people and tasks in a practical way. You can be sure that just the right combination of people and resources will be assigned to effectively complete the project when an Assimilator is involved in the planning. Assimilators are often most satisfied when they are working toward a concrete goal or providing a tangible product or service. One Assimilator describes this satisfaction:

"I enjoy doing electrical work. When the job is done, you flip a switch and see an immediate outcome. I like the problem solving, too. You have to carefully follow the current from start to finish to figure out what is wrong."

One Assimilator teaches physics in a way that typifies this practical focus. He makes sure that he provides concrete examples for all the principles he is teaching. He brings demonstrations into his class regularly. He has created videos on a roller coaster and gone bungee jumping to demonstrate the applications of physics principles. He excels at making abstract principles real for his students.

Assimilator Blind Spots
UNPREDICTABLE CHANGE

Since Assimilators are most comfortable working with the predictable and orderly, they may find it difficult to deal with change. Because they need to consider and understand all of the implications involved in a changing situation, they are sometimes slower to react to change than others may be. This will be especially true if the change is imposed externally without sufficient justification.

Assimilators are likely to see more value in making small, gradual improvements and revisions than in jumping into a totally new way of doing things.

They like to build and refine what exists rather than start over with something new. They can appear very stubborn and resistant to changes that are inconsistent with their experiences. Assimilators need to see practical reasons and examples of past success before they accept a change. Risk taking is seen as unnecessary and unproductive. They do not want to work on the cutting edge without some grounding in what they know from experience.

Snapshot: Assimilators' Natural Work Preferences

· 185 ·

Assimilators are at their best when they can use their natural work preferences. By focusing on your preferences, you will be able to better assess the types of work that will be personally satisfying. The following list describes characteristics and preferences of Assimilators. Check off the items that are true for you.

As an Assimilator, I am at my best when I can

- [ ] Organize people and resources and get the job done
- [ ] Collect and organize data and relate it to my past experiences
- [ ] Be guided and focused by a sense of what has worked in the past
- [ ] Take a practical and detailed approach
- [ ] Become a subject area expert in my field
- [ ] Attend to and organize the details
- [ ] Be exacting and precise
- [ ] Stick with what is tried and true
- [ ] Decide carefully
- [ ] Follow things through to their conclusion

- [ ] Follow procedures
- [ ] Approach tasks systematically
- [ ] Follow a sequential, step-by-step approach
- [ ] Stabilize and maintain systems
- [ ] Complete well-defined and well-structured tasks
- [ ] Have a plan in place before I start
- [ ] Receive clear directions and expectations
- [ ] Adhere to well-defined rules, procedures, and regulations
- [ ] Find long-term security and stability
- [ ] Preserve and work within a predictable environment
- [ ] Work at a steady pace

WHAT'S KEY FOR ME?
My Ideal Work Preferences

Look back at the snapshot for the work preferences for an Assimilator. From the items you have checked, jot down the points that best summarize your preferences. Feel free to add points that are not on the list.

My most important work preferences are...

....

....

....

....

....

....

....

WORK THAT ATTRACTS ASSIMILATORS

Assimilators can be found in many types of work. Here are some examples that use the Assimilator's natural way of working.

HEALTH CARE
Administrator—nursing
Community health worker
Pharmacist
Pharmacy technician
Physician
Veterinarian

Many of these occupations require attention to detail and careful decision making. If you enjoy the health-care field and like working with others, these careers may suit you.

SUPERVISION AND ADMINISTRATION
Administrator—social services, education
Corrections officer
Supervisor—variety of fields

Many Assimilators excel at supervising others or managing administrative details. If you especially like planning or supervising others, these careers may be for you.

OTHER SERVICES
Electrician
Legal assistant
Librarian
Real estate agent
Word processing

Assimilators often choose service occupations such as these that allow them to work with details in a practical way. Depending on your specific interests and skills, you may find one of these careers satisfying.

Of course, these are just some examples. There are many other types of work that Assimilators will enjoy. See the next sections for work that is specifically appealing to ISFJs and ISTJs.

HOW ASSIMILATORS FIND BALANCE

Assimilators are energized by working within the internal world, reflecting on and categorizing experiences. They continually take in and assimilate information, and over time, they develop a rich and detailed mental storehouse. They must balance this internal focus by making decisions and acting in the world around them. A well-developed decision-making approach helps Assimilators choose a focus for their observations as well as a purpose and direction for their actions. There are two approaches for evaluating information: a values-based approach and a logical approach. Personality type theory calls these two approaches Feeling (F) and Thinking (T). You may want to look back to Chapter 2 to discern which approach is most comfortable for you. The words *thinking* and *feeling* have many connotations that do not actually relate to how people evaluate information and make decisions. So, to avoid misconceptions, in this book Assimilators who prefer Feeling as a decision-making approach (ISFJs) are called Compassionate Assimilators, while Assimilators who prefer Thinking as a decision-making approach (ISTJs) are called Logical Assimilators.

Each approach has a different focus, but both allow the Assimilator an opportunity to make choices and act in the world. Over the course of their life, Assimilators will use and develop both approaches to help them make decisions and choose their actions. This natural development allows Assimilators to become more flexible decision makers over time.

Compassionate Assimilators naturally evaluate information on the basis of personal and human values. They act in a way similar to Practical Contributors, caring for and showing concern about people's immediate needs. Practical Contributors and Compassionate Assimilators deal with the world with the same personal and caring approach. They are often found in similar types of work and enjoy doing similar types of things. It is important to remember that, for Compassionate Assimilators, this focus on helping and understanding the situations of others is secondary to and supports their primary focus of expanding their understanding of the world around them.

Logical Assimilators, on the other hand, naturally use logical analysis to evaluate information. They act in a way similar to Practical Expeditors, work-ing efficiently toward practical goals. Practical Expeditors and Logical Assim-ilators both approach the world in a task-oriented way. They are often found in similar types of work and enjoy doing similar types of things. It is important to remember that, for Logical Assimilators, this focus on logical analysis is sec-ondary to and supportive of their primary focus of taking in and assimilating facts and data.

Practical Contributors and Practical Expeditors use their experiences to help guide their decision making, but, for them, past experience and stored data are secondary to decision making and action. Unlike Contributors and Expeditors, both types of Assimilators are more focused on the data and experiences they have collected than they are on deciding and acting.

As you go through this section, you may find it helpful to read about your most natural balancing approach first. Then read about the other approach to balancing to see what is in store for you as you mature and develop.

<table>
<tr>
<td>

☐ **I am most like ISFJ,**
so I am a Compassionate Assimilator.
I will initially balance my internal
focus on practical matters by
making values-based decisions.
As I mature and develop, I will
also learn to balance my approach
by incorporating more logical
analysis into decisions.

</td>
<td>

☐ **I am most like ISTJ,**
so I am a Logical Assimilator.
I will initially balance my internal
focus on practical matters by
making logical decisions.
As I mature and develop, I will
also learn to balance my approach
by incorporating values of others
and myself into decisions.

</td>
</tr>
</table>

BALANCING ASSIMILATING WITH COMPASSION

The latest research shows that about 13.8 percent of adults in the United States are Compassionate Assimilators (ISFJ). Compassionate Assimilators balance their internal focus on facts and experiences with an external focus on people and values. Like their extraverted counterparts, Contributors, they often are drawn to occupations that allow them to work within a group toward personally meaningful goals, coordinating, organizing, and helping in a variety of situations. Compassionate Assimilators tend to seek opportunities to contribute and to help others. They like to create and work within a positive, supportive, and harmonious working environment. As one Compassionate Assimilator explains,

"A team must communicate to work well together. Team members need a pat on the back and support from the team leader to work effectively."

Because Compassionate Assimilators have a personal and values-based focus as a balance for their attention to detail, they initially express their Assimilating way of working differently than Logical Assimilators do. However, Logical Assimilators in midlife may find that these values-based descriptions mirror the direction in which they are moving as they mature and develop.

What Compassionate Assimilators Do Naturally
HELP OTHERS
Compassionate Assimilators balance their wealth of experiences and astute observational skills with a focus on the needs of others. They are well suited

for practical, helping occupations and make good doctors and nurses. They are warm and caring to patients as they carefully and thoroughly assess their symptoms. They also may choose careers in other areas of the health-care field as dental hygienists, physical therapists, respiratory or radiological technologists, and speech pathologists or therapists.

Compassionate Assimilators like to be practical and help people meet immediate day-to-day needs. They may become child-care workers, hairdressers, orcashiers or may work in a number of other service occupations. They are also attracted to work in the helping fields, for example, social work, counseling, and teaching. One Compassionate Assimilator describes her personal view of others:

"I like and respect people. It is important to treat each one as an individual. Everyone should be recognized and appreciated for his or her contributions."

ENSURE THAT THINGS RUN SMOOTHLY

Compassionate Assimilators especially enjoy working with others on a one-to-one basis, being of service in an individual and personalized way. They often take on support roles as assistants or aides. Compassionate Assimilators are also good at organizing and managing details. They can arrange things, keeping track of a multitude of details. They will often work behind the scenes to ensure that events and projects run smoothly. One Compassionate Assimilator describes her role as a mediation assistant:

"During the mediations I sit back and listen for information. I have a good memory and will be able to recall verbatim what others have said. I am later able to share this information one-to-one with the negotiator to ensure that all of the important points are covered. I also enjoy preparing for the negotiations, collecting and organizing the necessary information. When needed, I am quickly able to access it and share it with the negotiator. I wouldn't want to do the up-front negotiating role. Staying in the background, listening, collecting details, and supporting the process are much more satisfying for me."

SUPPORT OTHERS

It is important for Compassionate Assimilators to give and receive positive feedback from others. They look for opportunities to support and nurture others and expect others to do the same. Preferring to stay in the background, they tend to listen more than talk and usually will not communicate a great deal about themselves. If they are not appreciated for their efforts, they can feel taken for granted. They may need to more actively step forward to share their successes or highlight their accomplishments.

Compassionate Assimilators like to be needed and will go out of their way to help someone who is in trouble or distress. They may seem overly eager to please or somewhat too dependent on external feedback. Compassionate Assimilators may feel very responsible and can base their decisions more on others' needs than their own.

MANAGE THE DETAILS

Compassionate Assimilators are comfortable following procedures and attending to details and may enjoy a range of technical or administrative work. They want procedures to be fair and easily implemented. One Compassionate Assimilator who works in a government agency helps clients manage the bureaucracy. This opportunity to utilize procedures as he helps others is very rewarding for him:

"I enjoy helping clients work their way through the paperwork necessary for returning to learning. I like to make the process as clear and simple as possible for them."

Snapshot: Ideal Work Environment for Compassionate Assimilators

By focusing on your personal preferences, you will be able to better assess the types of work that will be personally satisfying. The following list describes ideal work environments for Compassionate Assimilators. Check off the items that are true for you.

As a Compassionate Assimilator, I prefer a work environment that is

- ☐ Is supportive
- ☐ Is structured
- ☐ Provides opportunities to help or support others
- ☐ Is clear in its expectations and procedures
- ☐ Provides opportunities to administrate and manage details

Snapshot: Skills and Valued Activities for Compassionate Assimilators

By focusing on your personal preferences, you will be able to better assess the types of work that will be personally satisfying. The following list describes skills and activities valued by Compassionate Assimilators. Check off the items that are true for you.

As a Compassionate Assimilator, I value the following skills and activities:

☐ Administration

☐ Attention to detail

☐ Communication, especially listening

☐ Dependability

☐ Organization

☐ Time and task management

Work That Attracts Compassionate Assimilators

The following occupations are typically of interest to Compassionate Assimilators. When looking for career ideas, remember to also look at the work options listed for Assimilators earlier in the chapter, which are attractive to both Logical Assimilators and Compassionate Assimilators.

HEALTH CARE
Critical care nursing
Dental assistant
Dental hygienist
Dietitian or nutritionist
Health education practitioner
Health-service worker
Health technologist
Licensed practical nurse
Medical records administrator
Medical technologist
Nurse
Nursing aide
Nursing consultant

Nursing educator
Physical therapist
Physician—family, general practice
Public health nurse
Speech pathologist or therapist

Many Compassionate Assimilators choose careers in the health-care field. These careers allow them to blend their attention to detail with their compassion for others in a practical way. If you enjoy helping others and are comfortable around medical procedures, you may want to explore some of these careers.

COUNSELING, SUPPORTING, AND TEACHING
Counselor
Minister
Priest or spiritual advisor
Probation officer
Social worker
Teacher—elementary, reading, special education, preschool, religious
Teacher's aide

Compassionate Assimilators are often found in occupations that help the mind and spirit as well as the body. If you enjoy counseling and teaching, these careers may be of interest.

PERSONAL SERVICES
Child-care worker
Cosmetologist
Customer service representative
Food-service worker
Hairdresser
Optician

There are a number of occupations that provide a range of immediate services to others outside of health care, counseling, and teaching. Many of these jobs require attention to detail and a willingness to work with the public. Some, such as hairdressing and cosmetology, require a creative flair as well.

DATA MANAGEMENT
Aeronautical engineer
Bookkeeper
Cashier
Computer operator
Curator
Library assistant
Office—clerical worker
Secretary

Some Compassionate Assimilators are more content in the background, managing data. From creating highly technical aeronautical designs to creating effective business letters, they are "working the plan" behind the scenes. Depending on your interests, you may find one of these careers interesting.

CREATIVE OCCUPATIONS
Architect
Artist
Interior decorator
Musician

Assimilators sometimes seek creative expression. Their work is often very detailed and complex. If you have a creative flair, you may want to consider opportunities to work in an artistic career.

SUPERVISORY OR LAW ENFORCEMENT ROLES
Guard
Police detective
Site Supervisor

As mentioned for Assimilators in general, administration and supervision are often strengths. No matter what field you choose, you may find supervisory positions interesting. If you have a specific interest in the corrections field, a career in law enforcement might be something to consider.

Compassionate Assimilators as Leaders
Compassionate Assimilators bring unique strengths to the leadership role. They naturally lead and prefer to be led in a specific way.

SUPPORT AND ASSIST

Compassionate Assimilators are caring and unassuming leaders. They strive to create a mutually supportive environment in which individuals can complete their tasks in harmony. Compassionate Assimilators will be in touch with and focus on what the people in the organization need as well as the tasks that need to be accomplished.

Staying in the background, supporting, and assisting is how Compassionate Assimilators prefer to lead. Giving information and support rather than directions and commands is typical of their leadership style. Compassionate Assimilators strive to ensure that people have all the necessary resources and support available to do their work. They may, however, *assume* they know what people want, based on their storehouse of past experiences, rather than asking directly. Because of this, they may generalize and misunderstand people's needs. It is important for Compassionate Assimilator leaders to ask others what they need.

Compassionate Assimilators are likely to remember special occasions. They will celebrate others and uphold organizational traditions, especially those that validate and celebrate people. Through these types of activities, they will encourage a sense of connection and belonging within the organization.

WORK HARD AND FOLLOW THE RULES

Compassionate Assimilators have a strong work ethic. They follow the rules and expect others to do so as well. Compassionate Assimilators take their responsibilities very seriously and will do whatever it takes to meet their deadlines and get the work done. They can take it personally if others do not take their responsibilities seriously, fail to follow rules, or neglect to follow through on obligations. Compassionate Assimilators may take on additional duties themselves rather than chance conflict with others, to ensure that the work is completed.

AVOID CONFLICT

Compassionate Assimilators find it difficult to confront others and at first may not express their disappointment directly. After some time, however, they may become so frustrated that they may be overly critical or blunt with a poor performer. Ironically, they find this type of feedback personally unhelpful. Compassionate Assimilators are disheartened by and uncomfortable with conflict and disharmony. Confrontations and other expressions of discord are difficult for them to manage. Learning to provide direct and timely feedback can be an area of growth for Compassionate Assimilators. It can be difficult for them to recognize that dealing with conflict using a direct and assertive approach can have a positive influence on ongoing working relationships.

Snapshot: Compassionate Assimilators as Leaders

By focusing on your personal preferences, you will be able to better assess the types of work that will be personally satisfying. The following list describes the leadership preferences of Compassionate Assimilators. Check off the items that are true for you.

As a Compassionate Assimilator leader, I prefer to

- [ ] Create a mutually supportive environment
- [ ] Focus on what people need
- [ ] Stay in the background
- [ ] Support and assist
- [ ] Give information rather than commands
- [ ] Ensure that people have necessary resources and support
- [ ] Celebrate others and uphold organizational traditions
- [ ] Encourage a sense of connection and belonging within the organization
- [ ] Work hard and follow rules
- [ ] Meet deadlines and get the work done
- [ ] Avoid conflict

Compassionate Assimilators as Team Members

Compassionate Assimilators value camaraderie. They enjoy cooperating with others toward a common goal. As team members they are highly dependable and reliable. They complete their assigned duties accurately, thoroughly, and within the deadlines.

Compassionate Assimilators are negatively affected by discord on their team. They do not like to work in environments in which there is competition between individuals. Compassionate Assimilators value working together, as a team, toward a mutual goal rather than focusing on individual accomplishments. Collaboration is a key aspect of teamwork for this type. Preferring to stay in the background, they tend to support and assist rather than lead.

Giving and receiving positive feedback and support is important to Compassionate Assimilators. Although they do like to support others and stay in the background, they may feel taken for granted if they are not acknowledged. They do not always need to be singled out for praise; merely hearing others celebrate and appreciate the team's effort can be very rewarding. However, they also appreciate occasional positive feedback from the others they are supporting.

Snapshot: Compassionate Assimilators as Team Members

By focusing on your personal preferences, you will be able to better assess the types of work that will be personally satisfying. The following list describes how Compassionate Assimilators like to work within a team. Check off the items that are true for you.

As a Compassionate Assimilator team member, I

☐ Value camaraderie

☐ Enjoy cooperating with others toward a common goal

☐ Am highly dependable and reliable

☐ Complete assigned duties accurately and thoroughly

☐ Am negatively affected by discord

☐ Dislike working in competitive environments

☐ Meet deadlines

☐ Prefer to stay in the background

☐ Like to support and assist rather than lead

☐ Give positive feedback and support

☐ Appreciate positive feedback

Compassionate Assimilators as Learners

Compassionate Assimilators dislike information that is too theoretical, abstract, or presented in a disorganized manner. They find practical information with real-life applications to be far more useful. Because of their reflective nature, it is important to allow Compassionate Assimilators to relate information back to past experiences. Personal stories and detailed examples help them in this regard.

Compassionate Assimilators also prefer information that is presented clearly in a step-by-step manner. They like to have all of the facts and details, preferably within a well-organized framework. Compassionate Assimilators like structured learning environments that provide clear expectations and instruction. Knowing what is expected in the learning situation helps them set goals and manage their time, things that they naturally do well.

Compassionate Assimilators appreciate support and encouragement while learning. It is important for them to have an instructor or mentor who is interested in them and provides positive feedback. They appreciate having their learning efforts recognized and applauded by others.

Snapshot: Compassionate Assimilators as Learners

By focusing on your personal preferences, you will be able to better assess the types of work that will be personally satisfying. The following list describes the learning preferences of Compassionate Assimilators. Check off the items that are true for you.

As a Compassionate Assimilator learner, I

- ☐ Dislike theoretical, abstract, or disorganized information
- ☐ Want practical information with real-life applications
- ☐ Relate information back to my past experiences
- ☐ Like personal stories and detailed examples
- ☐ Like information presented clearly and step-by-step
- ☐ Prefer structured and supportive learning environments
- ☐ Seek clear expectations and instruction
- ☐ Like support, encouragement, and acknowledgment of effort

BALANCING ASSIMILATING WITH LOGIC

The latest research shows that 11.6 percent of people in the United States are Logical Assimilators (ISTJ). Logical Assimilators are outwardly decisive and logical. They are task oriented and focused on efficiently carrying out obligations and meeting goals. They are not averse to having nice possessions and being rewarded monetarily for their achievements. These external rewards help them maintain a sense of security and stability.

Logical Assimilators tend to be subject area experts and are drawn to opportunities to work in technical fields, often choosing to maintain and operate equipment and systems. They are excellent at seeing and correcting irregularities. Independent and thorough, Logical Assimilators do their best work when they are working within a structured environment, given clear expectations, and then left alone to get the work done.

Because Logical Assimilators have a logical approach as a balance to their focus on details, they initially express their Assimilating way of working differently than Compassionate Assimilators do. However, Compassionate Assimilators in midlife may find that these logic-based descriptions mirror the direction in which they are moving as they mature and develop.

What Logical Assimilators Do Naturally

FOLLOW THE RULES

Logical Assimilators are in tune with and are careful to follow rules and regulations. Wanting to conscientiously get the work done, they will carefully and precisely use existing policies and procedures to approach tasks as efficiently as possible. Logical Assimilators are able to work well doing routine tasks and repetitive work. They excel at concentrating and paying attention to detail. They do not like to be interrupted and can concentrate on a task for long periods. Being very organized and task focused, they dislike anything that gets in the way of their steady and deliberate approach. Environments with constant interruptions, meetings that are not short and to the point, and problems with work systems distract and frustrate Logical Assimilators. One Logical Assimilator meets his need for independence as a wildlife officer:

"I like going out to do fieldwork. I get a lot more done in the field than in the office. I am not interrupted by phone calls or meetings. When I drive, I can plan and organize what to do next."

BE PRECISE AND THOROUGH

Logical Assimilators are precise and thorough with facts and details. Occupations that require working with and accounting for money and statistics can be appealing to them. They often become accountants, actuaries, auditors, bankers, finance officers, insurance underwriters, or purchasing agents. One Logical Assimilator describes his approach:

"I am a stickler for details. I read things over carefully. It is important to take the time to understand something thoroughly."

ANALYZE AND DECIDE

Logical Assimilators are able to use logical analysis to make tough decisions. They see issues as black or white and make decisions that uphold the rules and maintain the integrity of the organization. Ambiguity and uncertainty are uncomfortable for them, and they would rather work with the facts and realities of the situation than with possibilities.

They like roles that allow them to administer or advise. They often become administrators and supervisors in a range of industries. They are reliable, dependable, and conscientious. They deal with others in a no-nonsense, practical, logical, and decisive manner. Logical Assimilators can be seen as independent, calm, and sometimes distant. However, they are genuinely concerned about and take responsibility for others and will often contribute to the community as volunteers or will become members of community organizations.

Logical Assimilators also use logical analysis and attention to detail to find and correct abnormal situations. Being careful to observe and maintain exacting standards, they can spot small deviations and discrepancies.

Snapshot: Ideal Work Environment for Logical Assimilators

By focusing on your personal preferences, you will be able to better assess the types of work that will be personally satisfying. The following list describes the ideal work environment for Logical Assimilators. Check off the items that are true for you.

As a Logical Assimilator, I prefer a work environment that

- [ ] Is stable and predictable
- [ ] Offers opportunities to use logic and decision making
- [ ] Is practical and routine
- [ ] Has clear expectations
- [ ] Allows uninterrupted time to concentrate
- [ ] Involves detailed and meticulous tasks
- [ ] Lets me direct others

> ## Snapshot: Skills and Valued Activities for Logical Assimilators
>
> *By focusing on your personal preferences, you will be able to better assess the types of work that will be personally satisfying. The following list describes the skills and valued activities of Logical Assimilators. Check off the items that are true for you.*
>
> As a Logical Assimilator, I value the following skills and activities:
>
> ☐ Analysis   ☐ Organizing
>
> ☐ Attention to detail   ☐ Planning
>
> ☐ Critical thinking   ☐ Precision
>
> ☐ Decision making   ☐ Time and task management

Work That Attracts Logical Assimilators

The following occupations are of interest to Logical Assimilators. When looking for career ideas, remember to also look at the work options listed for Assimilators earlier in the chapter, which are attractive to both Logical Assimilators and Compassionate Assimilators.

DATA MANAGEMENT AND ANALYSIS

Accountant

Actuary

Auditor

Banking and finance

Efficiency analyst

Information officer

Insurance underwriter

Purchasing agent

Researcher

Careers in data management and analysis provide opportunities to combine attention to detail with logical thinking. If you enjoy making detailed calculations or analyzing and interpreting facts, these careers may be of interest.

SCIENCE AND TECHNOLOGY
Chemist
Computer analyst
Computer technician
Dentist
Electrical or electronic engineering technician
Engineer
Engineering technologist
Geologist
Lab technologist
Meteorologist
Teacher—math, technical, trades
Technical writer

Scientific and technical careers can provide a good focus for Logical Assimilators. If you have an interest in learning how things work, investigation, and problem solving, these careers may be for you.

MANAGEMENT AND SUPERVISION
Consultant
Labor relations worker
Management consultant
Manager—law enforcement, government, business, executive, finance
Personnel
School principal

As mentioned for Assimilators in general, administration and supervision are often strengths. No matter what field you choose, you may find supervisory positions rewarding.

LAW AND REGULATORY ENFORCEMENT
Air force personnel
Detective
Judge
Military officer
Police officer
Pollution control specialist
Regulatory compliance officer

If you have a specific interest in the corrections field, a career in law enforcement might be something to consider. These careers provide opportunities to work within a structured system to ensure compliance to established rules. Many of these occupations also require an investigative and problem-solving focus.

TRADES AND OTHER HANDS-ON WORK

Cleaning service worker

Crafts worker

Farmer

Machine equipment or process operator

Mechanic

Steelworker

Hands-on work within a variety of trades and other occupations appeals to Logical Assimilators. These occupations provide opportunities to make immediate progress toward concrete goals. If you are mechanically or artistically inclined, some of these careers may suit you. Some may also be suitable if you prefer to be independent and work outdoors.

Logical Assimilators as Leaders

Logical Assimilators bring unique strengths to the leadership role. They naturally lead and prefer to be led in a specific way.

DIRECTIVE

Logical Assimilators are directive and authoritarian leaders. They follow rules and procedures and expect others to do the same. Logical Assimilators like to work within clearly defined hierarchical organizations, and they respect au-thority. It is important that they share their expectations and standards openly with others, since they tend to have much more exacting standards than others do. They like to manage and are often attracted to management positions, especially in structured and stable organizations.

TASK ORIENTED

Focused on tasks and deadlines, Logical Assimilators clearly define the duties and expectations they have for all staff. They value independence and give independence to those around them, assuming that others will carry out their tasks as prescribed. Logical Assimilators expect others to do their work carefully, thoroughly, and within the time limits given.

It is important for these leaders that things under their control proceed smoothly, efficiently, and on schedule. They are impatient with delays, especially those caused by others not following through with tasks they were assigned. Because of this task orientation, Logical Assimilators can be sticklers for details and may seem overly controlling in their leadership. The feedback they provide can seem harsh and overly critical to others. They are especially hard on those who shirk responsibilities, lack follow-through, or break the rules. Logical Assimilators often see the leadership role as a responsibility to help others work more efficiently.

Snapshot: Logical Assimilators as Leaders

By focusing on your personal preferences, you will be able to better assess the types of work that will be personally satisfying. The following list describes the leadership preferences of Logical Assimilators. Check off the items that are true for you.

As a Logical Assimilator leader, I prefer to

☐ Define expectations

☐ Follow rules and procedures

☐ Be independent and task oriented

☐ Respect authority

☐ Uphold exacting standards

☐ Attend to details

☐ Have others do their work carefully

☐ Help things proceed smoothly, efficiently, and on schedule

☐ Avoid delays

☐ Clearly define duties and expectations

Logical Assimilators as Team Members
Logical Assimilators are responsible and loyal team members. They are task oriented and prefer to work toward well-defined goals. It helps Logical Assim-

ilators if clear duties and expectations are established for each team member. Then all can accomplish what is expected as they work toward the goal.

Logical Assimilators may become impatient with spending time defining and building processes. They prefer a team to have a leader who can define goals and specify activities. Then everyone can follow the rules and get the job done. This, to Logical Assimilators, is the most efficient way to accomplish things.

Logical Assimilators dislike expending time and energy working out conflicts and dealing with personal issues. They may think that interpersonal conflict distracts people from the task at hand and should not be dealt with in the workplace. To other types, this task focus may seem overly abrupt.

Snapshot: Logical Assimilators as Team Members

By focusing on your personal preferences, you will be able to better assess the types of work that will be personally satisfying. The following list describes how Logical Assimilators like to work within a team. Check off the items that are true for you.

As a Logical Assimilator team member, I

☐ Am responsible and loyal

☐ Am task-oriented

☐ Prefer to work toward well-defined goals

☐ Want everyone to follow the rules and get the job done

☐ May become impatient with defining and building processes

☐ Like a team to have a leader who can define goals and specify activities

☐ Want clear duties and expectations established for each team member

☐ Dislike expending time and energy working out conflicts and dealing with personal issues

Logical Assimilators as Learners

Logical Assimilators want to learn relevant facts, in great detail. They want these facts presented in a logical, sequential manner by a qualified subject area expert. They learn well by observing and doing. Logical Assimilators have little interest in theory or discussion except when these things can be linked directly to a practical and immediate use. Concrete, specific, and detailed examples help them relate information to their experiences. It is important to allow Logical Assimilators time to link what they are learning to what they already know.

As in a work setting, Logical Assimilators want learning goals and expectations to be clearly defined. Learning activities and information should be directly and practically related to the learning goals. Logical Assimilators naturally and responsibly manage their time and meet their expected learning objectives.

Logical Assimilators like highly detailed and accurate reference materials. They will quickly see any errors or discrepancies in materials or presentations. They can interpret errors as a lack of rigor and may disengage or criticize information that is less than perfect. Logical Assimilators do not like to work with instructors who are disorganized or unprepared. For them, trying to learn under those circumstances is a waste of valuable time and energy.

· 206 ·

Snapshot: Logical Assimilators as Learners

By focusing on your personal preferences, you will be able to better assess the types of work that will be personally satisfying. The following list describes the learning preferences of Logical Assimilators. Check off the items that are true for you.

As a Logical Assimilator learner, I

- [ ] Want to learn relevant facts, in great detail
- [ ] Want facts presented in a logical, sequential manner
- [ ] Need qualified subject experts
- [ ] Learn well by observing and doing
- [ ] Have little interest in theory or discussion
- [ ] Need concrete, specific, and detailed examples
- [ ] Want time to link what I am learning to what I already know
- [ ] Want learning goals and expectations to be clearly defined
- [ ] Like highly detailed and accurate reference materials
- [ ] Have no tolerance for instructors who are disorganized or unprepared

The Assimilator's Greatest Challenges

Everyone has less-preferred activities and areas for growth and improvement. Assimilators are no exception. Here are two major developmental areas for both Compassionate Assimilators and Logical Assimilators, with tips on how to develop each one.

Managing Change

Assimilators are most comfortable in stable and structured environments. They are very grounded in and conscious of past experiences and current situations. They excel at maintaining the status quo. However, the world is rapidly changing, it is impossible to anticipate everything, and Assimilators need to develop flexibility. The status quo cannot always be maintained, and there will be times when it may be advantageous for an Assimilator to take a risk or to try new ways of doing things. A careful and cautious approach has some disadvantages. As one Assimilator describes it,

"My biggest challenge is starting a new project without having enough information. In the past I would hesitate. I am learning to jump in without all the information and make it work."

This is especially true as many organizations are flattening their organizational structures and changing the way they do business. Organizational chains of command are no longer as clear as they were, and operating procedures do not always solve problems encountered during times of change.

Tips for Managing Change

- Look for practical reasons behind the change. How can the change make your work easier or more efficient?
- Acquire information as far ahead as possible. Listen when others start talking about changes, even if their ideas seem far-fetched.
- Create a new structure that helps you work in the changed environment.
- Accept that change is a fact. Understand and accept that you cannot plan for everything.
- Work toward looking at the big picture and the future. Find information that discusses trends in your area and ask yourself, "What if this happened here?" Try to anticipate and prepare for change rather than react to it.

- Find out about your organization's long-range plans. Make sure you are aligning yourself with where the organization is heading.
- Now and then just jump in instead of planning your dive.

Learning to Enjoy the Moment

Because Assimilators are responsible and conscientious, they consistently put work before play. They find it difficult to leave a task undone. Assimilators often take on many responsibilities and work long and hard toward accomplishing goals. They can be very tough on themselves. Their sense of duty sometimes pushes them further than it is physically good for them to go. They have to work hard to maintain balance; otherwise they can find themselves experiencing burnout. One Assimilator uses his work ethic to his advantage:

"I find it relaxing to work around the house. Recently I built a fireplace. I enjoyed the mental stimulation of the problem solving and the change from my other work."

Using a similar strategy, another Assimilator coaches a running team as a way to wind down from her other responsibilities:

"I guess you could call coaching another type of work, but I find it highly enjoyable to work with motivated runners. It isn't my job to make them show up. I can simply enjoy their energy and commitment and encourage them to achieve their personal best. It's a very rewarding activity for me."

TIPS FOR ENJOYING THE MOMENT

- Use your observation and attention to detail as a means to focus on the here and now. Take time to use your senses to look carefully at a painting, smell a flower, or taste a meal.
- Take a break. Plan it if you must.
- Focus on your personal needs. What would be interesting and motivating for you to do right now?
- Indulge in a hobby, sport, or recreational interest on a regular basis.
- Focus on taking care of your body. Treat yourself to a massage, bubble bath, sauna, hot tub, or some other pampering activity.

KEY FOR ME: MANAGING MY CHALLENGES

Is managing change or learning to enjoy the moment a challenge for you? If so, which of the strategies explored in this chapter would be helpful to try? ....

....

....

....

....

....

....

....

FINAL TIPS FOR ASSIMILATORS: DOING WHAT COMES NATURALLY

An Assimilator naturally approaches the world of work in a practical and decisive way. Here are a few final tips that will help you choose and develop satisfying work.

Work the Plan

Find opportunities that allow you to complete tasks or provide practical services. You naturally are able to attend to detail and follow through responsibly to a goal, so use these powerful attributes to your advantage. Find opportunities to organize and manage projects or maintain systems.

Specialize

Your depth of information and practical experience, over time, will make you a subject area expert in your field. You may not even realize the extent of your comprehensive information base, or value it. Indulge your focus on and ability to collect and remember details. Share your practical knowledge with others who are interested in your area. When looking for a career path, identify the areas that you are naturally learning about and focusing on. Then think of ways to use your focus to generate income.

Attend to Details
Being meticulous and able to concentrate well for long periods of time allows you to complete a wide range of specialized tasks. For example, you can find errors and omissions in written materials, analyze and evaluate systems, diagnose problems, or administrate people and systems. All of these activities, and many others, require the close and careful attention to detail that you bring to work.

Organize and Manage
Because you approach the world in a task-oriented and organized way, you will likely enjoy managing people, projects, and resources. This is especially true because you are also focused on managing details. A combination of task orientation and attention to practical details is an excellent combination for organizing resources, moving forward, and getting the job done.

Adjust to Change
Remember that the status quo will change. Do not let the future sneak up on you. Find out what changes may be happening in the future, and start to prepare for them before they overtake you. Accept change as a part of life, and find ways to adjust. You may need to step outside of your preference for gradual change and improvement, taking giant leaps and risks to position yourself for the future.

Have Some Fun
Sometimes it is essential to step back from all your responsibilities and stop to enjoy the moment. Find ways to shed your sense of obligation for a short time and have some fun. You may need to plan and structure some recreation into your day.

Now that you have learned about your work preferences, please turn to Chapter 11 to begin planning your career path.

CHAPTER EIGHT

Visionaries
Interpret and Implement

PERSONALITY TYPES: INFJ AND INTJ

As a manager of a consulting business, I take great pride in getting the job done and doing a good job. I need to do things well. I feel a strong sense of commitment and responsibility to clients and staff.
—A Visionary

The latest research shows that about 3.6 percent of adults in the United States are Visionaries. Visionaries approach the world in a decisive way. They are interested in organizing people and resources to get the job done. At first glance, they may seem like Insightful Contributors if they are INFJs or Insightful Expeditors if they are INTJs. However, what you do not see at a casual glance is the Visionary's internal preference for focusing on the possibilities. Visionaries like to take in ideas and mold them internally to create new and unique mental frameworks; they can be powerful theorists, poets, and futurists. This internal focus is the guiding force of both INFJs and INTJs. As they work toward goals, Visionaries are constantly guided by and focused on their framework of ideas and possibilities. This internal focus on insight and ideas is their natural way of working.

Visionaries' insightful approach is immediate and automatic. It provides a way to interpret new information, thus allowing Visionaries to smoothly adjust their actions to their mental models. Visionaries may not necessarily explain the ideas they use to make their decisions. Appearing calm, quiet, and serious, they are content instead to use their knowledge as an internal guide that allows them to understand and interpret their current situation. Because of this internal focus, we are sometimes surprised by the Visionaries' actions, since we are not privy to all the ideas that direct their behavior.

VISIONARIES AT WORK
What Visionaries Do Naturally

LEARN AND INTERPRET
Visionaries naturally reflect on their knowledge, thinking of new and different ways to interpret what is known. This internal inspiration is their guide and primary focus. They will question the very frameworks in which information is presented and organized and will come up with new ways of thinking about that information. Nothing is set in stone for Visionaries. They will not hesitate to question basic assumptions of what is known or to view things in a completely new way. They can look at the same ideas in many different ways. Focusing on the world of ideas and possibilities, they are future and change oriented. It is not unusual to find them on the cutting edge. One Visionary commented,

"I graduated from university decades ago with a computer science major in the first year that a major in that subject was offered. I could see there was great potential in the field."

Visionaries will see no limits to what they can learn or to how learning can be applied to situations. They crave knowledge and ideas and are often strongly focused on lifelong learning. Visionaries can always come up with a number of things that they want to explore. They enjoy learning about and creating theory, putting ideas together in new ways, and finding new applications for existing information. They find it hard to stop processing information and to set limits to what they can imagine. They want to continuously learn more so that they can explore possible connections. Over time, it can become difficult for them to create order out of the immense number of ideas they have collected. This is a source of internal conflict. They want to learn as much as they can, and at the same time they are driven to apply what they already know and take action.

CREATE AND ORGANIZE IDEAS

Visionaries are attracted to work that allows them to research, learn about, and play with ideas. They work in a range of scientific careers, research, and consulting positions. They enjoy the academic environment and often become teachers and professors.

When working with ideas, Visionaries are independent and self-motivated. When inspired, they are strongly driven to make models and solve complex problems. Visionaries require time alone to process connections and possibilities, especially at the formative stages as they are conceptualizing and organizing their thoughts into a framework or plan. They need to be challenged intellectually and are motivated by complex problems. Visionaries often solve a problem by redefining the questions or changing the framework it is presented in. They are continually shifting paradigms and looking for ways to think outside the box. Routine work that does not allow them to tap into their inspiration bores them.

Visionaries need input to stimulate them and enjoy holding in-depth, one-on-one conversations that focus on ideas in an area of interest. They use metaphors, symbols, and other abstract figures of speech, and in doing so often struggle to put their ideas into words. They may have trouble explaining their ideas, as words alone cannot adequately reflect the complex patterns and possibilities they perceive.

Visionaries find themselves disagreeing with restrictions being put on thoughts. As soon as they are given information, they begin to think of new applications or alternative explanations. Often, they critique others' views as limited or one-sided. They can spend considerable time creating a unique and complex interpretation of the world, and, as a result, others can see them as strongly individualistic. It is very difficult to coerce Visionaries. They can be offered information and presented with theory and frameworks, but they will ultimately accept it or reject it on the basis of their own understanding of the world. One Visionary describes his educational experience this way:

"I don't remember dates or facts. I like to understand underlying ideas and syn-thesize the rest. Good learning is one 'aha!' moment after another. I have one big mental model the learning must fit into. If it doesn't fit, I need to take time to adjust my model."

FIND APPLICATIONS FOR IDEAS

Visionaries like to take action and find ways to use their ideas in the real world. Ideas without application hold little long-term attraction for them. To be mean-ingful, ideas must be used to improve something or create something better in the world. Planning and organizing are strengths that Visionaries use to put their ideas into action. This combination of creative ideas and a focus on prac-tical applications provides a strong impetus for the Visionary to move ahead.

Visionaries usually have an entire plan mentally mapped out before they begin to implement it. This plan can be very complex and detailed, but the details may not be available to the casual observer. Visionaries can become rather disconcerted if others want to modify their well-thought-out plans, since they have spent considerable mental energy conceptualizing and orga-nizing them.

Visionaries are internally motivated and demonstrate drive and integrity. Visionaries are results oriented and are highly responsible about meeting their obligations and completing their tasks. They need to get the work done well and on time. Visionaries like to create quality work and can be perfectionists. One Visionary, when asked if she was driven to meet deadlines, replied,

"I guess so—I've never missed one."

The idea of even considering missing a deadline was foreign to her.

Visionary Blind Spots

CHANGING PLANS IN MIDSTREAM

Visionaries put considerable time and energy into conceptualizing and creating workable plans. They are organized and effective when putting plans into action. They find it very difficult to change course midstream because it means they will have to revise their well-thought-out plans. This is especially true if the changes will slow down or derail some of the original intent of the project. It is not that Visionaries do not like change. In fact, they constantly work to improve, and they will often increase the scope of their plans. What is difficult for them is being forced to rethink an entire project because of an external influence. It is important to remember that Visionaries both are reflective and seek movement forward. They will often finish a project in their mind before they start acting on it. Changing the plan once it is started interferes with their need for closure. Rethinking the plan will take them considerable time and energy and will slow down or change their already well-thought-out process.

In a similar vein, Visionaries do not like to be taken off a project before it is completed. They can manage many things and manage them well, but if too many things are added to their plate they can become overwhelmed. They need to be careful about what they pile on, because they will work long and hard to meet their obligations. Visionaries like to take projects over the finish line. One Visionary explains,

"I become very uncomfortable if I am taken off the completion of one project to start a new one. I need closure, and I don't like leaving things up in the air. I really value that feeling of accomplishment associated with getting the project done."

COPING WITH ROUTINE

Visionaries find it difficult to complete routine activities unless those activities are linked to accomplishing long-term goals. Such tasks, being well defined, fail to provide opportunities to work with ideas and make decisions before taking action. Take away these key motivating aspects of their work and Visionaries will become disinterested. They must have opportunities to work with ideas and possibilities or they will feel stifled.

Visionaries find routine paperwork and administrative details especially unpleasant. One Visionary describes his least favorite activity:

"I don't like administrating things that are already established. I get too bogged down in detail, and I am unable to attend to the more conceptual work I enjoy."

Snapshot: Visionaries' Natural Work Preferences

Visionaries are at their best when they can use their natural work preferences. By focusing on your preferences, you will be able to better assess the types of work that will be personally satisfying. The following list describes characteristics and preferences of Visionaries. Check off the items that are true for you.

As a Visionary, I am at my best when I can

- ☐ Reflect on my knowledge
- ☐ Think of new and different ways to interpret what is known
- ☐ Question basic assumptions of what is known
- ☐ See many different ways of looking at the same ideas
- ☐ Focus on lifelong learning
- ☐ Enjoy learning about and creating theory
- ☐ Find a new application for existing information
- ☐ Be independent and self-motivated
- ☐ Make models and solve complex problems
- ☐ Use planning and organizing

- ☐ Have time alone to process connections and possibilities
- ☐ Be challenged intellectually
- ☐ Work on complex problems
- ☐ Redefine questions or change the framework they are presented in
- ☐ Avoid routine work
- ☐ Have in-depth, one-on-one conversations
- ☐ Use metaphors, symbols, and other abstract figures of speech
- ☐ Take action and find ways to use my ideas in the real world
- ☐ Improve something or create something better in the world

WHAT'S KEY FOR ME?
My Ideal Work Preferences

Look back at the snapshot for the work preferences for a Visionary. From the items you have checked, jot down the points that best summarize your preferences. Feel free to add points that are not on the list.

My most important work preferences are...

....

....

....

....

....

....

....

....

WORK THAT ATTRACTS VISIONARIES

Visionaries can be found in many types of work. Here are some examples that use the Visionary's natural way of working.

ARTS AND DESIGN
   Architect
   Artist
   Designer

These occupations provide Visionaries with opportunities to create products that reflect their ideas and insights. Opportunities for art and design are limited only by your imagination. You will need to determine if this is an interest area. If so, define the specific medium and situations in which art and design will be rewarding for you.

COUNSELING, HEALTH CARE, AND EDUCATION
   Educational consultant
   Occupational therapist
   Physician
   Psychiatrist

Psychologist
School administrator
Social scientist
Social services worker
Teacher—health, nursing, university or college professor

Many Visionaries use their insight to help others. If you especially enjoy learning about people and interacting with others, you may want to consider occupations in this area.

RESEARCH AND ANALYSIS
Attorney
Researcher
Writer

If you enjoy research or presenting ideas and information to others, some of these careers might suit you. You can learn, present viewpoints, and use analysis in these occupations.

Of course, these are just some examples. There are many other types of work that Visionaries will enjoy. See the next sections for work that is specifically appealing to INFJs and INTJs.

HOW VISIONARIES FIND BALANCE

Visionaries are energized by working within the internal world, reflecting on and categorizing experiences. They are continually taking in, creating, and relating ideas. Over time, they develop rich and detailed mental models of the world. They must balance this internal focus by making decisions and acting in the world around them.

A well-developed decision-making approach helps Visionaries sort, prioritize, and choose which inspirations to cultivate and develop; otherwise, they can become overwhelmed and overpowered by a multitude of ideas and possibilities. There are two approaches for evaluating information: a values-based approach and a logical approach. Personality type theory calls these two approaches Feeling (F) and Thinking (T). You may want to look back to

Chapter 2 to discern which approach is most comfortable for you. The words *feeling* and *thinking* have many connotations that do not actually relate to how people evaluate information and make decisions. So, to avoid misconceptions, in this book Visionaries who prefer Feeling as a decision-making approach (INFJs) are called Compassionate Visionaries, while Visionaries who prefer Thinking as a decision-making approach (INTJs) are called Logical Visionaries.

Each approach has a different focus, but both allow the Visionary an opportunity to make choices and act in the world. Over the course of their life, Visionaries will use and develop both approaches to help them make decisions and choose their actions. This natural development allows Visionaries to become more flexible decision makers over time.

Compassionate Visionaries naturally evaluate information on the basis of personal and human values. They act in a way similar to Insightful Contributors, seeing and developing human potential. Compassionate Visionaries and Insightful Contributors both deal with the world using the same personal and caring approach. They are often found in similar types of work and enjoy doing similar types of things. It is important to remember that, for Compassionate Visionaries, this focus on helping and understanding the situations of others is secondary to and supportive of their primary focus of expanding their understanding of the world around them.

Logical Visionaries, on the other hand, most naturally use logical analysis to evaluate information. They act in a way similar to Insightful Expeditors, working efficiently toward long-term goals. Logical Visionaries and Insightful Expeditors both approach the world in a task-oriented way. They are often found in similar types of work and enjoy doing similar types of things. It is important to remember that, for Logical Visionaries, this focus on logical analysis is secondary to and supportive of their primary focus of taking in and interpreting ideas to create possibilities.

Insightful Contributors and Insightful Expeditors also look to ideas and possibilities to focus their decision making, but ideas are secondary to their focus on decision making and action. Unlike the Contributors and Expeditors, Visionaries are more focused on the ideas and models they can create than they are on deciding and acting.

As you go through this section, you may find it helpful to read about your most natural balancing approach first. Then read about the other approach to balancing to see what is in store for you as you mature and develop.

☐ **I am most like INFJ,**
so I am a Compassionate Visionary.
I will initially balance my internal
focus on ideas by making values-
based decisions. As I mature and
develop, I will also learn to balance
my approach by incorporating
more logical analysis into decisions.

☐ **I am most like INTJ,**
so I am a Logical Visionary.
I will initially balance my
internal focus on ideas by making
logical decisions. As I mature and
develop, I will also learn to balance
my approach by incorporating
values of others and myself into
decisions.

BALANCING VISIONING WITH COMPASSION

The latest research shows that about 1.5 percent of people in the United States are Compassionate Visionaries (INFJ). Compassionate Visionaries focus on creating and implementing projects or other activities that will help people. Using a personal and caring approach, they like to work with others. They enjoy working on a team that is focused on meeting long-term goals. They learn about, appreciate, and utilize the special talents and skills of the people around them. They see potential in people and will be especially engaged in actualizing projects that will positively affect people. They are well organized and like to complete complex projects from start to finish.

Because Compassionate Visionaries have a personal and values-based focus as a balance to their internal focus on ideas, they initially express their Visioning way of working differently than Logical Visionaries do. However, Logical Visionaries in midlife may find that these values-based descriptions mirror the direction in which they are moving as they mature and develop.

What Compassionate Visionaries Do Naturally
CONNECT IDEAS TO PEOPLE AND VALUES

Compassionate Visionaries are most comfortable and at their best when they mentally conceptualize ideas and possibilities. At the same time, they take extra care to understand and validate the values of others around them. This creates a focus on possibilities for people. Harmony is an important goal for Compassionate Visionaries, and they will often find ways to conciliate people with opposing positions or change organizational structures to meet people's needs. They enjoy working in positions within an organization that allow them to influence people processes, such as human resources or organization development.

One Compassionate Visionary has focused her attention on understanding and promoting human diversity:

"There are several reasons why I enjoy working with and learning about human diversity. The area excites me because it engages my values, is grounded in my personal experience, has meaning and purpose for people, leaves a better world for my children, and is good for humankind in general."

· 227 ·

These reasons flowed naturally and easily for her as she described her passion in this area. This strong connection between ideas, values, and results is a common theme for the Compassionate Visionary.

CONNECT PEOPLE TO IDEAS AND VALUES

Compassionate Visionaries often develop excellent interpersonal communication skills. A strongly logical and impersonal environment can be a source of discomfort for them. It is important to Compassionate Visionaries that everyone feels included and validated. They will listen carefully to and affirm and support others, making sure everyone feels appreciated. One Compassionate Visionary describes how he enjoys facilitating groups:

"It is gratifying to see others discover something new about themselves and apply these new ideas to their lives. I find that my workshop participants are often grateful for the learning. I find it very rewarding to be thanked and appreciated for the insights I have helped others to find."

Compassionate Visionaries also like to be validated and appreciated themselves and will work well in organizations or with people who nurture and support others. This atmosphere of mutual support and encouragement is an important element that Compassionate Visionaries consider when looking for satisfying work. One Compassionate Visionary imagines,

"I would find great satisfaction creating a human resources department in which I could develop creative and nurturing compensation systems for the employees."

Compassionate Visionaries tend to form quick but accurate impressions of people and situations. They are highly attuned to nuances of speech and sensitive to nonverbal communications. They may not be able to explain the logical reasons or data behind the impressions, but they trust and want to act on them. Others may try to dissuade them, but Compassionate Visionaries will often trust and stick to their assessments.

LIVE THEIR VALUES

Compassionate Visionaries seek work that provides them with both a mental challenge and a sense of meaning. They enjoy working with people and are attracted to work that allows them to help or educate others. They may become psychologists, teachers, counselors, or consultants or work in the religious or spiritual fields. Compassionate Visionaries are very insightful in the areas of interpersonal relationships and the human experience. They often prefer one-on-one interactions or small-group work, although many successfully work as teachers and group facilitators. Those who do spend long periods of time facilitating groups or meeting multiple demands of others will require quiet time to regenerate at the end of the day. They also struggle when working in overly logical or critical environments. One Compassionate Visionary comments,

"I find it exhausting to work with people who aren't interested in validating others' views or who don't value my perspectives."

It is important for Compassionate Visionaries to find meaning and purpose in their work. They are strongly motivated and directed by taking actions to serve their values. Thinking about their values and using values to guide their career path can be a powerful exercise for Compassionate Visionaries. Often their sense of purpose will relate to others, by means of helping people develop or be more tolerant of their fellows. If Compassionate Visionaries do not feel a strong sense of purpose in their work, they can become disengaged.

Compassionate Visionaries have a uniquely and individualistic view of the world formed by their personal interpretation of information. Compassionate Visionaries share mainly the aspects that connect them to others, however, rather than sharing their idiosyncrasies. One Compassionate Visionary comments,

"The most important thing for me on the job is working with good people, whose values are congruent with mine. I want to be in an environment where people like to come to work and look forward to doing a good job. That, to me, is more important than the specific work I am doing."

ACTUALIZE THEIR VISIONS

Compassionate Visionaries work well within systems that provide them with opportunities to create ideas and the autonomy to carry the ideas through. They are able to work within rules and policies and can see them as helpful in letting people know what is expected. However, they abhor rules that limit or discourage growth of individuals within the system.

Compassionate Visionaries are hard workers and often hold high standards of performance for themselves. They have a need to follow through on projects they have started and will become unfocused if they cannot work an idea through from start to finish. They are often skilled at managing and organizing complex tasks, using their resources wisely. They will carefully consider people's needs and assign others to roles that will be best suited for them.

Compassionate Visionaries are distracted by interruptions and need time and space to plan and evaluate their progress. When working on a complex or meaningful problem or project, they can show powerful concentration, focus, and dedication. Because Compassionate Visionaries are driven to work diligently toward goals and because they strive to meet others' needs, they can become overcommitted or subject to burnout.

EXPRESS THEMSELVES

Because Compassionate Visionaries can envision powerful relationships, they can see the positive and potential in almost everyone and everything. They can become somewhat romantic or idealistic. Self-expression is important to them. They need to be genuine and are quick to see when others are posturing or insincere. One Compassionate Visionary comments,

"I would much rather do good than look good."

Compassionate Visionaries may express their idealistic and hopeful inner views in writing or by creating works of art. Their writing is often rich in images and metaphor and focused on the human experience.

· 223 ·

Snapshot: Ideal Work Environment for Compassionate Visionaries

By focusing on your personal preferences, you will be able to better assess the types of work that will be personally satisfying. The following list describes ideal work environments for Compassionate Visionaries. Check off the items that are true for you.

As a Compassionate Visionary, I prefer a work environment that is

- ☐ Supportive and affirming
- ☐ Collaborative
- ☐ Conceptual, with chances to learn and develop
- ☐ Meaningful, serving a higher purpose
- ☐ A source of opportunities to work with and implement ideas
- ☐ Focused on growth and development of people
- ☐ A source of opportunity to organize projects and follow through

Snapshot: Skills and Valued Activities for Compassionate Visionaries

By focusing on your personal preferences, you will be able to better assess the types of work that will be personally satisfying. The following list describes skills and activities valued by Compassionate Visionaries. Check off the items that are true for you.

As a Compassionate Visionary, I value the following skills and activities:

- ☐ Collaborating
- ☐ Communicating
- ☐ Creativity
- ☐ Facilitating
- ☐ Organizing
- ☐ Planning

Work That Attracts Compassionate Visionaries

The following list of occupations are of interest to Compassionate Visionaries. When looking for career ideas, remember to also look at the work options for Visionaries listed earlier in the chapter, which are attractive to both Logical Visionaries and Compassionate Visionaries.

COUNSELING AND EDUCATION

Corporate trainer

Counselor—crisis, career, alcohol and drug, mental health

Educational consultant

Mediator

Religious worker

Teacher—art, drama, English, music, high school, special education, early education

Compassionate Visionaries are often drawn to occupations that provide them with opportunities to teach and counsel. Depending on your specific interests and skills, you may want to consider some of these occupations if you enjoy providing support and direction to others.

HEALTH AND WELLNESS

Audiologist

Dental hygienist

Dietitian or nutritionist

Massage therapist

Medical assistant

Medical secretary

Occupational therapist

Pharmacist

Speech pathologist

Compassionate Visionaries are drawn to opportunities to help others in the areas of health and wellness. If you have an interest in science and like working in a medical setting, you may want to explore some of these occupations.

RESEARCH AND COMMUNICATION

Interpreter or translator

Librarian

Media specialist

Publicist

These occupations focus more specifically on books or on language. Many of the teaching and counseling occupations also use research and communication skills. One of these careers may be of interest to you if you have a love of books, an ear for languages, a talent for writing, or a creative flair.

BUSINESS AND MARKETING
   Management consultant
   Manager—human resources
   Marketing professional
   Organization development specialist
   Public relations specialist

Compassionate Visionaries are found in a variety of business settings, often seeking to help individuals within the organization learn and develop. Using their love of language and ability to understand others, they also are attracted to marketing positions. If you find these settings interesting, you may want to explore some of the occupations listed here.

Compassionate Visionaries as Leaders
Compassionate Visionaries bring unique strengths to the leadership role. They naturally lead and prefer to be led in a specific way.

DEVELOP HUMAN POTENTIAL
Compassionate Visionaries are advocates for developing human potential. The people within the organization or served by it are their primary concern. They bring a strong focus on interpersonal relationships to the leadership role and will work hard to create harmonious and functional work groups. They have a good understanding of how to motivate and validate others.

INTEGRATE ALL PERSPECTIVES
Compassionate Visionaries simultaneously focus on individual, group, and organizational needs. This multiple perspective ensures that all aspects and needs are respected and addressed, from the bottom-line profit motive of a company to the emotional needs of an employee. This broad focus can be both a gift and an area of potential distress for the Compassionate Visionary leader, since aligning these multiple needs is not always easy.

AVOID USING POWER AND AUTHORITY
Politics are not appealing to Compassionate Visionaries. They do not respect or seek positions of power. Compassionate Visionaries prefer to lead by example,

and they are much more likely to accommodate and cooperate than command. Sometimes they are offered rather than seek leadership. One Compassionate Visionary explains why his co-workers nominated him for a leadership position: They were impressed by his ability to meet the needs of the people around him as he adroitly managed projects.

Snapshot: Compassionate Visionaries as Leaders

By focusing on your personal preferences, you will be able to better assess the types of work that will be personally satisfying. The following list describes the leadership preferences of Compassionate Visionaries. Check off the items that are true for you.

As a Compassionate Visionary leader, I prefer to

- ☐ Advocate for developing human potential
- ☐ Focus on interpersonal relationships
- ☐ Integrate all perspectives
- ☐ Motivate and validate others
- ☐ Work hard to create harmonious and functional work groups
- ☐ Avoid using power and authority
- ☐ Lead by example
- ☐ Accommodate and cooperate rather than command

Compassionate Visionaries as Team Members

Compassionate Visionaries are warm, quietly inspiring, and actively supportive in a team environment. They are naturally attracted to the concept of teamwork and see collaboration as a valuable way to get the work done. Being such strong supporters of teamwork, they often take on and complete more than their share of duties.

When providing feedback, Compassionate Visionaries are careful to validate and appreciate others before providing suggestions for improvement. They prefer to receive feedback in a similar way. A logical list of improvements or criticism without some appreciation can be difficult for Compassionate Visionaries to hear. Normally accommodating and positive, they struggle to not react strongly and unfavorably toward others they see as uncaring or cold. Compassionate Visionaries do not work well in an environment of personal conflict.

Compassionate Visionaries are able to see situations from multiple perspectives and are good at linking people and finding common ground. They often play the role of mediator or conciliator in a team. They often bring a can-do attitude to a team.

Snapshot: Compassionate Visionaries as Team Members

By focusing on your personal preferences, you will be able to better assess the types of work that will be personally satisfying. The following list describes how Compassionate Visionaries like to work within a team. Check off the items that are true for you.

As a Compassionate Visionary team member, I

- [ ] Am warm
- [ ] Am actively supportive
- [ ] Take on and complete more than my share of duties
- [ ] Am careful to validate and appreciate others
- [ ] Have difficulty accepting critical feedback presented logically
- [ ] Struggle to not react strongly if others seem uncaring or cold

- [ ] Am accommodating and positive
- [ ] Do not work well in an environment of personal conflict
- [ ] See situations from multiple perspectives
- [ ] Am good at linking people and finding common ground
- [ ] Often play the role of mediator or conciliator

Compassionate Visionaries as Learners

Compassionate Visionaries enjoy ideas and the interchange of ideas, preferably in a supportive and personal learning environment. Interesting, conceptual lectures hold their attention. They take in and integrate information and see many ways to apply ideas. Much of their synthesis and connection of ideas must be done alone, in quiet time, after ideas have been presented. Once they have incorporated information in this way, they seek opportunities to apply con-

Snapshot: Compassionate Visionaries as Learners

By focusing on your personal preferences, you will be able to better assess the types of work that will be personally satisfying. The following list describes the learning preferences of Compassionate Visionaries. Check off the items that are true for you.

As a Compassionate Visionary learner, I

☐ Enjoy ideas and the interchange of ideas

☐ Prefer a supportive and personal learning environment

☐ See many ways to apply ideas

☐ Synthesize and connect ideas alone, in quiet time, after ideas have been presented

☐ Am intense and seek challenges

☐ Am not interested in regurgitating facts and details

☐ Need teachers to be genuine and approachable

☐ Like to develop a personal connection to the learning and the teacher

☐ Enjoy having a mentor, coach, or guide

☐ Bring high expectations to the learning situation

☐ Am conscientious and determined

☐ Seek opportunities to apply concepts and ideas in new ways in the world around me

☐ Dislike disorder

☐ Like learning to occur in an organized and focused way

· 229 ·

cepts and ideas in new ways in the world around them. Regurgitating facts and details holds very little interest for the Compassionate Visionary.

Teachers, to be respected, need to be genuine and approachable. The Compassionate Visionary prefers to develop a personal connection to both the learning and the teacher. A mentor, coach, or guide is the type of teacher the Compassionate Visionary seeks.

Compassionate Visionaries bring high expectations to the learning situation and are conscientious and determined learners. They seek learning that is intense and challenging. Compassionate Visionaries dislike disorder and prefer learning to occur in an organized and focused way.

BALANCING VISIONING WITH LOGIC

The latest research shows that about 2.1 percent of people in the United States are Logical Visionaries (INTJ). Logical Visionaries trust and naturally use logical analysis to help them sort through ideas to find the most expedient way of solving a problem or improving a system. They are future and goal oriented. Logical Visionaries like to create and work with complex models of processes and enjoy systems thinking. They like to work on and complete complex, long-range projects.

Because Logical Visionaries have an outward focus on logical reasoning and decision making as a balance to their internal focus on ideas, they initially express their Visioning way of working differently than Compassionate Visionaries do. However, Compassionate Visionaries in midlife may find that these logic-based descriptions mirror the direction in which they are moving as they mature and develop.

What Logical Visionaries Do Naturally

CREATE NEW THEORY OR TEST IDEAS

Logical Visionaries are drawn to work that allows them to create new theory or test ideas using logical analysis. Science, mathematics, linguistics, and medicine are examples of arenas that may appeal to them. They are independent thinkers and careful decision makers. Once their decisions and timelines are made, they are very task and deadline oriented.

Logical Visionaries will take a new piece of information, look at it in a number of ways, test its limitations, and then decide whether it has merit. They question everything and will discard or discount information that is limited in application or incongruent with their internal understanding. When an idea is presented to them, they will critique it rather than simply accept it at face value. Others may find this approach overly skeptical, cynical, or judgmental. However, no matter how critical Logical Visionaries appear, internally they are open to and willing to consider any idea they think may be useful.

SOLVE COMPLEX PROBLEMS

It is important for Logical Visionaries to find real-world applications for their ideas. They are drawn to work that requires them to solve complex, challenging problems, and they are good at all components of problem solving: conceptualizing, testing, and following through by planning and implementing solutions. They naturally seek knowledge, understanding, and insights. They abhor inefficiency and will quickly move to improve processes and remove bottlenecks that slow a project or an organization down. Logical Visionaries can become disengaged and lose motivation at work if they lack a complex problem to solve, a system to improve, or a long-term goal to achieve.

One Logical Visionary comments,

"I like to be rewarded for successful problem solving or project management by being given a slightly more complex problem or project. Change, complexity, and challenge are powerful motivators for me."

Logical Visionaries like to take charge of and control the world around them by planning and implementing. As one Logical Visionary comments,

"Either you control the world or the world controls you."

Logical Visionaries like to take time to think before they set goals and begin to implement a project. They enjoy setting processes, developing strategies, and creating a conceptual view of a project from start to finish. Their mental planning is intense and complex. They internally plan for possible problems, develop contingencies, and have backup plans in place.

IMPLEMENT PLANS

Once they have mentally outlined a process from start to finish, Logical Visionaries are good at organizing resources and implementing their plan. Once the plan is complete, their focus turns to following through and actualizing their vision. They are able to conceive and operationalize plans that have far-reaching implications and meet long-term or distant goals. They need time to work alone when conceptualizing ideas and like to have a quiet and contained workspace where they can concentrate.

Logical Visionaries often map, diagram, or create flowcharts for their plans. Although they are not strongly sequential in process, they do need to see the logical flow of a process. Work such as writing computer software, completing a computer systems analysis, or helping develop a telecommunication system are examples of types of work that allow them to design and plan in this logical way. They are able to maintain a good balance between seeing a system or process in its entirety and drilling down to the detail level to plan and implement. However, as strong as this ability is, Logical Visionaries are so focused on the world of ideas and possibilities that they can miss some of the facts.

Snapshot: Ideal Work Environment for Logical Visionaries

By focusing on your personal preferences, you will be able to better assess the types of work that will be personally satisfying. The following list describes the ideal work environment for Logical Visionaries. Check off the items that are true for you.

As a Logical Visionary, I prefer a work environment that

☐ Allows opportunities to generate and implement ideas

☐ Values independence

☐ Is competency driven

☐ Allows me to work with others who are competent

☐ Provides opportunities to use logical analysis

☐ Lets me work with models or systems

☐ Provides complex problems to solve

Snapshot: Skills and Valued Activities for Logical Visionaries

By focusing on your personal preferences, you will be able to better assess the types of work that will be personally satisfying. The following list describes the skills and valued activities of Logical Visionaries. Check off the items that are true for you.

As a Logical Visionary, I value the following skills and activities:

☐ Creativity

☐ Critical thinking

☐ Logical analysis

☐ Organizing

☐ Planning

☐ Problem solving

Work That Attracts Logical Visionaries

The following list of occupations are typically of interest to Logical Visionaries. When looking for career ideas, remember to also look at the work options for Visionaries listed earlier in the chapter, which are attractive to both Logical Visionaries and Compassionate Visionaries.

ARTS AND DESIGN
  Actor
  Composer
  Curriculum designer
  Entertainer
  Environmental planner
  Inventor
  Musician
  Photographer

Many Logical Visionaries enjoy creating and designing. If you have a creative flair, you may want to consider occupations that allow you to design or express your ideas.

DATA MANAGEMENT AND ANALYSIS
  Auditor
  Business analyst
  Consultant
  Credit investigator
  Economist
  Editor
  Financial planner
  Information services specialist
  International or investment banker
  Journalist
  Judge
  Reporter

If your focus is more toward analysis and research, you may find some of these occupations interesting. They require analytical skill as well as, in some cases, an ability to manage and organize multiple details. Some of these occupations involve a good deal of objective decision making.

SCIENCE AND TECHNOLOGY
  Biologist
  Chemist
  Computer programmer
  Computer systems analyst

Dentist
Electrical or electronic technician
Engineer
Mathematician
Telecommunications expert

Some Logical Visionaries choose to express their natural way of working by entering the fields of science and technology. In these fields, objective analysis and decision making are valued and encouraged. Often there are complex problems to solve.

MANAGEMENT

Management consultant
Manager—executive, human resources, sales, government
School principal
Strategic planner

Being organized and efficient, Logical Visionaries are often drawn to management positions. If you have a strong vision to share and like to lead others, management might be an area to consider.

Logical Visionaries as Leaders

Logical Visionaries bring unique strengths to the leadership role. They naturally lead and prefer to be led in a specific way.

STRATEGIC PLANNING

Logical Visionaries are the ultimate strategic planners. Being future and change oriented, they see and work toward broad long-term goals. They may be so focused on the future that they do not see immediate needs or allow time to solve small or immediate problems. They often share their visions with others in the form of complex and abstract models or schematics. They may need to learn to bring these models down to earth so that they make sense to those with more practical ways of working. Reducing visions to the detail level can be tedious for Logical Visionaries, so they need to work with others who can map out and attend to specific details.

FOCUS ON COMPETENCY AND PERFORMANCE

Logical Visionaries value competency and performance. Position authority is less meaningful to them than what people demonstrate they can do. Logical Visionaries are driven to learn and implement new ideas. They will expect others to do the same and may be surprised if others are not independent in thought or action. One Logical Visionary describes his view:

"I don't like to take accountability for the actions of someone else. I can't guarantee that."

They respect those who show vision and foresight. It is important that Logical Visionaries share ideas and get input before they start implementing a plan, since discussing ideas and obtaining agreement on strategies will not be a focus for them once they have chosen a path forward. It may be difficult for Logical Visionaries to find words that succinctly and clearly describe their plan.

TASK ORIENTATION

Logical Visionaries can become completely immersed in a complex project and can be very task and deadline oriented as they move toward actualizing an important vision. This is a strength that can also cause communication difficulties. One Logical Visionary leader notes that others have seen him as secretive and manipulating:

"I don't intend to come across as secretive. I make a complex plan in my mind, and sometimes I guess I don't take the time to explain it. When others try to discuss a next step or course of action, I admit I am quick to direct them to the already-thought-out step I have decided on."

This leader recognizes that he needs to get input earlier, while he is conceptualizing a plan, since he finds it hard to be patient and discuss things when, in his mind, the course of action is obvious. He also recognizes that he needs to share more of his vision and be open to modifying his plan, even if the process slows him down. Otherwise, the team members who are carrying out the plan will lack commitment and ownership.

Snapshot: Logical Visionaries as Leaders

By focusing on your personal preferences, you will be able to better assess the types of work that will be personally satisfying. The following list describes the leadership preferences of Logical Visionaries. Check off the items that are true for you.

As a Logical Visionary leader, I prefer to

☐ Plan strategically

☐ Focus on the future

☐ See and work toward broad long-term goals

☐ Work with competent, committed people

☐ Learn and implement new ideas

☐ Work with others who are independent in thought or action

☐ Lead people who show vision and foresight

☐ Immerse myself in a complex project

☐ Accomplish tasks and meet deadlines

Logical Visionaries as Team Members

Logical Visionaries are not naturally drawn to teamwork. They like input and discussion at the initial idea formulation stage and can see the value of teamwork once a plan is made and the team is focused and working efficiently toward a goal. Once they know where they want to go, they will be impatient with any processes that take time and energy away from getting the work done.

Logical Visionaries are not naturally focused on giving positive feedback. They tend to evaluate themselves internally and expect that others will do the same. In general, their communications are brisk, to the point, and directive. Small talk and developing rapport do not come easily to Logical Visionaries.

Logical Visionaries often have high expectations both for themselves and for those around them. They can be self-critical as well as critical of others if expectations are not met. Because of these aspects of their communication style, others may see the Logical Visionary as arrogant or uninterested. One Logical Visionary describes her biggest work challenge:

"I need to develop networks and rapport with others. This is difficult for me because I am naturally independent and self-sufficient. I'm also not very good at small talk. I can do the weather for a couple of minutes, and then I don't know what else to say."

Snapshot: Logical Visionaries as Team Members

By focusing on your personal preferences, you will be able to better assess the types of work that will be personally satisfying. The following list describes how Logical Visionaries like to work within a team. Check off the items that are true for you.

As a Logical Visionary team member, I

☐ Need time and space to conceptualize ideas

☐ Like input and discussion at the initial idea formulation stage

☐ See the value of teamwork once a plan is made

☐ Like the team to be focused and working efficiently toward a goal

☐ Am impatient with processes that take time and energy away from getting the work done

☐ Am not naturally focused on giving positive feedback

☐ Tend to evaluate myself internally, and expect that others will do the same

☐ Am not adept at small talk and developing rapport

☐ Have high expectations for myself and for those around me

☐ Can be self-critical and critical of others

Logical Visionaries as Learners

Logical Visionaries seek opportunities to learn new ideas and theories. They are systems thinkers and need to understand the whole picture before learning the details. Spending time alone processing new information helps them organize and integrate it with what they already know. Independent learners, they may find reading or attending lectures good ways to take in ideas. Logical Visionaries are serious and intensely focused learners. They have high standards and will meet the goals they set for themselves.

These critical thinkers need to validate information, questioning and challenging everything before they accept (or reject) it. They like to debate ideas and may be critical, calm, and cool. Others may find debate uncomfortable, but for Logical Visionaries it is a logical exercise that allows them to validate and explore ideas. They prefer to learn from highly competent and knowledgeable instructors. Logical Visionaries often research courses and instructors before committing their time and energy.

Snapshot: Logical Visionaries as Learners

By focusing on your personal preferences, you will be able to better assess the types of work that will be personally satisfying. The following list describes the learning preferences of Logical Visionaries. Check off the items that are true for you.

As a Logical Visionary learner, I

☐ Seek opportunities to learn new ideas and theories

☐ Am systems focused

☐ Need to understand the whole picture before learning the details

☐ Need time alone to process information

☐ Am independent

☐ Am serious and intensely focused

☐ Naturally have high standards

☐ Meet the goals I set for myself

☐ Am a critical thinker

☐ Need to validate information before I accept (or reject) it

☐ Question and challenge everything

☐ Want highly competent and knowledgeable instructors

☐ Like to debate ideas

THE VISIONARY'S GREATEST CHALLENGES

Everyone has less-preferred activities and areas for growth and improvement. Visionaries are no exception. Here are two major developmental areas for both Compassionate Visionaries and Logical Visionaries, with tips on how to develop each one.

Paying Attention to the Here and Now

Because Visionaries are future focused and driven to complete tasks, they can have trouble stopping to enjoy the moment. When working in their inspired mode, they can become so caught up in a project that they neglect their physical needs for a healthy diet, exercise, and time off. They can become exhausted and unhealthy. As well, their trusted ability to generate ideas can, at its worst, create so many options that Visionaries become overwhelmed and unfocused.

If Visionaries fail to find ways to regenerate, they can lose their energy and enthusiasm. Even then, they still find it hard to stop thinking about their projects. This is perhaps the most difficult developmental step for Visionaries: to learn to pay attention to their immediate environment and become more practical. They recognize that inspiration needs to be balanced with an understanding and appreciation of their physical needs and limitations. Visionaries are susceptible to burnout and may need to set limits to what they expect from themselves. One Visionary describes her experience:

"Burnout was a serious problem for me a few years ago. I was putting in long days and long weeks. I can become extremely overcommitted in my need to satisfy my obligations. I now make a conscious effort to play more and work less."

Many Visionaries in midlife learn to consciously pay more attention to and appreciate the physical world. Their focus on future rewards and accomplishments begins to blend with a more present and practical focus on their immediate environment and their immediate needs.

TIPS FOR PAYING ATTENTION TO THE HERE AND NOW

- Attend to the physical basics: a healthy diet, plenty of sleep, and regular exercise. The earlier Visionaries can notice their physical limits being stretched, the less likely they are to experience physical exhaustion and resulting illnesses.
- Learn to stop and "smell the roses" by taking time to enjoy your immediate environment and sensory experiences.
- Take time to focus on your many accomplishments rather than only on the tasks that still need to be completed.
- Pursue creative leisure activities, such as writing, performing, and making artwork, as a change from work commitments.

Developing Flexibility in Planning

Visionaries have a powerful combination of approaches that allows them to see the big picture and then create a way to actualize their vision. They will conceptualize and organize a complex and detailed plan. However, this strength can create some tension as they attempt to put their well-developed plans into action. Visionaries are internally focused and, in the case of the Logical Visionary, fairly independent. They will often map out their plan mentally, on their own, before sharing it with others. Others, of course, will at that point want to offer input and may often seek to influence and modify the Visionary's plan.

Visionaries can find it difficult to change course once their plans are mapped out. If others jump in with new and different ideas after the Visionary has conceptualized a plan, the Visionary may ignore them. Or, alternatively, the Visionary can go to great lengths to reconceptualize a plan. The first option is not satisfactory for the co-worker, and the second option is not satisfactory for the Visionary. Other ways must be found that allow the Visionary the freedom to conceptualize a path forward, while taking into account ongoing input from others.

TIPS FOR DEVELOPING FLEXIBILITY IN PLANNING

- Recognize when others will have an investment in your plan, and expect that they will want to have input. This can help you develop contingencies for the plan. Share your plan openly in its rough stages. This may feel uncomfortable, but it will let you understand how others may react.
- Seek input early on, while the plan is still relatively undeveloped. Explain to people that you would like input up front and that you will use it to formulate your plan.
- Accept that the plan will change. Schedule extra time for unexpected changes.
- Review your plan as it is being implemented, and ask for feedback along the way.

KEY FOR ME: MANAGING MY CHALLENGES

Is paying attention to the here and now or developing flexibility in your planning a challenge for you? If so, which of the strategies explored in this chapter would be helpful to try? ....

....

....

....

....

....

....

FINAL TIPS FOR VISIONARIES: DOING WHAT COMES NATURALLY

A Visionary naturally approaches the world of work by creating and implementing ideas. Here are a few final tips that will help you choose and develop satisfying work.

Find Opportunities to Learn

Visionaries are most stimulated when they are learning. Make sure that you find and take opportunities to learn more about the areas that interest you. This does not need to be formal education. You may prefer to read, take on new and more complex duties, find a mentor, or surf the Internet. The modality of learning is less important than the stimulation that comes from being exposed to new ideas. When choosing work options, consider the learning opportunities associated with each option.

Create and Organize Ideas

Visionaries are engaged when they can play with ideas, sorting them, thinking about things from a variety of perspectives, and otherwise connecting ideas. Take time to allow yourself to play with ideas in new and unusual ways. Find work opportunities where you can deal with concepts as well as realities.

Apply New Ideas to Real Situations

Visionaries are not happy simply creating ideas and models in their heads. They will need to find ways to use their creativity. This might be managing a project, making a process manual to share with others, writing, creating a work of art, or changing a system so that it works more effectively.

Learn to Enjoy the Moment

Being very responsible and task driven, it can be difficult for Visionaries to stop working and enjoy the moment. Find opportunities to take time off from your work to enjoy the things around you.

Hold Your Plans a Little More Loosely

Planning and task completion are your strengths, and you can use them to efficiently obtain goals. It can be helpful, sometimes, to step back and allow the plan to flex and bend. Getting it all done in a specific way on a specific timeline can be stressful. Build flexibility and opportunities to regroup within your plan so that you create some breathing room and lessen the possibility of burnout.

Now that you have learned about your work preferences, please turn to Chapter 11 to begin planning your career path.

CHAPTER NINE

Analyzers
Examine and Evaluate

PERSONALITY TYPES: ISTP AND INTP

My work in the safety field provides me with autonomy and troubleshooting, two things I really enjoy. I like being presented with an incident to investigate. It gives me a problem that it is my job to solve. I like talking to and working with people one-on-one, asking questions and finding solutions. —An Analyzer

The latest research shows that about 8.7 percent of adults in the United States are Analyzers. Analyzers approach the world in an open-ended, exploratory way. They like to solve problems or generate ideas. At first glance they may seem like Logical Responders if they are ISTPs or Logical Explorers if they are INTPs. However, what you do not see at a casual glance is the Analyzer's internal preference for understanding and logically interpreting the world. This internal analytical focus is the guiding force of both ISTPs and INTPs. As they solve problems or explore new ideas, they are constantly guided by and focused on logical thinking. This focus on examining and evaluating the world internally is their natural way of working.

Analyzers' logical approach is immediate and automatic. It provides a way to make decisions and allows Analyzers to smoothly adjust their actions as they examine situations. Analyzers may not necessarily show their logical thought process or explain the reasons behind their actions. They are content to use their logic as an internal guide to interpret and decide about situations. Because of this internal focus, we are sometimes surprised by Analyzers' actions, since we are not privy to the thought processes that direct their behavior.

ANALYZERS AT WORK
What Analyzers Do Naturally

USE LOGICAL ANALYSIS

Whatever type of work Analyzers choose, it is important that they have opportunities to use their natural logical approach to situations. Analyzers need to understand how and why things work. They need to see the logic behind decisions and actions before they will jump into action. One Analyzer describes this use of logic as a tendency to look at every situation as a problem:

"I often find myself reacting to situations by automatically using logic to ask myself a number of questions: What is the problem here? What information do I need? What are my alternatives? What are the consequences of each alternative? What will I do?"

Logical conclusions, for Analyzers, are based on their principles, experience, and knowledge. Everything Analyzers see, hear, read, touch, and experience is examined and critiqued. Analyzers do not just accept information or directions at face value. They do well in occupations that allow them to make judgments and sometimes work as lawyers, judges, investigators, and analysts.

One Analyzer who works as a nurse describes one of her favorite work duties as doing ergonomic assessments. She enjoys being able to carefully analyze the factors involved and make a judgment:

"I am able to start with a problem, logically evaluate the situation, provide recommendations, and then move on to another problem. I also enjoy the freedom and variety that come from moving on to something new and different."

FOCUS ON COMPETENCY AND SELF-EVALUATION

Analyzers naturally critique and evaluate both their own performance and that of others. They set and hold very high standards for themselves and find it difficult to work in environments where others are incompetent.

Their internal sense of how they are doing prompts Analyzers to adjust their personal behavior. One Analyzer notes that he has very little need for external feedback or rewards:

"I know I have messed up when I find myself thinking, 'If I were my employer, I'd fire me.' This is my cue to change."

Because they have a strong internal sense of how well they are performing, Analyzers are usually not devastated by negative feedback from others. This is especially true if the competency of the person evaluating them is in doubt. If Analyzers know their performance was poor, they have likely already been self-critical. If instead they know that their performance was justified or appropriate, Analyzers may ignore or minimize external feedback that opposes their self-assessment.

ADAPT AND GO WITH THE FLOW

Although Analyzers use their logical thinking as an internal guide and focus for their decision making, they approach the world around them in an open and flexible way. Usually not dominating or directive, they tend to be somewhat quiet, detached, impersonal, adaptable, and curious. Although they do like to solve problems, they may put off making decisions as they play with possible courses of action.

Analyzers enjoy coming up with ideas or solutions to problems and are usually quite happy to let others worry about directing projects, implementing solutions, and following through. The process of figuring out how to solve the problem holds much more interest for them than taking the course of action they have decided on. One Analyzer comments that he has to be careful in this regard:

"When I have a problem to solve, I find myself automatically testing and evaluating solutions in my mind. When I choose a course of action, I may actually forget about the problem. In my mind, it has already been dealt with. I have learned that I need to write down my solution as a way of making sure that I don't simply move on to something else without implementing the solution."

To maintain their interest, it is important for Analyzers to work on a variety of tasks or projects. They especially like to work on new and unusual problems and situations where the results and consequences are unknown. This allows them to engage and challenge their thinking skills. One Analyzer comments,

"As soon as a job becomes repetitious or routine, I get bored and need to do something different. I actually become uncomfortable when I know a job well. My energy level goes down and I find myself feeling complacent and sleepy. These are my cues to move on to something different."

WORK INDEPENDENTLY

Analyzers prefer to solve their own problems and set their own pace. They need independence, flexibility, and control over their work. An overly structured environment or dictated procedures will not allow them to maneuver. Although some Analyzers are good immediate problem solvers, they often need time and space to think a problem through. One Analyzer explains,

"I like jobs that don't have a job description. I can define what I need to do as the job evolves around the project or problem at hand."

Analyzer Blind Spots

FOLLOWING SOCIAL NORMS

Analyzers can become impatient when others focus too much on social rules and responsibilities. They are not fans of protocol and cannot see the practical or logical value of social conventions. Hospital visits, writing thank-you notes, calls to keep in touch, social functions, and staff celebrations are activities they would rather avoid than attend to. Analyzers tend to dislike small talk and often feel uncomfortable engaging in it, preferring to stay in the background in social situations. They do not naturally or casually network to share their ideas. Indeed, the idea of having to sell or promote themselves is uncomfortable. However, this said, Analyzers will learn to adapt and react to these situations when necessary.

COMMUNICATING THEIR THOUGHTS

Analyzers do not like to be slowed down. It takes time and energy to share with others their complex, logical thought processes. They are not likely to offer explanations regarding their decisions, and they tend to focus on the task they are completing rather than the people they are working with. This can result in communication that is brisk, objective, and impersonal. Other people can find this communication style alienating. An Analyzer may not see the importance of developing interpersonal skills or feel a need to do so.

To Analyzers, emotions get in the way of thinking. They can be very uncomfortable dealing with emotional situations at work, feeling that it is a waste of time and energy. They may absent themselves from these situations as a coping strategy.

Providing feedback to others that is not overly critical can be a difficult task for Analyzers. They automatically critique and see flaws rather than appreciate and see strengths. They are also impatient with the process of stating and explaining the obvious. These attributes can get in the way when others are seeking feedback from the Analyzer.

DEALING WITH RULES AND REGULATIONS

Because Analyzers like to solve problems, act spontaneously, and deal flexibly with situations, they can find that regulations and procedures limit their freedom of action. They will follow the rules as long as they can still work toward their results. However, if the rules get in the way, they will not hesitate to break or circumvent them. Freedom to determine the direction of their actions is very important to Analyzers. Routine tasks do not motivate or hold their interest for long. One Analyzer explains his need for freedom of action, using a map and a compass as an analogy:

"If I have to go somewhere, all I need is a compass. Having a general sense of moving forward, I can navigate my way around the barriers in whatever way works best at the time. I don't like to have to follow a map, taking only very clearly defined, established paths. The pathway may work at times, but it doesn't allow the flexibility to bushwhack my way around the barriers."

Snapshot: Analyzers' Natural Work Preferences

Analyzers are at their best when they can use their natural work preferences. By focusing on your preferences, you will be able to better assess the types of work that will be personally satisfying. The following list describes characteristics and preferences of Analyzers. Check off the items that are true for you.

As an Analyzer, I am at my best when I can

- ☐ Approach situations using logic
- ☐ Critique and see flaws
- ☐ Work on new and unusual problems and situations
- ☐ Come up with ideas or solutions to problems
- ☐ See the logic behind decisions and actions
- ☐ Set my own pace
- ☐ Have time to observe and reflect on problems
- ☐ Work independently with opportunities for spontaneity
- ☐ Uphold the high standards I set for myself

- ☐ Work in environments where others are competent
- ☐ Approach the world in an open and flexible way
- ☐ Do a variety of tasks
- ☐ Let others worry about directing, implementing, and following through
- ☐ Have control over my work
- ☐ Have time and space to think a problem through
- ☐ Avoid overly structured, routine, or rigid work tasks or environments
- ☐ Not have to sell or promote myself

WHAT'S KEY FOR ME?

My Ideal Work Preferences

Look back at the snapshot for the work preferences for an Analyzer. From the items you have checked, jot down the points that best summarize your preferences. Feel free to add points that are not on the list.

My most important work preferences are ....

....

....

....

....

....

....

....

WORK THAT ATTRACTS ANALYZERS

Analyzers can be found in many types of work. Here are some examples that use the Analyzer's natural way of working.

SCIENCE AND TECHNOLOGY

Computer analyst

Computer programmer

Computer software designer and developer

Computer specialist

Economist

Electrical or electronic technologist

Engineer

Machine operator

Network integration specialist

Surveyor

These occupations focus on objective, scientific principles, investigation, and problem solving, which are of interest to the Analyzer. If you have an interest in working with electronics, computers, or equipment, you may want to consider some of these occupations.

LEGAL AND MEDICAL
>   Attorney
>   Investigator
>   Judge
>   Legal assistant
>   Physician
>   Respiratory therapist

The legal and medical fields also provide opportunities to use investigation and problem solving. If you are interested in figuring out medical problems or dealing with the legal system, these occupations might be worth considering.

Of course, these are just some examples. There are many other types of work that Analyzers will enjoy. See the next sections for work that is specifically appealing to ISTPs and INTPs.

How Analyzers Find Balance

Analyzers are energized by working within the internal world of reflection and analysis. They are continually using logic to organize and evaluate the world. They must balance this internal focus by taking in new information and acting in the world around them. Without new information, their analysis can lack perspective. To acquire information, Analyzers ask questions, generate options, and generally take a flexible, curious approach to situations.

There are two approaches for taking in information: attending to practical details and seeing possible patterns. Personality type theory calls these two approaches Sensing (S) and Intuition (N). You may want to look back to Chapter 2 to discern which approach is most comfortable for you. The words *sensing* and *intuition* have many connotations that do not actually relate to how people take in information. So, to avoid misconceptions, in this book Analyzers who prefer Sensing as a way to take in information (ISTPs) arc called Practical Analyzers, while Analyzers who prefer Intuition as a way to take in information (INTPs) are called Insightful Analyzers.

Practical Analyzers naturally focus their attention on the current facts, details, and practical applications. They tend to initially work toward immediate results rather than systemic changes. Insightful Analyzers naturally take in information as patterns and possibilities. They balance their logical decisiveness with input, in the form of ideas and possibilities. Each approach has a different focus, but both allow Analyzers to expand and validate their logical decision-making process. Over the course of their life, Analyzers will use and develop both approaches to help them collect information and deal with the world around them. This natural development allows Analyzers to become more flexible in what they focus on over time.

Practical Analyzers focus on collecting facts and details to understand and deal with immediate situations. They act in a way similar to Logical Responders, acting and adapting in the immediate world. Practical Analyzers and Logical Responders approach the world with the same active, problem-solving approach. They are often found in similar types of work and enjoy doing similar types of things. It is important to remember though that, for Practical Analyzers, this focus on action and troubleshooting is secondary to and supportive of their primary focus on logic and analysis.

Insightful Analyzers focus on ideas and possibilities as ways to help them analyze theories and integrate ideas. They act in a way similar to Logical Explorers, innovating and initiating in the world of ideas and possibilities. Insightful Analyzers and Logical Explorers approach the world with the same open-ended look at possibilities. They are often found in similar types of work and enjoy doing similar types of things. It is important to remember that, for Insightful Analyzers, this focus on finding and exploring creative options is secondary to and supportive of the primary focus on logic and analysis.

Logical Responders and Logical Explorers use analysis as a secondary focus to guide them as they take in information from the world around them. Unlike Responders and Explorers, both types of Analyzers are first internally focused on logical analysis and then have a secondary focus on exploring or responding in the world around them.

As you go through this section, you may find it helpful to read about your most natural balancing approach first. Then read about the other approach to balancing to see what is in store for you as you mature and develop.

☐ **I am most like ISTP,**
so I am a Practical Analyzer.
I will initially balance my
analysis in a practical way.
As I mature and develop, I will
also learn to balance my analysis
with insights.

☐ **I am most like INTP,**
so I am an Insightful Analyzer.
I will initially balance my
analysis with insights. As I
mature and develop, I will also
learn to balance my analysis in
a practical way.

BALANCING ANALYZING WITH PRACTICALITY

The latest research shows that about 5.4 percent of adults in the United States are Practical Analyzers (ISTP). Practical Analyzers like to troubleshoot and solve problems. They enjoy dealing with immediate situations and are most engaged when analyzing the details and specifics of a concrete problem. Practical Analyzers like to think problems through carefully and reflect before they act. They tend to have a good memory and will look back to past experiences to help them solve a current problem or deal with an immediate situation. Practical Analyzers are good at improvising and jury-rigging solutions. They are independent and flexible, and they use analysis in an immediate and pragmatic way. They are often initially attracted to occupations involving hands-on, practical activities that require precision and technical knowledge.

Because Practical Anlyzers have a practical, detail-oriented focus as a balance to their analytical nature, they initially express their Analyzing way of working differently than Insightful Analyzers do. However, Insightful Analyzers in midlife may find that these detail-oriented descriptions mirror the direction in which they are moving as they mature and develop.

What Practical Analyzers Do Naturally
ATTEND TO DETAILS
Practical Analyzers balance their approach of internal logical analysis with an external focus on the realistic and matter-of-fact. Like their extraverted counterparts, the Responders, they often are drawn to occupations that allow them to work with details and solve practical problems. Practical Analyzers tend to

accumulate a large storehouse of facts that they can use in their day-to-day activities. One Practical Analyzer describes this natural accumulation of facts:

"I am excellent at trivia games and have earned the nickname 'Data' from my co-workers. When anyone at the office is trying to remember some obscure fact, I will be the first person they will ask."

Practical Analyzers are good at using their logic and practical focus to sort out facts and details. They work well with data and statistics and are attracted to careers in accounting, economics, banking, and securities.

· 253 ·

TROUBLESHOOT

Practical Analyzers like to know how and why things happen, and they often have interests in practical and applied sciences and technology. For example, they are attracted to work in computer programming, analysis, and software development as well as a range of technical occupations, including electrical, electronic, and medical technology.

Practical Analyzers are impatient with and uninterested in theory unless they see practical and immediate applications. They like to see concrete results as they solve real problems; they do not like to work in ambiguous situations toward abstract goals. Practical Analyzers are not big fans of goal setting in general, but if prompted they will set immediate and practical goals. However, they are not likely to make an action plan to meet their goals and will wait to take advantage of any opportune events. They tend to avoid long-range goal setting and planning, finding these processes too far removed from their direct experiences. One Practical Analyzer comments,

"I like to do research and collect data, but I would not be interested in taking the data back to an office and trying to see patterns and relate the information to the bigger theoretical picture. For the same reason, I dislike working on committees that require me to imagine what will be happening in five to ten years. I prefer working directly with what I can see and experience."

DEVELOP PHYSICAL DEXTERITY

Practical Analyzers prefer hands-on work. Because they are attuned to the immediate environment, they tend to develop and master physical skills for operating, repairing, and maintaining tools and equipment. For example, many work as mechanics, technicians, operators, builders, and repairers. They are often skilled at making things work and fixing things, using whatever materials they have at hand. They are excellent improvisers in the world of practical things. Some Practical Analyzers use their physical skills to become skilled trades workers or artisans.

ADD SOME EXCITEMENT

Practical Analyzers can be risk takers and sometimes seek activities that are physically challenging and maybe even dangerous. They are action oriented and work well in crisis situations. Practical Analyzers are often caught up in and energized by dealing with immediate problems. They work well under tight timelines and can be attracted to work that requires an immediate response to a crisis. They may become race-car drivers, emergency medical technicians, firefighters, and police officers. One Practical Analyzer describes a job he had as a railroad station officer as one of his favorites:

"I was responsible for making sure trains were moving on the right tracks. The job was a huge, complicated chess game, with all the pieces moving all the time at different speeds and going different directions. I liked the fact that all this action was happening in real time with real trains and tracks. I spent the day actively problem solving and putting together a very complex, logical puzzle. I quit the job, however, because the organization I worked for was far too structured. At the time, it promoted by seniority, rather than competency. I could not fathom why someone who was hired one month or even one day ahead of me would always be considered ahead of me for promotions or new opportunities."

Practical Analyzers seek opportunities to be active and have fun at work. They do not like to sit or stay inside all day and will look for opportunities to move around and work outside. They like maneuvering around problems and finding shortcuts for getting things done. One Practical Analyzer describes herself, quite proudly, as lazy. She explains,

"I find it a challenge to complete my work with the greatest amount of efficiency and the least amount of energy."

This playful and practical approach to work can, indeed, be seen by others as lazy or unmotivated. To the Practical Analyzer, however, it is simply the best way to get the job done.

Snapshot: Ideal Work Environment for Practical Analyzers

By focusing on your personal preferences, you will be able to better assess the types of work that will be personally satisfying. The following list describes ideal work environments for Practical Analyzers. Check off the items that are true for you.

As a Practical Analyzer, I prefer a work environment that is

- ☐ Hands-on
- ☐ Focused on practical problem solving and concrete results
- ☐ Conducive to my being autonomous
- ☐ A source of varied activities
- ☐ Physically challenging
- ☐ Geared toward tight timelines
- ☐ Focused on immediate and perhaps risky response to a crisis
- ☐ Active
- ☐ Fun and playful
- ☐ Outdoors

· 255 ·

Snapshot: Skills and Valued Activities for Practical Analyzers

By focusing on your personal preferences, you will be able to better assess the types of work that will be personally satisfying. The following list describes skills and activities valued by Practical Analyzers. Check off the items that are true for you.

As a Practical Analyzer, I value the following skills and activities:

- ☐ Analysis
- ☐ Improvising
- ☐ Maintaining
- ☐ Operating
- ☐ Precision
- ☐ Repairing
- ☐ Technical knowledge
- ☐ Troubleshooting
- ☐ Working with data and statistics
- ☐ Working with details

Work That Attracts Practical Analyzers

The following occupations are typically of interest to Practical Analyzers. When looking for career ideas, remember to also look at the work options for Analyzers listed earlier in the chapter, which are attractive to both Practical Analyzers and Insightful Analyzers.

TRADES AND CRAFTS
Carpenter
Cleaning-service worker
Commercial artist
Computer repair technician
Construction worker
Cook
Crafts worker
Farmer
Laborer
Mechanic
Steelworker

Analyzers often enjoy the hands-on demands of trades and crafts occupations. Depending on your specific interests and skills, you may want to consider an occupation that provides opportunities to make practical products.

SCIENTIFIC AND MEDICAL
Dental assistant
Dental hygienist
Marine biologist
Medical technologist
Optometrist
Physical therapist

These occupations involve working with equipment and collecting data, as well as interacting with others. If you like helping others and are interested in science or the medical field, you may want to consider one of these occupations.

LAW ENFORCEMENT AND EMERGENCY RESPONSE
Corrections officer
Detective
Emergency medical technician
Firefighter
Guard
Intelligence agent
Military officer

Police officer
Probation officer
Park ranger

These occupations provide immediate opportunities to respond to and solve problems. If you are action oriented and enjoy taking risks, some of these occupations might be appealing.

DATA MANAGEMENT AND ANALYSIS

Accountant
Purchasing agent
Securities analyst

If attending to detail and using your logic to make decisions about financial matters is appealing to you, these types of occupations might be attractive.

EQUIPMENT OPERATOR

Pilot
Race-car driver
School-bus driver
Transportation operator

Some risky and some more secure, these occupations provide an opportunity to operate equipment. Like emergency response work, the immediate sensory component of these occupations is attractive to some Analyzers.

MANAGEMENT AND TEACHING

Manager—small business, utilities, government
Teacher—adult education, coach
Technical trainer

Some Analyzers prefer to use their practical analytical skills to teach or manage others. Management careers are usually secondary to establishing an area of expertise. Some entrepreneurial Analyzers start their own business.

Practical Analyzers as Leaders

Practical Analyzers bring unique strengths to the leadership role. They naturally lead and prefer to be led in a specific way.

LEAD BY EXAMPLE

Practical Analyzers tend to not get too excited about things. As leaders, they prefer to act rather than talk, expressing themselves precisely and concretely in as few words as possible. They see themselves as someone who can offer solutions rather than someone who directs and guides. Practical Analyzer leaders tend to be understated and lead by example.

One exception to this is when Practical Analyzers talk about a specific area of expertise. Then, thanks to their great depth of knowledge, they enjoy talking extensively and in great detail.

CREATE EFFICIENT, IMMEDIATE SOLUTIONS

Practical Analyzers like working in a crisis and are most satisfied in a leadership role that gives them the opportunity to deal with a number of different problem situations. Leadership roles that require intense political positioning and an ability to sell ideas are less attractive than those that allow Practical Analyzers to act independently. They usually dislike sitting in meetings, finding them to be a waste of time unless they are short and to the point. They quickly become impatient with ongoing discussion and rehashing of information.

Practical Analyzers can always see more than one way to solve a problem. They can see many possible solutions as workable and want to provide independence and allow others to choose the one that is most appropriate. This can make the leader seem noncommittal. As one Practical Analyzer explains,

"I hear from my staff that I am 'indecisive.' I like to reframe that label as 'flexible.' I can see many ways to reach a goal and can endorse two totally different solutions that achieve the same end."

Practical Analyzers do not like to expend any more energy than necessary and look for the easiest way to get the job done. They enjoy finding or creating shortcuts, bypasses, or quick fixes. These quick fixes may, at times, get in the way of finding long-range solutions. However, Practical Analyzers find it difficult to slow down enough to consider future consequences. They become bored leading in highly structured and traditional organizations where maintaining and stabilizing are the primary leadership functions.

This immediate, hands-on task orientation can create some tension and frustration for other people involved in the project. Sometimes the other people will not be considered, and personal needs and input will take a backseat to the project at hand.

DEMONSTRATE COMPETENCY

For the Analyzer, competency is a key component of leadership. Leaders are not automatically followed simply because of their position or power. Instead, they must demonstrate their competency by achieving results. Practical Analyzers believe that leaders must show an ability to solve problems and think on their feet, so leaders who demonstrate their competency are respected and listened to. Practical Analyzer leaders are more likely to give instructions than information. Taking action is their prime focus. Rather than explain tasks or count on others, they may choose to do it all themselves. A Practical Analyzer explains,

· 259 ·

> "I have trouble delegating. I want to decide what I have to do. It's important to work it all out myself. I'm reluctant to explain everything and give away the work. However, if I don't delegate, things start to become unacceptably deferred."

Snapshot: Practical Analyzers as Leaders

By focusing on your personal preferences, you will be able to better assess the types of work that will be personally satisfying. The following list describes the leadership preferences of Practical Analyzers. Check off the items that are true for you.

As a Practical Analyzer leader, I prefer to

- ☐ Remain quiet and calm
- ☐ Act rather than talk about matters
- ☐ Express myself precisely and concretely in as few words as possible
- ☐ Give instructions rather than information
- ☐ Offer solutions rather than direct and guide
- ☐ Focus on what is efficient, immediate, and practical
- ☐ Solve immediate and concrete problems
- ☐ Look for the easiest way to get the job done

Practical Analyzers as Team Members

Analyzers value prize achievement and, because of that, may have less inclination to take a team approach than some of the other personality types. They like to do their own thing and will add the most value to a team by being allowed to independently complete a specific task. They can commit to and contribute to teamwork as long as their needs for independence and freedom are appreciated and accommodated.

When not directly engaged in a problem or situation, Practical Analyzers tend to sit back and observe the proceedings, objectively examining and evaluating the information. Because of this, others may see Practical Analyzers as cool or detached.

Practical Analyzers are impatient with processes that force them to deal with and resolve interpersonal issues, which they feel are not relevant to the work at hand. Understanding and dealing with the causes of issues may seem to Practical Analyzers to be a waste of time. They will ignore or minimize feedback that opposes their self-evaluation.

· 260 ·

Snapshot: Practical Analyzers as Team Members

By focusing on your personal preferences, you will be able to better assess the types of work that will be personally satisfying. The following list describes how Practical Analyzers like to work within a team. Check off the items that are true for you.

As a Practical Analyzer team member, I

- [ ] Value personal achievement
- [ ] Prefer to take a specific task and complete it independently
- [ ] Sit back and observe the proceedings
- [ ] Like to do things my own way
- [ ] May be seen as cool or detached
- [ ] Am impatient with processes that force me to deal with and resolve interpersonal issues

Practical Analyzers as Learners

As Practical Analyzers experience the world, they are constantly examining and evaluating. They like to test their analyzing by trying things. They do not like to read instructions, preferring to learn in a hands-on, practical, logical trial-and-error way. They seek fun, flexibility, and action when learning.

As in their work, they find structure and routine confining when learning. Classroom settings are too structured for them. They seek opportunities to solve real problems and apply their learning immediately. They prefer information that is presented sequentially and logically, and they want to learn theory in relation to practical applications. They are quick to critique and find any errors in materials. They respect teachers who have in-depth knowledge of a topic. One Practical Analyzer who works as a biologist notes,

"I find it extremely difficult to learn from books or manuals. I remember my poor study skills in school. I was disorganized, took sloppy notes, and didn't read my textbooks. Now I learn by doing. I recently purchased a Global Positioning System. I went out in the field and pushed the buttons until I understood how it worked. I did refer to the manual, but only briefly to help me solve a problem."

· 261 ·

Snapshot: Practical Analyzers as Learners

By focusing on your personal preferences, you will be able to better assess the types of work that will be personally satisfying. The following list describes the learning preferences of Practical Analyzers. Check off the items that are true for you.

As a Practical Analyzer learner, I

- ☐ Am hands-on
- ☐ Prefer the concrete to the abstract
- ☐ Need to see practical links to theoretical information
- ☐ Like immediate applications and results
- ☐ Want to have some fun and action

- ☐ Use logical trial and error
- ☐ Find structure and routine confining
- ☐ Like to solve real problems and apply learning immediately
- ☐ Prefer information that is presented sequentially and logically

BALANCING ANALYZING WITH INSIGHT

The latest research shows that about 3.3 percent of adults in the United States are Insightful Analyzers (INTP). Insightful Analyzers are naturally attracted to opportunities to independently analyze and solve complex problems. They seek time alone to analyze and evaluate ideas in depth.

Because Insightful Analyzers have a focus on ideas, theories, and systems as a balance to their analytical nature, they initially express their Analyzing way of working differently than Practical Analyzers do. However, Practical Analyzers in midlife may find that the descriptions of Insightful Analyzers mirror the direction in which they are moving as they mature and develop.

What Insightful Analyzers Do Naturally
PLAY WITH THEORIES AND MODELS

Insightful Analyzers tend to use their focus on generating ideas and their logical framework to explore possibilities and find creative solutions to problems. They enjoy working with theoretical ideas and seek knowledge and insights that help them objectively understand the world around them. Everything is subject to their critique and can be improved and modified. Insightful Analyzers often come up with solutions or ideas that are outside of conventional ways of thinking and may create and develop new theory in the process. They are often found in occupational fields that require theoretical knowledge, such as science and technology. New and cutting-edge areas are especially attractive to Insightful Analyzers.

Manipulating abstract ideas, building models, and solving complex problems with innovative solutions are motivating activities for Insightful Analyzers. They prefer to understand a problem or area of interest in depth, exhibiting great absorption and focus when their curiosity is stimulated. One Insightful Analyzer who works as a performance consultant describes this depth:

"When I look at improving a system, I start by making flowcharts and overviews of the work processes. I find it hard to look at just a piece of the process or to put boundaries on the systems. Everything links together at some level."

Insightful Analyzers enjoy learning and integrating ideas from a variety of sources and sometimes become inventors, scientists, or researchers or work in jobs that combine research and development. Many become teachers of the abstract, working with theoretical subjects such as mathematics. One Insightful Analyzer explains,

"One of my favorite work activities is facilitating groups. I like to go through processes with people. I find it rewarding when people get insights. I always learn something from the group, too."

THINK LONG RANGE

Insightful Analyzers like to work with abstract possibilities, using a strategic focus. They seek opportunities to spend time alone reflecting on and processing ideas. They naturally focus on the long-term impacts and consequences of actions. They are open to new ideas, yet are also skeptical, constantly looking for evidence that will prove or disprove ideas. Making improvements and developing new systems for the long term are powerful motivators for Insightful Analyzers. They may work as strategic planners and managers. One Insightful Analyzer describes how she prefers to look at long-range impacts and solve problems:

"I like to look to the future and make sure that I consider solutions that are 'outside the box.' The best solutions may seem impractical in the short term and may challenge accepted norms, but in the long run it is these creative solutions that will position the organization for success."

CREATE, NOT IMPLEMENT

The follow-through and implementation stages of a project are not as interesting for Insightful Analyzers as the conceptualization stage. Although they may have many idealistic long-term goals, they may stumble when it comes to creating an action plan. In fact, Insightful Analyzers may find it more enjoyable to modify, refine, elaborate, and broaden their model than to actually make or follow an implementation plan. This can be very irritating to others with a more task-oriented way of working, who may be waiting for some direction and action. One Insightful Analyzer explains,

"In a perfect world, once I had a general plan to solve a problem, I would have someone else attend to the plan and manage the details and realities. I would then be free to move on to conceptualizing another model and solving a new challenge. The analyzing process is much more engaging for me than the end result."

Snapshot: Ideal Work Environment for Insightful Analyzers

By focusing on your personal preferences, you will be able to better assess the types of work that will be personally satisfying. The following list describes the ideal work environment for Insightful Analyzers. Check off the items that are true for you.

As an Insightful Analyzer, I prefer a work environment that is

☐ Focused on ideas, theories, and systems

☐ Conducive to working independently

☐ A source of abstract subjects and complex problems

☐ A source of opportunities to have time alone to analyze and evaluate ideas in depth

☐ Open to finding creative solutions to problems

☐ Geared toward developing, improving, or modifying systems or processes

☐ A place where I can work outside of conventional ways of thinking

☐ Focused on new and cutting-edge areas

☐ Set up so that someone else manages the details

☐ Organized so I can initiate rather than follow through

Snapshot: Skills and Valued Activities for Insightful Analyzers

By focusing on your personal preferences, you will be able to better assess the types of work that will be personally satisfying. The following list describes the skills and valued activities of Insightful Analyzers. Check off the items that are true for you.

As an Insightful Analyzer, I value the following skills and activities:

☐ Abstract analysis

☐ Building conceptual models

☐ Creating innovative solutions

☐ Long-range, strategic thinking

☐ Manipulating abstract ideas

☐ Solving complex problems

Work That Attracts Insightful Analyzers

The following occupations are typically of interest to Insightful Analyzers. When looking for career ideas, remember to also look at the work options for Analyzers listed earlier, which are attractive to both Practical Analyzers and Insightful Analyzers.

SCIENCE AND TECHNOLOGY
Biologist
Chemist
Electrician
Mathematician
Social scientist

Insightful Analyzers enjoy the theoretical focus and logical analysis that scientific pursuits encourage. If one of these subject areas interests you, you may want to research the work opportunities in that area.

MEDICAL AND HEALTH CARE
Dentist
Health practitioner
Laboratory technician
Occupational therapist
Pharmacist
Plastic surgeon
Veterinarian

If you like working with and helping people, you may find that the medical and health-care fields provide opportunities to use your natural way of working.

ARTS AND DESIGN
Actor
Architect
Entertainer
Fine artist

Inventor
Musician
Photographer

If you have a creative flair, you may choose to pursue a career in the arts and design field. You can create ideas and express yourself in a variety of ways.

COMMUNICATIONS

Editor
Interpreter or translator
Journalist
Legal mediator
Public relations specialist
Writer

If you enjoy the precision of language, a communications career may suit you. You may want to focus on written or oral language, or on a combination of both. Some of these occupations also require negotiation skills.

DATA MANAGEMENT

Financial planner
Investment banker
Researcher

If you prefer to use your investigation skills as a primary focus, you may want to consider an occupation that provides opportunities to research and analyze data.

TEACHING AND COUNSELING

Counselor—suicide, crisis, runaway youth
Psychiatrist
Psychologist
Teacher—mathematics, university

Some Insightful Analyzers use their natural focus to teach and counsel others. If you like to share your subject expertise or you are interested in helping people solve problems, these careers may be of interest to you.

MANAGEMENT
Administrator—college
Manager
Strategic planner

Some Insightful Analyzers like to use their long-range focus and planning ability in leadership and administrative roles. If you are skilled at leading others and sharing your visions, you may enjoy an occupation in these areas.

Insightful Analyzers as Leaders

Insightful Analyzers bring unique strengths to the leadership role. They naturally lead and prefer to be led in a specific way.

FOCUS ON THE FUTURE
Because creating and sharing an overview of their vision is a key part of their leadership role, Insightful Analyzers are future focused. Since they also value independence of action, they tend to let others decide their own course of action. Insightful Analyzers do not want to get bogged down in day-to-day details. Those looking for clear and precise directions will not likely get them from an Insightful Analyzer leader. Insightful Analyzers are much more likely to share schematics, flowcharts, and diagrams than specific facts, details, or concrete applications. Insightful Analyzers are rarely interested in supervising others directly, but prefer to work independently and let others work that way as well.

GET ON WITH THE TASK
Grounding and explaining their visions is a tedious process for Insightful Analyzers. Since they have integrated many ideas into a complex mental model, they can be impatient with the effort needed to explain the entire system. They are susceptible to two types of communication misunderstandings. On the one hand, they may give an overview so abbreviated that others cannot follow, or, on the other, they may overwhelm people with too many technical and complex ideas. Ironically, Insightful Analyzers are often skilled at using precise and exact language to help them conceptualize ideas, but knowing what amount and level of information to share and suiting the information to others' backgrounds are challenges for Insightful Analyzers. Perhaps, if they state what to

them is obvious, they will be working at the level needed by their typical listener.

DO IT THEMSELVES

Insightful Analyzers may complete tasks or solve problems themselves, rather than take the time to try to delegate them, especially if they are unsure of others' skills and competency. One Insightful Analyzer leader describes as a trap her tendency to jump in with solutions:

· 268 ·

"When one of my staff approaches me with a problem, my first impulse is to quickly analyze the situation and come up with a solution. I find it difficult to see others struggle to find a solution that, to me, is painfully obvious. However, by throwing out solutions, I realize I am not allowing others to solve problems themselves. One of my goals, as a leader, is to learn to back off and guide, rather than direct others in problem solving."

Snapshot: Insightful Analyzers as Leaders

By focusing on your personal preferences, you will be able to better assess the types of work that will be personally satisfying. The following list describes the leadership preferences of Insightful Analyzers. Check off the items that are true for you.

As a Insightful Analyzer leader, I prefer to

☐ Focus on the future

☐ Let others decide their own course of action

☐ Get on with the task rather than talk about it

☐ Not get bogged down in day-to-day details

☐ Share information in schematics, flowcharts, and diagrams

☐ Not have to focus on specific facts, details, or concrete applications

☐ Not supervise others directly

☐ Work independently

☐ Use precise and exact language to help conceptualize ideas

☐ Do it myself rather than delegate

Insightful Analyzers as Team Members

Insightful Analyzers are quite independent and may find it difficult to work in a team unless they are allowed flexibility and freedom of action. They may avoid interpersonal conflict and hope it will go away, rather than work it out. When they must work through conflicts, they want to do so in a calm and impersonal way. They are not swayed by emotional responses, needing to approach these problems, like all others, in a logical and analytical way. At their worst, they can become sarcastic and highly critical.

Snapshot: Insightful Analyzers as Team Members

By focusing on your personal preferences, you will be able to better assess the types of work that will be personally satisfying. The following list describes how Insightful Analyzers like to work within a team. Check off the items that are true for you.

As a Insightful Analyzer team member, I

- ☐ Prefer to be independent
- ☐ Need flexibility and freedom of action
- ☐ Am calm and impersonal
- ☐ Am not swayed by emotional responses
- ☐ Approach problems in a logical and analytical way
- ☐ Avoid interpersonal conflict
- ☐ Can become sarcastic and critical when frustrated

Insightful Analyzers as Learners

Insightful Analyzers constantly seek to acquire knowledge and competencies. They like to work with abstract, ambiguous, and complex ideas. They are able to conceptualize relationships and find logical connections among a wide variety of topics. They seek competent and knowledgeable teachers and will critically evaluate the information they present. Insightful Analyzers need time and space to process complex information and integrate it into their logical framework. They are not focused on or good at memorization or repetition of facts and details. They can find structured learning confining and will do better if given complex independent projects to complete.

Snapshot: Insightful Analyzers as Learners

By focusing on your personal preferences, you will be able to better assess the types of work that will be personally satisfying. The following list describes the learning preferences of Insightful Analyzers. Check off the items that are true for you.

As a Insightful Analyzer learner, I

- [ ] Seek to acquire knowledge and competencies
- [ ] Like abstract, ambiguous, and complex ideas
- [ ] Am able to conceptualize relationships and find logical connections
- [ ] Seek competent and knowledgeable teachers

- [ ] Need time and space to process complex information
- [ ] Do not like and am not good at memorization or repetition of facts and details
- [ ] Find structured learning confining
- [ ] Like complex independent projects

THE ANALYZER'S GREATEST CHALLENGES

Everyone has less-preferred activities and areas for growth and improvement. Analyzers are no exception. Here are two major developmental areas for both Practical Analyzers and Insightful Analyzers, with tips on how to develop each one.

Developing Rapport and Connecting with Others

Because Analyzers are logically and analytically focused, they may not take the time to appreciate others. For them, it is easier to critique than to connect.

Engaging in small talk, sharing personal experiences, and providing others with ongoing support and positive feedback may not be as important to Analyzers as they are to others.

Analyzers evaluate their performance internally and are not dependent on others for support or feedback. They assume that others prefer to operate this way as well. It can come as a surprise to them to realize that others may need significantly more support and encouragement. One Analyzer describes how difficult it is for him to give positive feedback:

"I feel like I am overstating the obvious when I give positive feedback. People must surely know they did a good job. It feels phony and contrived to pat them on the back."

· 277 ·

Analyzers are usually their own worst critics and feel broadsided if they receive negative feedback about behaviors that they have not already evaluated internally. This is especially true if feedback is given without evidence to back up the opinion. An Analyzer will struggle to accept information that seems illogical or not well thought out. One Analyzer explains,

"I can get crippled inside when I get criticized out of the blue. That is especially true if the criticism is related to something I hadn't thought about or if it has no evidence to support it."

TIPS FOR DEVELOPING RAPPORT AND CONNECTING WITH OTHERS

- Do not assume that others are as independent of external feedback as you are. Offer positive feedback when it is deserved.
- Before offering negative feedback or expressing disagreement with an idea, offer positive feedback or mention points of agreement.
- Listen to others, and learn to understand and appreciate other ways of working.
- Include people and personal factors in the logical decision-making model as important factors to consider.
- Find ways to develop your ability to engage in small talk and chitchat. These communication skills can help you connect with others. Think of a few topics to talk about and questions you can ask.

- Use empathic statements in your conversations. If a person describes a negative experience, a simple supportive comment can be very important for developing rapport.
- Monitor and limit your tendency to critique or be cynical. Remember that others may be uncomfortable with this type of communication.

Following Through

Analyzers like to solve problems, but they usually do not enjoy the follow-through. They would rather turn their logical thinking toward a new problem than implement a solution. Unfortunately, few types of work allow them to move from conceptual stage to conceptual stage. They will often need to implement the solution to one problem before moving on to another one. This stage of the process is not highly motivating for the Analyzer. As one Analyzer explains,

"I quickly lose interest in a problem once I think of a solution. I detest all the finite details of organizing and implementing solutions. I get worried that I'll forget some important detail."

TIPS FOR FOLLOWING THROUGH

- Set deadlines for yourself. Recognize your tendency to do things at the last minute, and allow extra time close to the deadline to get the work done.
- Use time- and task-management strategies. Write things down. Set priorities. Organize your time.
- Negotiate with others to follow through so that you can move on to a new challenge. Find opportunities to move on to other projects.
- Look for ways to improve or modify your solution as you implement it. This will keep your interest level higher.
- Make and follow a step-by-step implementation plan. This will provide a greater challenge.

KEY FOR ME: MANAGING MY CHALLENGES

Is developing rapport and connecting with others or following through a challenge for you? If so, which of the strategies explored in this chapter would be helpful to try? ....

....

....

....

....

....

....

FINAL TIPS FOR ANALYZERS: DOING WHAT COMES NATURALLY

An Analyzer naturally approaches the world of work in an open and exploratory way. Here are a few final tips that will help you choose and develop satisfying work.

Engage in Logical Analysis

Key to a sense of satisfaction for the Analyzer is having an opportunity to assess information. Find work that provides both new and interesting situations and opportunities to make logical decisions.

Solve Problems

Analysis is often most satisfying when it is applied to real-world problems and situations. Seek opportunities to use your ingenuity and innovation to think outside the box, finding creative and useful solutions to a wide range of problems. Solving problems will keep you challenged and engaged mentally at work.

Find Independence and Flexibility

Avoid organizations and situations that require a constant focus on inflexible rules, routines, and standard operating procedures. You will find these environments very confining and unrewarding. Instead, look for opportunities to work independently, preferably in a rapidly changing, dynamic environment.

Develop Rapport

As you adapt to your work, find ways to link with and develop a resource network of people. You may find it rewarding if you stop to appreciate and support the important people around you. Find ways to express yourself and use empathic and nurturing communication skills.

Now that you have learned about your work preferences, please turn to Chapter 11 to begin planning your career path.

Chapter Ten

Enhancers
Care and Connect
PERSONALITY TYPES: ISFP AND INFP

As a carpentry shop assistant I am constantly working behind the scenes to make sure everyone has what they need. I also take on a variety of projects fixing and building customized products when needed. I enjoy the variety and knowing that doing my work helps everything run smoothly.   —An Enhancer

The latest research shows that about 13.2 percent of adults in the United States are Enhancers. Enhancers approach the world in an open-ended, exploratory way. They like to solve problems or generate ideas. At first glance they may seem like Compassionate Responders if they are ISFPs, or Compassionate Explorers if they are INFPs. However, what you do not see at a casual glance is the Enhancer's preference for choosing actions on the basis of personal values and priorities. This internal personal focus is common to both ISFPs and INFPs. As they solve problems or explore new ideas, they are constantly guided by and focused on what is personally important. Enhancers' natural way of working is to live by their values.

Enhancers' personal approach is immediate and automatic. It provides a way to make decisions that allows Enhancers to smoothly adjust their actions as they consider how to respond to situations. Enhancers may not necessarily explain to others the reasons behind their actions. They are content to use their values as an internal guide to interpret and decide about situations. Because of this internal focus, we are sometimes surprised by Enhancers' actions, since we are not privy to the thought processes that direct their behavior.

ENHANCERS AT WORK
What Enhancers Do Naturally

LIVE BY THEIR VALUES

Enhancers' actions must be in harmony and aligned with their personal values and the values of those who are important to them. Often working behind the scenes or in the background, Enhancers focus on what is good for the people involved in a situation. When making decisions, they will evaluate every situation individually. Each situation is unique, and the individuals and values involved must be considered. Enhancers strive to treat all people with respect and dignity.

Work is personal for Enhancers. Whatever work they choose, they express themselves in a unique and individual way. They share a part of themselves in what they do, and it is essential that they work in an environment that validates and supports individual effort and expression. They may leave a job rather than stay in a situation that violates what they feel is right. As one Enhancer explains,

"I worked many extra hours as a construction supervisor to develop good rapport with subcontractors and tradespeople who built houses. I created a cohesive group that cared about the quality of their work and that worked well together. When the construction company I worked for expanded to take on a large project, they hired a manager. It soon became obvious that the new manager would not allow me to continue the same quality of construction and relationships with tradespeople I had worked so hard to develop. I quit rather than work under the new manager, who did not share my values."

EXPRESS THEMSELVES

Enhancers strive to express themselves in a personal, unique, and individual way. They will find a number of flexible and creative ways to express who they are to the world. Everything Enhancers make, do, or do not do is an expression of what is personally important to them. Work that is most attractive to Enhancers allows them to express their work values and live in a meaningful way. One Enhancer explains,

"I work hard if my heart is there, but I lose interest in something very quickly if I'm not committed. Without commitment I don't stick to it."

The ways Enhancers express themselves and their values can vary, but are often related to appreciating or improving the world around them. They are attracted to work that they can put their heart and soul into. They may change jobs frequently as they move through their lives. What they do is not as important to them as being true to who they are. As one Enhancer comments,

"I have worked in a number of occupations. Each type of work allowed me to be creative and express what was personally important. I was able to put a part of myself into everything I've done. Above all, in each case, I was able to work in an independent and flexible way, which are two of my core work values."

APPRECIATE AND AFFECT OTHERS

Appreciating human values is a core focus of Enhancers' natural way of working. They are idealistic and often strongly devoted to people or causes. They have a strong sense of purpose and will ensure that their life reflects and serves their inner direction. This inner purpose will not be obvious to the casual observer, and Enhancers are unlikely to share their highly personal motivators. Rather, Enhancers show their values by helping others, creating things, or finding creative solutions to problems.

Enhancers are drawn to work that will help people, in either a practical or a developmental way. They are more likely to listen than talk. They do not necessarily work with people directly, but may create a product that others find helpful, beautiful, or interesting.

DEFINE AND NURTURE THEIR VALUES

Enhancers' personal values evolve over time. They will spend considerable time reflecting, defining, and carefully nurturing what is important to them. The resulting set of values will be individual, deep, and well defined. Enhancers may not be able to articulate their values system to others, but it will clearly and consistently define their course of action. They are often intensely loyal to the people or causes they are attached to.

Each Enhancer's set and hierarchy of values is unique, but all contain a common theme that relates to respect for and appreciation of the human experience. Money and status are less important motivators for the Enhancer than personal values. One Enhancer explains,

"I took a 30 percent pay cut to move into work that was personally more satisfying. I miss the additional money, but I don't regret the decision. I find it much easier to get up and go to work every day."

APPROACH THE WORLD IN A FLEXIBLE WAY

Enhancers approach work in an open and adaptable way. It is important for them to have variety in their work. They are flexible and enjoy taking things as they come. They do not seek to make complex plans or follow through in a structured way. Enhancers can struggle to figure out exactly how to express themselves in the world. They can appear very comfortable in a number of roles, without being personally satisfied.

Enhancers enjoy flexibility and freedom in their world. However, their important personal values are not flexible, and they will refuse to carry out any actions that will put them in conflict with their internal sense of purpose and direction. Stepping on the Enhancer's values will create a situation in which he or she can become stubborn, closed, and inflexible.

WORK IN HARMONY

Enhancers seek a harmonious and friendly working environment. They are content to work quietly in collaboration with others who are pleasant and sup-

· 278 ·

portive. Competitive or critical environments very quickly wear them out, as will interpersonal conflict.

Enhancers like to give and receive positive feedback. Being so invested in emotions and values, they can be easily hurt by negative feedback, especially if it is presented in an overly cool, logical, or critical way. Sometimes, the person giving feedback may be unaware of the impact the information has. Naturally quiet and wanting to maintain harmony, Enhancers may keep the peace by not expressing their feelings or needs. One Enhancer describes this reluctance:

"I have a habit of not speaking up when something bothers me. That would be okay if I would just let the feeling go, but I hold my emotions in. I usually don't speak up until something has bothered me for a long time. By then I am usually very angry, hurt, and frustrated. The most frustrating thing of all is that the other person may be completely unaware of the situation."

Enhancer Blind Spots

ALWAYS MEETING OTHERS' NEEDS

Enhancers need work that they can believe in and that contributes to their values and inner purpose. They tend to sacrifice their personal needs to meet the needs of others. For example, a specific job that provides an Enhancer with lots of time to share with family will align with the Enhancer's need to be involved as a partner and parent. However, the job itself may be unsatisfying in terms of the Enhancer's personal values. In this situation, the Enhancer has put family needs ahead of his or her own needs. One working Enhancer comments,

"My main focus has been on my family for so many years that I'm not sure I even have what someone might call a career."

Enhancers do not like to impose on others and feel uncomfortable with conflict and disharmony. They genuinely want to meet the needs of others and feel distressed when this causes internal conflict. Because of these characteristics, Enhancers may choose not to voice their personal needs, and others may be unaware of how overloaded they are. Over time Enhancers may feel taken for granted. Dealing with this type of situation is difficult for them.

Snapshot: Enhancers' Natural Work Preferences

Enhancers are at their best when they can use their natural work preferences. By focusing on your preferences, you will be able to better assess the types of work that will be personally satisfying. The following list describes characteristics and preferences of Enhancers. Check off the items that are true for you.

As an Enhancer, I am at my best when I can

- ☐ Live by my values
- ☐ Work behind the scenes or in the background
- ☐ Focus on what is good for the people involved
- ☐ Express myself in a personal, unique, and individual way
- ☐ Appreciate or make improvements in the world around me
- ☐ Share a part of myself in what I do
- ☐ Be in a harmonious and friendly working environment
- ☐ Treat all people with respect and dignity

- ☐ Appreciate and make an impact on others
- ☐ Help others, create things, or find unique solutions to problems
- ☐ Listen more than talk
- ☐ Contribute to something meaningful
- ☐ Have variety in my work
- ☐ Take things as they come
- ☐ Have freedom to act autonomously
- ☐ Work in environments that validate and support individual effort and expression

WHAT'S KEY FOR ME?

My Ideal Work Preferences

Look back at the snapshot for the work preferences for an Enhancer. From the items you have checked, jot down the points that best summarize your preferences. Feel free to add points that are not on the list.

My most important work preferences are ....
....
....
....
....
....
....
....

WORK THAT ATTRACTS ENHANCERS

Enhancers can be found in many types of work. Here are some examples that use the Enhancer's natural way of working.

HEALTH AND WELLNESS
    Dietitian
    Nutritionist
    Personal coach or trainer
    Therapist—physical, occupational, massage

Enhancers are interested in encouraging the health and well-being of others. If you like supporting others as they work toward improving themselves, you may enjoy these types of careers. Personal coaching is becoming a popular work option.

ARTS AND DESIGN
    Architect
    Designer
    Media specialist

You may find satisfaction in a career that allows you to use your creativity. Depending on your skills and interest, you may find it rewarding to design buildings, clothing, landscapes, or web sites.

COUNSELING
Counselor—runaway youth, child welfare, alcohol and drug
Social worker

You may be drawn to occupations that provide opportunities to look out for others. Often empathic and supportive, Enhancers can find great satisfaction helping others.

SCIENCE, TRADES, AND TECHNOLOGY
Biologist
Carpenter
Cook
Engineer
Laboratory technologist
Surveyor

Some of these areas allow independence and provide opportunities to solve problems. If you have a creative flair for cooking, or if you find it rewarding to work with tools, a trade or technical area may suit you. Practical Enhancers are especially drawn to trade and technical occupations.

SUPPORT ROLES
Administrative assistant
Executive secretary

Some Enhancers enjoy behind-the-scenes tasks and supporting the work of others. If you enjoy variety, challenge, and adding your personal touch to make things run smoothly, you may find these types of work appealing.

Of course, these are just some examples. There are many other types of work that Enhancers will enjoy. See the next sections for work that is specifically appealing to ISFPs and INFPs.

How Enhancers Find Balance

Enhancers are energized by working within their internal world of reflection and analysis and use their values to organize and evaluate their external world. They must balance their internal focus by taking in new information and acting in the world around them. Without new information, their evaluation of the situation can lack perspective.

To acquire information, Enhancers ask questions, generate options, and generally take a flexible, curiosity-driven approach to situations. There are two approaches that can be used to seek new ideas: a focus on current realities or a focus on ideas and possibilities. Personality type theory calls these two approaches Sensing (S) and Intuition (N). You may want to look back to Chapter 2 to discern which approach is most comfortable for you. The words *sensing* and *intuition* have many connotations that do not really relate to how people take in information. So, to avoid misconceptions, in this book Enhancers who prefer Sensing as a way to take in information (ISFPs) are called Practical Enhancers, while Enhancers who prefer Intuition as a way to take in information (INFPs) are called Insightful Enhancers.

Each approach has a different focus, but both allow Enhancers to expand and validate their values-based decision-making process. As Enhancers develop throughout their life, they will learn to focus on both current realities and ideas and possibilities as ways to take in information. This natural development allows them to be more flexible over time.

Practical Enhancers focus on collecting facts and details to understand and deal with immediate situations. They act in a way similar to Compassionate Responders, acting in and adapting to the immediate world. Practical Enhancers and Compassionate Responders approach the world in the same active, problem-solving way. They are often found in similar types of work and enjoy doing similar types of things. It is important to remember, though, that, for Practical Enhancers, this focus on action and troubleshooting is secondary to and supports their internal personal focus.

Insightful Enhancers, on the other hand, focus on patterns and possibilities to help them analyze theories and integrate ideas. They act in a way similar to Compassionate Explorers, innovating and initiating in the world of ideas and possibilities. Insightful Enhancers and Compassionate Explorers are often found in similar types of work and enjoy doing similar types of things. It is important to remember that, for Insightful Enhancers, this focus on finding and exploring creative options is secondary to and supports their internal personal focus.

Compassionate Responders and Compassionate Explorers use a values-based decision-making process similar to that of Enhancers, but the analysis is secondary to a focus on the facts and possibilities themselves. Unlike Responders and Explorers, Enhancers are more focused on interpreting and sorting the data they collect through a framework of personal values.

As you go through this section, you may find it helpful to read about your most natural balancing approach first. Then read about the other approach to balancing to see what is in store for you as you mature and develop.

☐ **I am most like ISFP,**
so I am a Practical Enhancer.
I will initially balance my personal approach in a practical way. As I mature and develop, I will also learn to balance my approach with insights.

☐ **I am most like INFP,**
so I am an Insightful Enhancer.
I will initially balance my personal approach with insights. As I mature and develop, I will also learn to balance my approach in a practical way.

BALANCING ENHANCING WITH PRACTICALITY

The latest research shows that about 8.8 percent of adults in the United States are Practical Enhancers (ISFP). Practical Enhancers naturally enjoy and find ways to connect to and be in harmony with the moment. They are kind and considerate and appreciate the people and things around them. Quietly supportive, they remain in the background and find practical ways to enhance. They often express themselves by providing a useful service or creating a tangible product that others can use immediately, finding comfort or pleasure in what the Practical Enhancer provides.

You are not likely to hear about what is important to Practical Enhancers. They will focus the conversation on you and do more listening than talking. They are quick to focus on the needs of others.

Because Practical Enhancers have a spontaneous, action-oriented focus as a balance to their values-based individual approach, they initially express their Enhancing way of working differently than Insightful Enhancers do. However, Insightful Enhancers in midlife may find that the descriptions of Practical Enhancers mirror the direction in which they are moving as they mature and develop.

What Practical Enhancers Do Naturally

LIVE IN AND APPRECIATE THE MOMENT

Practical Enhancers are practical and easygoing. They approach the world in a casual, open-ended way, looking for opportunities to express themselves or help others. Practical Enhancers are able to live mostly in the present moment, appreciating and affecting the world around them directly. Action oriented, they want to be able to respond freely to situations as they occur. They strongly resist and avoid highly structured or routine tasks. One Practical Enhancer who works as a substitute teacher comments,

"One thing I enjoy about the job is that I can walk in and then, at the end of the day, walk out. I like to jump in and take the class for a day or two. I can do the work and then, at the end of the day, be finished."

Practical Enhancers are drawn to work that provides opportunities to make immediate and practical responses. They value having fun and enjoying the moment and seek opportunities to take time to appreciate the world around them. They express themselves by engaging in the task at hand and completing it in a creative and unique way.

MAKE AN IMMEDIATE AND PERSONAL CONTRIBUTION

To engage their values, Practical Enhancers often help others by providing a practical service. Often these services are personal and focused on making people feel good. For example, a Practical Enhancer might enjoy giving a massage, helping someone through a medical procedure, styling hair, or fitting a customer with glasses.

Practical Enhancers want to personalize these services to individuals and are inclined to help people one at a time. They do not enjoy providing standardized or routine assistance to others, since part of their natural way of working is to understand and appreciate individual differences. The work they do must be worthwhile both to them and to those around them. One Practical Enhancer describes her work as a teacher of adults who are learning to read:

"I am able to work with students individually. I listen to their needs and provide them with support and encouragement. I customize my approach for each student, using reading materials that reflect his or her interests and goals. I enjoy helping each student in a unique and personal way. I also experience satisfaction as I see students' skills develop."

EXPRESS THEMSELVES

Practical Enhancers may have a love of nature. They may seek to express that value by working outdoors. They may choose to experience, improve, and enhance the natural world by working as botanists, foresters, or gardeners.

They may also choose to express themselves by creating a practical or artistic product. They are observant and use their senses to see and create beauty. Practical Enhancers often combine the artistic and unique with the practical. The result is a functional and beautiful product. They can become very skilled artisans. They can also be attracted to work as fashion, interior, and landscape designers. One Practical Enhancer who works as an interior designer explains,

"I like to pay attention to the colors and textures. I can blend pieces together in a very appealing way while still staying within the price range my client can afford."

Practical Enhancers are attracted to work that allows them to express their values, and the values they express can be diverse. If you want to find the specific work that will be most appealing to you as a Practical Enhancer, first identify what values you want to express. Then look for opportunities to express those values in a practical, friendly, and flexible environment.

TROUBLESHOOT

Focused on the immediate, Practical Enhancers are creative problem solvers. They prefer to solve problems using the materials at hand, and they like to improvise to improve or fix things. One Practical Enhancer finds his troubleshooting skills to be very handy when working as a child-care worker:

"I often need to find ways to solve conflicts that occur when children are playing with a limited number of toys. I enjoy coming up with spur-of-the-moment ways to keep the kids happy. I have learned a few magic tricks, and I will quietly take an upset child aside and distract him or her. I enjoy being able to contribute to making the atmosphere more harmonious."

Snapshot: Ideal Work Environment for Practical Enhancers

By focusing on your personal preferences, you will be able to better assess the types of work that will be personally satisfying. The following list describes ideal work environments for Practical Enhancers. Check off the items that are true for you.

As a Practical Enhancer, I prefer a work environment that is

- [ ] Focused on the practical and immediate
- [ ] Supportive and harmonious
- [ ] Flexible and autonomous
- [ ] A source of opportunities to enjoy the moment
- [ ] A place where I can make an immediate and personal contribution
- [ ] A place where I can express myself
- [ ] Focused on solving practical problems

Snapshot: Skills and Valued Activities for Practical Enhancers

By focusing on your personal preferences, you will be able to better assess the types of work that will be personally satisfying. The following list describes skills and activities valued by Practical Enhancers. Check off the items that are true for you.

As a Practical Enhancer, I value the following skills and activities:

- [ ] Adapting
- [ ] Communication—listening
- [ ] Creativity
- [ ] Customer service
- [ ] Empathy
- [ ] Observing
- [ ] Troubleshooting

Work That Attracts Practical Enhancers

The following occupations are typically of interest to Practical Enhancers. When looking for career ideas, remember to also look at the work options for Enhancers listed earlier in the chapter, which are attractive to both Practical Enhancers and Insightful Enhancers.

PERSONAL SERVICES
    Animal groomer
    Beautician
    Bookkeeper
    Cleaning service
    Customer service and sales
    School-bus driver
    Veterinarian assistant
    Waitperson

Opportunities to provide immediate and helpful services attract Practical Enhancers. If you are customer-service oriented, you might consider one of these occupations. Note that this category includes options that require various amounts of contact with people.

HEALTH AND WELLNESS
    Child-care worker
    Dental assistant
    Dental hygienist
    Health or medical technologist
    Health-service worker
    Licensed practical nurse
    Lifeguard
    Medical assistant
    Nursing aide
    Optician
    Optometrist
    Pharmacy technician
    Physician
    Public health nurse

Recreational attendant
Registered nurse
Respiratory therapist

Many Practical Enhancers are drawn to opportunities to work in the health and wellness area. These occupations provide immediate and meaningful contact with others, often in situations in which clients are anxious or uncomfortable. If you enjoy comforting and assisting others, these occupations may be of interest.

OFFICE SUPPORT
Administrative assistant
Clerical supervisor
Clerk
Computer operator
Legal assistant
Secretary

If your interests lie in the area of managing facts and details, you may want to consider providing office support.

SCIENCE, TRADES, AND TECHNOLOGY
Botanist
Construction worker
Electrician
Electronic technician
Forester
Gardener
Geologist
Machine operator
Marine biologist
Mechanic

Practical Enhancers are drawn to hands-on occupations. If you like work that provides opportunities for working outdoors or making an immediate product, some of these occupations may appeal to you.

ARTS AND DESIGN
Crafts worker
Fashion designer
Interior design
Landscape designer

Here are some occupations that appeal to the Practical Enhancer's creative side. If you have a flair for design or creating artistic products, there are a number of occupations that you might enjoy.

TEACHING AND COUNSELING
Corrections officer
Crisis hotline operator
Teacher—grades K–12
Teacher's aide

Some Practical Enhancers find satisfaction helping others. If you enjoy groups or working one-on-one with someone dealing with personal issues, you might enjoy teaching or counseling.

LAW ENFORCEMENT
Police detective
Police officer

Practical Enhancers bring a personal and supportive side to police work. If you like variety and action, you may want to consider law enforcement.

Practical Enhancers as Leaders
Practical Enhancers bring unique strengths to the leadership role. They naturally lead and prefer to be led in a specific way.

SOLVE PROBLEMS
Practical Enhancers are engaged by and focused on the problems of the moment. They are likely to ignore rules and procedures, especially if they can

see shortcuts, and will find a creative and individualistic solution to any immediate problem. They lead by example, solving problems themselves rather than
delegating responsibility. They do not enjoy the long-range planning aspects of
leadership and may need to take more time to consider the long-term impact of
some of their creative short-term solutions.

STAY IN THE BACKGROUND

Practical Enhancers are often easygoing and personable in a quiet and understated way. They prefer to stay in the background. They are motivated to help
others and believe that letting people work independently rather than providing direct supervision shows respect.

Autonomy and freedom are frequently at the top of Practical Enhancers' list
of important values. They have little interest in controlling, organizing, and
directing others. They rarely seek leadership positions. They do not lead by
using authority and do not respect leaders who do. Politics, policies, and protocol have no place in a Practical Enhancer's world.

Snapshot: Practical Enhancers as Leaders

*By focusing on your personal preferences, you will be able to better assess the types
of work that will be personally satisfying. The following list describes the leadership preferences of Practical Enhancers. Check off the items that are true for you.*

As a Practical Enhancer leader, I prefer to

- ☐ Deal with situations as they come up
- ☐ Focus on the problems of the moment
- ☐ Ignore rules and procedures
- ☐ Find a creative and individualistic solution
- ☐ Avoid long-range planning
- ☐ Be easygoing and personable
- ☐ Stay in the background
- ☐ Avoid direct supervision of others
- ☐ Lead by example

Practical Enhancers as Team Members

Practical Enhancers enjoy contributing to a team. A collaborative working environment is important to them, although they often stay in the background being quietly supportive. Practical Enhancers are kindhearted and will do whatever they can to help others. They are attuned to others on the team, helping them deal with immediate problems. They work more through actions than words, physically helping people or creating a product that will help them. They can be very generous and thoughtful.

Practical Enhancers like to give and receive positive feedback, and they are uncomfortable with interpersonal conflict or confrontation. They avoid these situations when possible. It may be difficult to convince Practical Enhancers to look to the root of interpersonal problems. Abstract thinking about problems seems to be a waste of time. They would prefer to focus on what can be done in the immediate situation.

Snapshot: Practical Enhancers as Team Members

By focusing on your personal preferences, you will be able to better assess the types of work that will be personally satisfying. The following list describes how Practical Enhancers like to work within a team. Check off the items that are true for you.

As a Practical Enhancer team member, I

- [ ] Enjoy working with others
- [ ] Am good at troubleshooting
- [ ] Find practical solutions to immediate problems
- [ ] Stay in the background
- [ ] Will do whatever I can to help others
- [ ] Am attuned to and like to help others on the team
- [ ] Work more through actions than words
- [ ] Am kindhearted
- [ ] Am generous and thoughtful
- [ ] Like to give and receive positive feedback
- [ ] Am uncomfortable with interpersonal conflict or confrontation

Practical Enhancers as Learners

Practical Enhancers like to learn practical information just in time to solve a problem. They prefer to learn as they work, in a hands-on, practical way. They are not likely to read manuals or written resources. They are observant and pay attention to detail.

Theory and abstraction bore Practical Enhancers. They seek facts that will help them accomplish their immediate task more effectively. They dislike the formality and structure of the classroom, preferring a more flexible, individual approach to learning. They like to control the pace of their own learning.

Practical Enhancers like individual support and encouragement as they are learning. They like to work alone or within a small group when possible. As with other situations, they are friendly and quiet, often staying in the background.

· 293 ·

Snapshot: Practical Enhancers as Learners

By focusing on your personal preferences, you will be able to better assess the types of work that will be personally satisfying. The following list describes the learning preferences of Practical Enhancers. Check off the items that are true for you.

As a Practical Enhancer learner, I

- [ ] Like to learn practical information
- [ ] Learn just in time to solve a problem
- [ ] Prefer hands-on learning
- [ ] Am not likely to read manuals or written resources
- [ ] Learn by doing
- [ ] Am bored by theory and abstraction
- [ ] Seek facts to help me accomplish immediate tasks
- [ ] Dislike the formality and structure of the classroom
- [ ] Prefer a flexible and individual approach to learning
- [ ] Prefer to learn alone or in a small group
- [ ] Need a supportive environment

BALANCING ENHANCING WITH INSIGHT

The latest research shows that about 4.4 percent of adults in the United States are Insightful Enhancers (INFP). Insightful Enhancers have an outward orientation that appreciates people, ideas, and possibilities. They will work to help others achieve their goals. They are quietly supportive of others and appreciate and seek positive feedback themselves. They dislike being underestimated or undervalued. Insightful Enhancers express their creative ideas in personal and innovative ways. They do not like structure and routine and work best when allowed flexibility and independence.

Because Insightful Enhancers have an insightful focus on possibilities and potential as a balance to their values-based individual approach, they initially express their Enhancing way of working differently than Practical Enhancers do. However, Practical Enhancers in midlife may find that the descriptions of Insightful Enhancers mirror the direction in which they are moving as they mature and develop.

What Insightful Enhancers Do Naturally

GROW AND DEVELOP

Insightful Enhancers can find many ways to express who they are in a wide range of work. They look at things holistically and can find it difficult to articulate what, specifically, is important to them. For Insightful Enhancers, work is an ongoing way to develop themselves and learn what, for them, is important. They like to learn and develop new skills throughout their life and may try many different kinds of work.

SUPPORT AND ADVOCATE

Insightful Enhancers can have strong impressions about others, which are usually accurate. They may not be able to explain where the impression came from, but they know it can be trusted. They naturally see the potential in others, and then support and encourage them to develop that potential. They are attracted to counseling and teaching roles that provide them with opportunities to mentor and foster others' development. They can be very dedicated in these roles. They also seek long-term growth and development in their personal relationships. Work is intensely personal for the Insightful Enhancer.

Insightful Enhancers are good listeners and will devote their attention to understanding and appreciating another's situation and point of view. They are unusually perceptive, aware of emotions and values, and able to read people well. One adult math instructor describes typical interactions with his students:

"I often have students come to my office with math anxiety or a lack of confidence. They tell me about their experiences. By listening well, I can get a better understanding of their needs and find ways to help them overcome their problems."

CHAMPION CAUSES

Insightful Enhancers champion causes as well as people. They are attracted to work that allows them to endeavor toward something that is personally meaningful and important. They are very loyal to the organization they work for. If the organization betrays their values, Insightful Enhancers will feel personally betrayed. In the same way, they expect genuineness and honesty in personal relationships and will not take kindly to those who are insincere or deceptive.

BE CREATIVE

Insightful Enhancers express their values and creativity by creating works of art, entertaining, or working in the design field. Whichever outlet they choose to express their values, the result is personal and individual. An Insightful Enhancer will not teach any two children in exactly the same way and is unlikely to mass-produce a standard piece of art. Each person and object is treated uniquely. Insightful Enhancers focus on quality, not quantity, in their work.

Insightful Enhancers often have a gift for language and expression. Their insight provides them with ideas, while their values provide them with passion and direction. This combination tends to produce individuals who are very expressive. However, due to their quiet and personal nature, Insightful Enhancers are often most comfortable with written rather than spoken communication.

WORK ONE-ON-ONE

Because Insightful Enhancers invest the time and energy needed to individualize their contacts with others and work one-on-one, they can become drained if they have to interact with many people over a short period, especially if the people involved are needy. All Insightful Enhancers need time alone to regenerate their energy, especially those working in the helping fields. Insightful Enhancers in counseling fields may need to take significant breaks from their work if they are to retain their motivation.

AVOID RULES AND STRUCTURE

Their focus on the individual and the situation predisposes Insightful Enhancers to dislike rules and structure, which take away their freedom to operate in an individualistic way. They tend to work in bursts of creative energy and can feel confined in a regular day job that requires a steady pace. One Enhancer who works as a farmer comments,

"I love the independence and natural rhythms of farming. I enjoy having the freedom to choose when I do things. I hate rigidity."

STRUGGLE WITH DETAILS AND FOLLOW-THROUGH

Insightful Enhancers can generate many ideas and see many possibilities, and may be drawn toward multiple projects. They are not strong on follow-through, however, and may leave projects half-finished. In times of stress, they can feel overwhelmed by this lack of follow-through.

In a similar way, they can omit or not attend to important details. A self-employed Insightful Enhancer found that even though he had the expertise to complete contracts, he often came in second when competing for work with other independent contractors. His proposals, though, were imaginative and full of good ideas, and when he began to include more facts and details, his proposals were chosen more often.

Work That Attracts Insightful Enhancers

The following occupations are typically of interest to Insightful Enhancers. When looking for career ideas, remember to also look at the work options for Enhancers listed earlier in the chapter, which are attractive to both Practical Enhancers and Insightful Enhancers.

ARTS AND DESIGN

Actor

Architect

Artist

Composer

Entertainer

Fine artist

Graphic designer

Musician

Snapshot: Ideal Work Environment for Insightful Enhancers

By focusing on your personal preferences, you will be able to better assess the types of work that will be personally satisfying. The following list describes the ideal work environment for Insightful Enhancers. Check off the items that are true for you.

As an Insightful Enhancer, I prefer a work environment that is

☐ Supportive and nurturing

☐ Creative

☐ A source of opportunities to generate ideas

☐ Flexible and independent

☐ A source of one-on-one people contact

☐ A source of opportunities to learn

☐ A place where I can mentor others

Snapshot: Skills and Valued Activities for Insightful Enhancers

By focusing on your personal preferences, you will be able to better assess the types of work that will be personally satisfying. The following list describes the skills and valued activities of Insightful Enhancers. Check off the items that are true for you.

As an Insightful Enhancer, I value the following skills and activities:

☐ Adapting

☐ Advocating

☐ Communicating—Listening

☐ Creativity

☐ Empathy

☐ Innovating

Insightful Enhancers with a creative flair are drawn to occupations that allow them to express their ideas and feelings. For some Insightful Enhancers, these artistic pursuits are hobbies. For others, they are their main source of income.

COUNSELING AND TEACHING

Counselor—rehabilitation, educational, vocational, crisis
Educational consultant
Human resources specialist
Psychiatrist
Psychologist
Public health nurse
Religious worker
Social scientist
Teacher—art, drama, English, reading, religion, special education,
  early childhood
Therapist

Insightful Enhancers often find the helping professions rewarding. These occupations provide them with an opportunity to foster the growth and development of others.

RESEARCH AND COMMUNICATIONS

Editor
Journalist
Librarian
Reporter
Researcher
Translator or interpreter
Writer

Written language provides a medium for Insightful Enhancers to express their ideas and feelings. If you have a flair for the written word, a career in communications may be of interest. Or, you may enjoy the new ideas and insights you can find when completing research.

Insightful Enhancers as Leaders

Insightful Enhancers bring unique strengths to the leadership role. They naturally lead and prefer to be led in a specific way.

PROVIDE A PERSONAL TOUCH

Insightful Enhancers focus on those they lead, like all others they connect with, on a personal and individual basis. They are highly supportive and encourage others to do their best. Because of this personal focus, they can become distracted from the task at hand by the problems and situations of those who work for them. Supporting people may become more important than completing the task.

UPHOLD ETHICS

Insightful Enhancers see leadership as an ethical role that requires authenticity. They do not enjoy politics or respect positions of power. For an Insightful Enhancer, respect for a leader is given on the basis of how ethically the leader behaves.

SUPPORT OTHERS

Insightful Enhancers do not command or direct others. They believe that people will naturally work well and commit to the organization if they are understood, valued, and supported. Insightful Enhancers see their role as supporting and setting up flexible systems and processes that will allow people to meet their potential and complete their work more effectively.

Snapshot: Insightful Enhancers as Leaders

By focusing on your personal preferences, you will be able to better assess the types of work that will be personally satisfying. The following list describes the leadership preferences of Insightful Enhancers. Check off the items that are true for you.

As an Insightful Enhancer leader, I

☐ Connect with others on a personal and individual basis

☐ Encourage others to do their best

☐ See leadership as an ethical role that requires authenticity

☐ Do not enjoy politics or respect positions of power

☐ Do not command or direct others

☐ Am supportive

Insightful Enhancers as Team Members

Insightful Enhancers are very supportive of team members. They appreciate others by listening carefully and showing that they understand their ideas. This ability to empathize is greatly appreciated and tends to create a positive team environment.

Insightful Enhancers are usually positive, optimistic, and somewhat idealistic. They expect that others will operate on the basis of compassion and kindness, and they expect the best from others.

They can personalize feedback and can be very hurt by feedback that is presented in an overly critical manner. Insightful Enhancers are uncomfortable with and may avoid interpersonal conflict, striving to maintain harmony even at the risk of leaving their own needs unmet. However, if pushed too far, they may offer a full and frank description of exactly how they have felt for years. Other team members may be taken aback by these revelations, since nothing was said previously.

Snapshot: Insightful Enhancers as Team Members

By focusing on your personal preferences, you will be able to better assess the types of work that will be personally satisfying. The following list describes how Insightful Enhancers like to work within a team. Check off the items that are true for you.

As a Insightful Enhancer team member, I

- ☐ Am supportive of team members
- ☐ Appreciate others by listening carefully
- ☐ Create a positive team environment
- ☐ Expect the best from others
- ☐ Am positive, optimistic, and somewhat idealistic
- ☐ May avoid interpersonal conflict
- ☐ Strive to maintain harmony
- ☐ Can personalize feedback

Insightful Enhancers as Learners

Insightful Enhancers want to learn about ideas. They especially like personal stories of inspiration and seek opportunities to learn how others have managed adversity or solved problems. Theories and possibilities are more interesting to them than facts and details.

Insightful Enhancers prefer to learn about things that are directly connected to their values. Because they approach learning in a personal way, they can be significantly affected by their relationship with the instructor. An instructor who provides encouragement and positive feedback will bring out the best in an Insightful Enhancer.

Insightful Enhancers like to learn independently and work best alone or in small groups. They prefer flexibility and feel confined in highly structured learning environments. One Enhancer summarizes her perspective on learning:

"What I like about learning are the ideas, possibilities, and new ways of thinking. What I dislike are the structure, rigidity of thought, formality, and right-or-wrong answers."

Snapshot: Insightful Enhancers as Learners

By focusing on your personal preferences, you will be able to better assess the types of work that will be personally satisfying. The following list describes the learning preferences of Insightful Enhancers. Check off the items that are true for you.

As an Insightful Enhancer learner, I

- ☐ Want to learn about ideas
- ☐ Like personal stories of inspiration
- ☐ Want opportunities to see how others have managed adversity or solved problems
- ☐ Prefer theory to facts and details
- ☐ Can be significantly affected by my relationship with the instructor
- ☐ Appreciate support and encouragement from the instructor
- ☐ Approach learning in a personal way
- ☐ Learn independently
- ☐ Need flexibility
- ☐ Work well alone or in a small group

THE ENHANCER'S GREATEST CHALLENGES

Everyone has less-preferred activities and areas for growth and improvement. Enhancers are no exception. Here are three major developmental areas for both Practical Enhancers and Insightful Enhancers, with tips on how to develop each one.

Meeting Their Own Needs

Enhancers are very aware of and sensitive to the needs of people around them. It is their nature to strive to help others; they will be there to help someone in a crisis, spend time with family members who need attention, and nurture all their relationships in general. The needs of others become personally important to them.

Although helping others may provide a sense of satisfaction for Enhancers, they may find that there is little time left at the end of the day to nurture their own personal needs. Over time, this can create frustration and a sense of being taken for granted. One Enhancer describes her goal in this respect:

"I would like to learn to be more outgoing so that people will see the inner me. I feel that I am often underestimated and that my needs are often not recognized."

TIPS FOR MEETING THEIR OWN NEEDS

- Remember that you will be better at helping others when you are feeling good about yourself. Taking care of yourself is not a selfish behavior. Do it for those around you!
- Focus each day on a small, positive thing that you can do for yourself. It need not cost a lot of money or take a lot of time.
- Build small, satisfying times into your day. Stop to have a cup of tea, take a leisurely bath instead of a shower, and so on.
- Focus on defining exactly what your needs are. Take time to write them down or to share them with someone close to you.

Using a Logical Approach

A values-based approach can become lopsided if it is not balanced with logic. Logic and analysis can help Enhancers avoid decisions that they may later regret. This balance is important, especially if the decisions are being made at emotional times or about emotional matters. Subjective decisions can be very emotional and focused only on a short-term outcome or a particular value. However, these decisions can have significant consequences in both the long and short term. One Enhancer describes how she struggles to keep her emotions at bay:

"My biggest challenge is keeping my emotions under control at work. Sometimes I become so passionate about something that I can get emotional just thinking or talking about it. It can embarrass me."

TIPS FOR USING A LOGICAL APPROACH

- When making a decision, stop to weigh the pros and cons of options. List them and look at them with an objective eye.
- Follow each option through to its logical conclusion. Focus on the specific implications of your decisions in both the long and short term.
- Make sure your options are reasonable as well as appealing.
- Imagine trying to explain and justify your decision to someone who is highly logical. What questions would he or she ask? How would you answer?
- Defer a decision if you are emotional or upset. Take time to think logically about what you are feeling.

Not Taking Things Personally

Enhancers may miss out on opportunities for growth and improvement because they find it hard to listen to and incorporate critical feedback. This is, in part, related to the way they like to give and receive feedback themselves. Enhancers, being naturally affirming and supportive, usually give negative feedback gently and with great care for a person's feelings. They often mention a positive attribute first and then add a suggestion for improvement. They are careful not to make global statements that might hurt a person's feelings or self-esteem.

Enhancers want to receive feedback in the same way they like to give it. However, not everyone appreciates their approach. Many people prefer a direct, no-nonsense sharing of areas for improvement. When Enhancers receive this type of feedback, they feel hurt and personally attacked. They may globalize the information and feel that the person giving the feedback does not like or respect them.

At their worst, Enhancers may feel criticized by a suggestion or comment that is not even intended as feedback. For example, imagine that someone walks into an office and says, "I really like the way the furniture in the room is arranged now." An overly sensitive Enhancer might think that they are indirectly criticizing the way the furniture was arranged *before*. This, of course, is an overly dramatic example, but it does capture the subjective and personal way an Enhancer can interpret feedback from others. Enhancers are more likely to react sensitively to feedback when they are under stress or unsure of themselves.

· 304 ·

TIPS FOR NOT TAKING THINGS PERSONALLY

- Consistently remind yourself to separate critical feedback of behaviors and performance from an attack on you as a person.
- Make your new mantra "All good people make mistakes."
- When you start to feel criticized, remember that not all people affirm and support as a way of communicating. Remember that there are other ways of relating, and accept feedback in the spirit in which it is given.
- Minimize your chances of misunderstanding by clarifying what you hear. Ask the person providing feedback to specify what he or she means and to give examples.
- Ask for additional positive feedback. Acknowledge the negative feedback, and then ask if there was anything that worked or was done well. You may be pleasantly surprised by the positive feedback that the person did not bother to mention.
- If you find yourself taking things more personally than usual, you may be in a particularly stressful or uncomfortable situation. Try to lower your stress level or to back away from the situation and assess what is different. Take time to understand whether your values are being challenged and what you can do about it.
- If you work in a helping occupation, find ways to keep from taking on all the problems of the people around you. It can be very difficult for an Enhancer to stay uninvolved. Although it is valuable to become involved and care about others, it can lead to burnout. Some detachment can be essential for your own health and well-being.

KEY FOR ME: MANAGING MY CHALLENGES

Is meeting your own needs, using a logical approach, or not taking things personally a challenge for you? If so, which of the strategies explored in this chapter would be helpful to try? ....

....

....

....

....

....

....

FINAL TIPS FOR ENHANCERS: DOING WHAT COMES NATURALLY

An Enhancer naturally approaches the world of work by expressing personal values. Here are a few final tips that will help you choose and develop satisfying work.

Identify Your Key Values

Enhancers are internally and powerfully driven to live by and express their values in their day-to-day life. Stop to assess what key values are important to you, since these values provide an inner guide to the type of work that will be satisfying. Once you have identified important values, assess whether you are expressing them in your work.

Express Your Key Values

Find work that provides you with opportunities to express your individuality. The possible options are diverse, from artist to veterinarian. Whatever work you do, ensure that it touches your heart and soul. At the end of the day, you want to be able to say that you made a contribution to something that is personally important and meaningful.

Work with Supportive People

Enhancers seek to give and receive positive feedback. It is important to find an environment in which you are supported and encouraged. The work you do is an expression of yourself. Sharing your work with others is sharing a piece of yourself. In a negative or overly critical environment, you will feel hurt and unappreciated.

Be Yourself

Find an environment that allows you the flexibility, autonomy, and space to be yourself. Stay away from work that boxes you in or stifles your individuality.

Now that you have learned about your work preferences, please turn to Chapter 11 to begin planning your career path.

PART FOUR

Making Better Career Choices

Chapter Eleven
Taking Stock

Career satisfaction looks different to different people. Knowing your natural way of working is a good start in learning what will make a career satisfying for you. But you are more than just a developing personality type. You express your natural way of working through a unique combination of interests, values, skills, constraints, knowledge, and work experiences. Furthermore, you are in a specific situation that, in most cases, involves others and their needs as well as your own. Now, to find that ideal career, you need to make an accurate summary of what career satisfaction looks like to you.

This chapter will show you how to express your natural way of working. You will assess your skills, values and interests, and lifestyle and constraints. This assessment will provide the information you need to start shaping your career. In Chapter 12 you will use this self-assessment information to find work that will be meaningful and rewarding. Let's begin with a few tips to help you use your natural preferences when completing a self-assessment.

Tips for Self-Assessment
Responders

- Try to be patient with theory and the concept of self-assessment. The information you collect will help you in a practical way.
- Find practical reasons and applications for your self-assessment. Think of how you can use this information right away. Keep career planning practical.
- Assess by doing; try things out.
- Rather than completing inventories, try card sorts and other more active assessment tools.

Explorers

- Look for patterns, and make connections between your natural way of working, interests, values, and lifestyle.
- Involve others in your self-assessment process. Ask for feedback, and discuss your thoughts.

Expeditors

- Make your assessment logical. Critically analyze your experiences. Find out what you did not like and what did not fit, and then figure out why.
- Focus on your skills and competencies. Think of what you want to be most competent at.

Contributors

- Find support for your self-assessment. Share the process with someone who knows you well and can coach or encourage you.
- Remember that your values and the impact of your career choice on others are critical factors to consider.
- Learn from your personal experiences and reactions as well as the experiences of others.

Assimilators

- Use your mental storehouse of past experiences to help you focus your self-assessment.
- Capture your experience by listing some of your more enjoyable work, tasks, and skills. Then look for themes and patterns, rather than focusing on individual facts and details.

Visionaries

- Seek and use metaphors and images to guide your planning. Capture your dreams and visions. Make a picture of yourself in an ideal future.
- Remember to focus on facts and details as well as themes and meanings.

Analyzers

- You have likely already critically analyzed yourself and your work. You may need to also focus on your strengths. List your best skills and competencies.

- Reflect on your self-assessment information. Does it all fit together in a logical way? Are any conclusions evident?

Enhancers
- Focus on the values of the people around you. Whom are you supporting, and what does that mean in terms of your career?
- Focus on your own values. What is important to you personally?
- Take these two focuses—others' needs and your own—and look for a balance. Are you getting a chance to meet your needs?

COMMON SELF-ASSESSMENT PITFALLS

No matter what your natural way of assessing yourself is, here are some common traps that *all* people can fall into. Try to avoid these pitfalls.

Equating What You Can Do with What You Prefer to Do

Sometimes people describe their work when they assess themselves, rather than looking inward to evaluate what parts of their work suit or fail to suit them. This is especially true when they have been doing a specific type of work for many years. One can develop the skills to do the work to such a high degree that it becomes hard to determine where the work ends and the person starts. As well, we can get trapped into thinking that we should continue to do what we have always done because that seems the fastest and easiest way through the transition.

It can be hard not to jump right back into comfortable and familiar tasks. However, transition is an opportunity to take stock of what you can learn to do and be. No matter what your age and situation, you can always change your path if it will help you get what you need from your life. On the other hand, the work you were doing may have been just right for you personally. If so, jump back in and carry on shaping your career by finding opportunities to maintain all that you enjoyed.

Being Overly Concerned with the Opinions of Others

Some skills, values, and preferences may not be as popular or have the same status as others, but they may be perfect for you. Remember that the opinions of others are often based on what they see as best for *them*, not you. Also, it is difficult for some people to understand that entirely different things can motivate others. Family members, co-workers, and friends may judge your success by their own standards, rather than seeing what is important for you. In some families there are strong expectations and pressures to follow, or not follow, in the footsteps of those who came before you. However, taking over the family farm, business, or legacy may not meet your career needs; getting the education or pursuing the profession that your parents wish they had may not be your path either.

Collecting Data Without Processing It

Career self-assessment typically involves completing a number of inventories, checklists, and questions. Often these data are simply data: a bunch of information. It is important to find ways to make the information personal and practical. Ask yourself, "So what?" What does it mean, to you, to have a certain interest or value? How will interests or values make a difference when you are choosing between two jobs or deciding what to learn or do? Focus on what the data mean, which are important, and what relevant themes or patterns emerge.

Focusing on Only One Aspect of Your Self-Assessment

Self-assessment requires integration skills. You need, for example, to consider whether your interests fit your lifestyle. You may be a single parent and crave risk and adventure. How do those pieces of information relate to and affect each other? If you have difficulty processing the information you collect, you may want to consult a career planning professional who can help organize your information into a coherent whole.

USE WHAT YOU ALREADY KNOW

To begin your self-assessment, reflect back on what you already know. If you are just starting out, looking for your first job, this might consist of simply reflecting on the school subjects and leisure activities you enjoy or dislike. If you are a midlife career-changer, reflection on your experiences can be a very powerful tool for self-understanding. You have likely already collected lots of information about what suits you. Answer the following questions as a way to help you reflect.

What associations, clubs, or groups are you a member of? Why?

....

....

How do you like to spend your time?

....

....

Do you like to read books? What types?

....

....

Do you like to watch TV shows or movies? What types?

....

....

Are you involved in your community or in volunteer activities?

....

....

What courses have you taken recently? Why did you take them?

....

....

What do you like learning about? How do you like to learn?

....

....

What topics of discussion interest you?

....

....

What do people say when they describe you or the way you work?

....

....

Have you done work that you especially liked? What did you like about it?

....

....

Have you done work that you especially disliked? What did you dislike about it?...

....

....

What recreational activities do you enjoy?

....

....

This information can help you focus on your skills, values, interests, lifestyle, and personal preferences. You may want to write down a career/life history. This exercise may not be as useful if you are just starting out, but even young people can make a record of their activities. Include jobs such as babysitting, paper routes, helping with the family business, sports, especially enjoyable field trips or internships, and the like. List what you have done over the years, in chronological order. Now review your history by looking for themes and asking yourself questions such as these:

What activities do I enjoy?
What do I dislike?
Why did I take that course or choose that activity?
Why did I change jobs?
What things are showing up as important to me over time?

USE YOUR NATURAL WAY OF WORKING

One of the most helpful pieces of self-information, as emphasized throughout this book, is your *natural way of working*. These personality preferences and natural inclinations can be used as the starting point for your self-assessment. As you read the chapter describing your preferences, you likely agreed with some of the statements and disagreed with others. This is a common experience since everyone expresses his or her personality in a unique way.

Flip back to the chapter that best describes your natural preferences. Now is the time to apply the information to complete the "So what?" part of the learning. Reread the information in the chapter. Pay special attention to the items you checked in the various lists. Ask yourself questions such as, "Is this characteristic really true of me? Is it important to me? Can I use this information in a practical way to shape my career? Do I need to incorporate more (or less) of this into my career? Does this help me focus on what to look for in my next work?" These questions are only samples; the general idea is to apply the content of the chapter to your unique situation. You may want to highlight, underline, jot notes in the margin, make a set of index cards with notes, or write in a notebook. However you complete the task, the idea is to make this information real for *you*, today.

Also think about your stage of development. What are you using now to balance your natural way of working? Are you in the process of moving into new ways of finding balance? Remember, each person's situation is unique. For example, Expeditors and Analyzers tend to communicate in a task-oriented, brisk way. However, they will obviously learn, to a greater or lesser degree, to relate to people using empathy. An Expeditor or Analyzer who has taken the time and energy to learn about and work in the human services arena may have a different way of working from one who has worked independently in a technical field.

Now you are ready to apply your natural preferences to your situation. Describe the key things that you want from work. Do not list jobs; instead, describe your personal preferences. Using your chapter review, complete the following statements. You may want to look back to the introductions to the introverted and extraverted ways of working and consider the points covered there.

Keep your top preferences in mind as you complete the next exercises.

For me, the ideal work will provide opportunities for me to

....

....

....

....

....

My preferred work environment is

....

....

The specific skills or activities I would like to use are

....

....

I would like to lead and be led by

....

....

I would like to contribute to a team by

....

....

I would like to learn and grow by

....

....

Skills

Your skills provide the expertise you need to perform work well. They are a key component of your self-assessment process and the ultimate job security. Taking a careful look at your skills will help you assess and increase your competitive advantage. Matching skills that you have, enjoy, or want to develop with work opportunities can help you shape your career path.

Your skills often, but not always, relate to your natural way of working. For example, an Expeditor, who thrives on getting the work done efficiently, tends to develop organizational and time-management skills. An Enhancer, who thrives on attending to and meeting the needs of others, tends to develop listening and empathic skills. However, an Expeditor may choose to become a psychiatrist and take time to develop listening and empathic skills to best serve his or her patients. An Enhancer, seeking autonomy, may develop time- and task-management skills that will allow him or her to set up and manage a small business.

Skill assessment can occur in a variety of ways. If you are currently working within an organization, ask what tools are available to help you in your self-assessment. Your organization may have skill or competency gap analysis tools, which are highly specific comparisons of a person's skills with the skills needed to perform the tasks in a particular position. These tools are very helpful in pinpointing specific strengths and areas for improvement in different types of work opportunities as well as in your current position. You also may use your job description or any performance feedback you have received to assess your skills. At the same time, you can let others know that you are interested in enhancing your skills. Starting a dialogue with your co-workers will help you negotiate learning opportunities and assignments that facilitate skill development.

If you own a business, you may want to survey your customers to find out what they expect from you and your staff. As well, associations and certification boards in your skill area may provide you with a specific set of skills or qualifications. You may be able to align your professional development needs to meet specific market demands.

If you are not currently working, reflect back to work you have done in the past. Ask yourself questions such as these.

What do I do well?

....

....

What type of task or activity gives me satisfaction?

....

....

Why would someone have me work with or for them?

....

....

The following exercise is a tool you can use to assess nine general skill sets. Each skill set has ten contributing skills. The general skills are needed to accomplish virtually any type of work. The specific skills—the ones that reflect your education, training, and experience—will help you pinpoint or refine your career path.

COMPREHENSIVE SKILLS ANALYSIS

To thoroughly assess a contributing skill, it is important to consider whether you use, enjoy, and want to develop it. By analyzing the contributing skills using these three criteria, you can clearly define your career and development path. The categories for assessment in this exercise are

Use: Do I use this skill?
Enjoy: Do I enjoy using this skill?
Develop: Do I want to develop this skill in the future?

For each skill, place a check mark in the relevant boxes. If appropriate, you may check all three boxes for any one skill. After completing a skill set, add up the number of check marks in each column and record it in the totals boxes at the bottom of each set. At the end of the skills assessment, summarize your results.

CHANGE MANAGEMENT SKILLS	USE	ENJOY	DEVELOP
Adapt behaviors appropriately			
Challenge accepted ways			
Create new ideas or inventions			
Think flexibly, fluently, and creatively			
Deal with ambiguity (uncertainty or multiple meanings)			
Orient to future; anticipate and create changes for self and business			
Increase scope of endeavors			
Originate new ways to accomplish tasks			
Observe market trends and accommodate them			
Prepare for changes in personal and professional requirements			
Total			

COMMUNICATION SKILLS	USE	ENJOY	DEVELOP
Clarify situations and communications			
Tactfully converse to explore possibilities (display a keen sense of what and when to do or say things)			
Explain thoughts clearly			
Listen carefully and respond appropriately			
Present information or ideas to a group			
Ask questions for information, instructions, or understanding			
Read for information, instructions, or understanding			
Share information appropriately			
Summarize and integrate information			
Write to express and explain self clearly			
Total			

LEADERSHIP SKILLS	USE	ENJOY	DEVELOP
Coach others to meet personal and business needs			
Confront issues, seeking win-win resolutions			
Coordinate resources to reach goals			
Commit to visions and values (plan strategically to actualize visions)			
Experiment and take risks (learn from mistakes; help others to do same)			
Facilitate and support development of teams/members			
Initiate action			
Manage stress (perform and cope in difficult situations)			
Model expected behaviors (demonstrate integrity of personal and business values)			
Develop vision with a team			
Total			

LEARNING SKILLS	USE	ENJOY	DEVELOP
Acquire skills to increase performance			
Adapt plans based on results			
Align learning to business and personal performance needs			
Assess current/future learning and career development needs			
Develop learning strategies			
Manage information using effective learning strategies			
Monitor progress			
Plan for learning; use and accommodate learning preferences in a development plan			
Take responsibility for actions and results			
Set objectives for learning			
Total			

Numerical Data Skills	USE	ENJOY	DEVELOP
Budget money and other resources			
Calculate using basic arithmetic			
Estimate size or cost accurately		/	
Understand math terms and symbols (math literacy)			
Measure to determine quantities			
Reason numerically to interpret numbers or statistics			
Use, meet, or verify accurate and exact specifications (precision)			
Keep records in an organized and efficient manner			
Sort information into categories			
Use computers and calculators to manage data (technical literacy)			
Total			

Problem-Solving Skills	USE	ENJOY	DEVELOP
Analyze problems and categorize information into components and likely causes			
Clarify possibilities			
Decide on effective courses of action			
Develop measurement criteria			
Evaluate information to make decisions			
Generate possible solutions			
Identify deviations from the norm			
Integrate information into a whole			
Predict potential problems			
Research to gather relevant information			
Total			

RESULTS ORIENTATION SKILLS	USE	ENJOY	DEVELOP
Compile relevant data to measure results			
Plan tasks effectively; reliably complete what is required (efficiency)			
Evaluate progress and success			
Take initiative to achieve personal and business results			
Measure results			
Organize activities to achieve goals			
Plan the sequence and timing of multiple events to meet long-term goals			
Prioritize multiple time and task demands in and outside of work or school			
Set goals to guide planning			
Complete tasks to systematically achieve goals			
Total			

TEAMWORK SKILLS	USE	ENJOY	DEVELOP
Align work and goals with those of team members			
Collaborate to accomplish goals			
Cooperate to reach common goals			
Coordinate people and resources to reach goals			
Celebrate success of self and others			
Be sensitive to the needs of others (empathy)			
Encourage efforts of team members			
Provide feedback that is positive and constructive			
Resolve conflicts in a win-win context			
Accept and accommodate individual differences (diversity)			
Total			

Thinking Skills	Use	Enjoy	Develop
Reason abstractly; work with symbols and concepts			
Apply common sense (practical judgment)			
Logically analyze and evaluate information (critical thinking)			
Deal with complexity; manage multiple variables			
Manage information systematically			
Strive for self-awareness, assessment, evaluation, and adaptation (metacognition)			
Retain facts, figures, and events accurately			
Plan long-term sequences of effective actions (strategic thinking)			
Integrate information (synthesize)			
Relate and integrate processes (systems thinking)			
Total			

Comprehensive Skills Analysis Summary

Now that you have analyzed your skills, you can begin to use this knowledge to shape the direction of your career path. Summarize your scores in the following chart. A total of ten is possible for each box within each skill set.

Skill Set	Use	Enjoy	Develop
Change Management			
Communication			
Leadership			
Learning			
Numerical Data			
Problem-Solving			
Results Orientation			
Teamwork			
Thinking			

Focus on shaping your career path and your future skill use and development by answering the following questions to help you interpret this exercise.

Which skill sets do you use most?

....

....

Which skill sets do you enjoy most? (If these are significantly different from the ones you use most, you may need to redirect your career!)

....

....

If you are currently working, which skill sets would you like to develop to enhance your current job performance?

....

....

Which skill sets would you like to use more often in the future? How might you be able to use them?

....

....

Which skills within each set would you most like to develop now or in the future? You may want to refer back to the list of general skills to see which contributing skills you checked.

....

....

What are some ways that you might be able to develop those skills?

....

....

OCCUPATION-SPECIFIC SKILLS ANALYSIS

In addition to the nine clusters of general skills you just assessed, occupation-specific skills contribute to your employability. These are the skills that focus on your specific area(s) of expertise. You may be an expert by virtue of your experience or qualifications, or a combination of the two. Occupation-specific skills are usually related to a subject area or to work expertise, so we often think of them in terms of what we do at work: accounting, engineering, carpentry, teaching, selling, driving, and so forth.

These occupation-specific skills demonstrate what areas of expertise we operate within and often define the type of work we may do. Many people are experts at more than one occupation-specific skill. Think about your education and work experiences, and then list your occupation-specific skills. For example, if you have worked as a nurse, your occupation-specific skills might include nursing, educating, and counseling.

· 325 ·

If you are new to the workforce, you may not have many occupation-specific skills. You will want to consider developing both general and specific skills.

My occupation-specific skills are ....

....

....

Choose three of your occupation-specific skills to assess. Check the box if the statement is true for you.

One of my occupation-specific skills is ....

In this area, I

❏ Have a good knowledge base

❏ Am aware of new developments

❏ Apply leading-edge practices

❏ Identify and use my competitive advantage

❏ Acquire new information in unfamiliar yet related areas

❏ Use my expertise to achieve business results

Another occupation-specific skill is ....

In this area, I

❑ Have a good knowledge base

❑ Am aware of new developments

❑ Apply leading-edge practices

❑ Identify and use my competitive advantage

❑ Acquire new information in unfamiliar yet related areas

❑ Use my expertise to achieve business results

Another occupation-specific skill is ....

In this area, I

❑ Have a good knowledge base

❑ Am aware of new developments

❑ Apply leading-edge practices

❑ Identify and use my competitive advantage

❑ Acquire new information in unfamiliar yet related areas

❑ Use my expertise to achieve business results

If you are unable to check the boxes, you may want to consider whether this occupation-specific skill is one you intend to use as you travel along your career path. If you decide it is, you may need to spend time strengthening that skill.

You may need to identify your areas of specific expertise to understand what you need to learn or do. For example, if you are a computer expert, in what area is your competitive advantage? It may be word processing applications, hardware maintenance and repair, computer-assisted design, networking, web page design, and so forth.

You will also need to compare your general skills and your specific skills. For example, if you enjoy analysis and problem solving, there are a million things that you can analyze and a million problems to solve. This is where occupation-specific skills can help you define your career path. For example, you may choose to develop skills in troubleshooting electronic systems and move in a career direction that includes electronic technology, appliance repair, or instrumentation. Or, the same general skills of analysis and problem solving can be used to help people. You may then choose to learn counseling strategies and other specific information that can head you toward a career in social work, counseling, or nursing.

Focus on shaping your career through your future skill use and development by answering the following questions.

Which occupation-specific skill area am I most interested in?

....

....

What specific areas of knowledge and experience relate to this skill?

....

....

How can I enhance this skill area?

....

....

You may want to repeat this process for other occupation-specific skills. If you have many skills you want to develop, you can work on them one at a time by choosing your priorities as you shape your career path.

VALUES AND INTERESTS

Values and interests are prime motivators at work. The following list can help you focus on what makes work satisfying for you. It lists work and personal values and interests, which you can rate according to their importance to you and then use to facilitate a suitable career decision. Read each value and then rate it on a scale of 1–4 as follows: 1 = essential, 2 = important, 3 = neutral, 4 = not important.

· 328 ·

———— Action (moving to different places or being active during work)

———— Advancement (having potential for increased pay and responsibility)

———— Adventure (having opportunities for excitement and travel)

———— Aesthetics (appreciating beauty and artistic skills)

———— Belonging (being part of a well-known group or organization)

———— Collaboration and teamwork (being part of a functional team)

———— Community involvement (making a meaningful contribution to the community)

———— Competition (comparing your performance with that of others)

———— Contact with people (having regular contact with others)

———— Creativity (generating new ideas, programs, or procedures)

———— Data management (recording and organizing data)

———— Decision making (influencing or controlling decision making)

———— Developing new skills (learning and trying new skills)

———— Emotional expression (performing, or creating ideas or products)

———— Expertise (being known for specialized knowledge or skills)

———— Friendships (developing new friends and fostering existing relationships)

———— Hands-on activities (using tools or operating equipment)

———— Helping others (showing compassion for aspirations of others)

———— Helping society (making beneficial contributions to society)

———— Independence (working with little direction or supervision)

———— Intellectual challenge (understanding and developing new concepts)

———— Leisure activities (pursuing hobbies, recreation, and relaxation)

_____ Money (earning a high income or gaining material goods)

_____ Moral principles (acting within ethical standards of conduct)

_____ Organization (organizing events or people)

_____ Parenting (being involved with children and their activities)

_____ Partnering (being involved with a spouse or significant other)

_____ Personal development (learning about and developing oneself)

_____ Physical fitness (maintaining a healthy body through diet and exercise)

_____ Power and authority (directing and influencing others)

_____ Precision (being exact or maintaining a high degree of accuracy)

_____ Problem solving (using thinking skills to solve problems)

_____ Recognition (receiving recognition and appreciation for work)

_____ Routine (preferring recurring duties)

_____ Security (needing employment protection and reasonable pay)

_____ Solitary work (having little contact with others)

_____ Spiritual development (observing and developing deep-set beliefs to live by)

_____ Stability (having routine and predictable work responsibilities)

_____ Status (performing work that leads to respect from others)

_____ Supervision (managing others)

_____ Time and freedom (scheduling own work and hours)

_____ Variety (having changing responsibilities and duties)

Analyzing your values and interests can help you decide how to structure your work so that you can spend time and energy on the things that are important to you.

List the values and interests you rated as *essential* (1)

....

....

....

List the values and interests you rated as *important* (2)

....

....

....

LIFESTYLE AND CONSTRAINTS

Understanding lifestyle and constraint factors helps you integrate your work with the other factors that affect your life. Fill in your personal preferences in each of the following categories.

When and how much you work (hours . . . days . . . structure . . .)

....

....

Where you work (inside, outside, moving to another center . . .)

....

....

Physical limitations (vision . . . lifting . . . sitting . . .)

....

....

Health considerations (illness . . . allergies . . . fitness . . .)

Psychological factors (stress . . . pressure . . . demands . . .)

How much money you make (salary . . . pension . . . benefit . . .)

Other roles (home . . . parenting . . . caring for aging parents   )

Leisure or hobbies (groups . . . associations . . . sports . . .)

When considering lifestyle and constraint factors, it is helpful to separate "must have" from "want to have." Put a star beside the factors that are necessities, to distinguish them from the factors that would merely be nice to have.

SELF-ASSESSMENT SUMMARY

Now you are ready to integrate all the components of your self-assessment. Read what you have written in this chapter for each of the self-assessment areas. Summarize the information by listing your most important points in the box on page 332. You may want to discuss your self-assessment with someone else. You may also have other sources of information you want to include. For example, you may have filled out other inventories or obtained useful feedback from others that will add to this summary.

I have reflected on my history and realized that these things are important to me ....

....

Learning about my natural way of working led me to identify these things I want from work ....

....

I enjoy and want to develop these general and specific skills ....

....

....

These values and interests are essential or very important to me ....

....

....

My lifestyle and constraints add these additional parameters to my career choice ....

....

The information you have gathered is most useful if you translate it into concrete statements describing what you need or want from work. Imagine that you have lucked into finding a recruiting organization that has several hundred types of work they need to fill. They ask you to describe what key things you want from work, so that they can find the right type of work for you. They do *not* want you to tell them about your preferred jobs—they just want you to tell them about your personal preferences, skills, interests, values, lifestyle, and constraints. They will then fit you to an appropriate job. Thinking about the self-assessment work you have done so far, what would you say?

In the space below, summarize what you would tell the recruiter. Use the questions to help you write your answer. Do you see any patterns or themes emerging in your self-descriptions? What natural approaches to work would you use? When would you work? Where? What tasks and responsibilities would you have? Whom would you work with? How would the day-to-day tasks unfold? Use list or sentence form, whichever is more natural.

My ideal type of work would be

....

....

....

....

....

....

....

....

· 333 ·

Now, highlight three to five pieces of information from your description that are the most important. Let this description be a reference for you when you consider or evaluate possible work opportunities or options.

....

....

....

....

....

....

With your work preferences in mind, you are ready to move to Chapter 12 to shape your career path.

Chapter Twelve
Shaping Your Career

To shape your career, you need to generate options, research, decide, and then take action. Each step takes you closer to your goal of finding satisfying work.

Generate Options

Once you have a picture of career satisfaction, you need to think of possible work that will match your preferences and situation. It is important not to jump too quickly into making a work choice: stop to consider all the options. You can save yourself a lot of grief if you expand your horizons and consider a wide range of options *before* you choose a career direction.

To ensure that you have covered all possibilities and work opportunities, you need to identify different types of work that will meet your needs. If you are new to the world of work, look around and familiarize yourself with all the various types of work that are available in your community or region.

Depending on your situation and preferences, you may need to think outside the box for different ways to work. For example, if you need to accommodate lifestyle constraints or other factors, you might look for a career that offers a flexible schedule. The following are some options you might consider as alternatives to full-time permanent employment:

- Casual work
- Consulting
- Contract work
- Hobbies that pay
- Job sharing
- Making products
- Part-time job(s)
- Providing services
- Selling products
- Temporary work

If you are specifically looking for a change within an organization, you may want to reflect on the available opportunities there. Some examples might include a different position or work site, a developmental assignment, flex time or working at home, progression up (or down) the ladder, and different tasks within your current position. Remember that a "promotion" is not always a solution. Different roles may require different hours and very different responsibilities. Some people find that a move back down rather than up the corporate ladder enhances their work satisfaction!

One way to generate career options is to brainstorm possibilities. Be open to any ideas that pop into your head. There will be time later to weed out the impractical ideas. If you have always thought it would be interesting to be a brain surgeon, write it down. Later you can figure out what specific need makes that option appealing. Perhaps it's the status . . . money . . . saving lives? Focus initially on the general rather than the specific, the broad rather than the narrow.

If you are not a fan of brainstorming, you may prefer a more concrete way to generate options:

- Review the occupations listed in the chapter that describes your way of working. Remember, there are three different occupation lists in every chapter.
- Look through job postings.
- Observe the workplace for opportunities.
- Look through the yellow pages of the phone book.
- Read a newspaper that has a lot of job ads (Sunday is usually a good day).
- Ask someone who knows you to help generate ideas.
- Do research at a career center.
- Ask your alumni association if it has job resources.
- Search a topic on the Internet.
- Look for opportunities in your daily activities.
- Volunteer. For example, if you think you might want to work in the medical field, volunteer at a hospital.
- Pick up books at the library that discuss career fields that interest you.

Work Options to Consider

Use the space below to write down some work options you would like to consider, keeping your self-assessment in mind. Open your mind and think of as many work options as you can that would be interesting. One way to open up your options is to take yourself out of the picture. Look at your self-assessment and ask, "What work might suit a person with those characteristics?" Be creative and write down anything that comes to mind.

Themes

Look for themes in your options and list them below. Compare the themes you have written down with your self-assessment summary. For example, if your brainstorming list includes selling cars, marketing books, and selling office equipment, perhaps you would like to pursue a career in sales and marketing. Themes can help you generate more related options and can also provide you with a focus for research now, and for learning and skill development later.

Tips for Generating Options

Here are some tips to help you generate options that are specifically related to your natural way of doing things.

RESPONDERS
- Choose a theme or type of work and brainstorm variations.
- Generate options actively; try this while doing something else (walking . . . swimming . . . doodling).
- Use practical, here-and-now options that are easy for you to imagine.
- Go out and look around. Observe what people are doing.

EXPLORERS
- Stretch to include here-and-now as well as future-oriented options.
- Use your ability to see possibilities and potential. Use your strong focus on the possibilities to brainstorm options.
- Use your ability to focus on the future and imagine what could be.

EXPEDITORS
- Generate options on a logical theme.
- Be careful not to ignore options that do not immediately seem logical. Turn off your analysis for a short while as you explore.

CONTRIBUTORS
- Use personal examples of others for inspiration.
- Brainstorm with others who are imaginative and supportive.

ASSIMILATORS
- Stretch yourself by considering unfamiliar as well as familiar options.
- Brainstorm in a group, or find lists of options.
- Generate as many options as you can.

VISIONARIES
- Stretch to include here-and-now as well as future-oriented options.
- Use your ability to see possibilities and potential. Use your strong focus on the possibilities to brainstorm options.
- Use your ability to focus on the future and imagine what could be.

ANALYZERS

- Generate options on a logical theme.
- Be careful not to ignore options that do not immediately seem logical. Turn off your analysis for a short while as you explore.

ENHANCERS

- Look for occupations and organizations that are values based.
- Think of ways to express your important personal values.

RESEARCH

By now you will have generated a number of options. You may be wondering why you spent time and energy brainstorming or otherwise identifying options when you likely will not have time to research them all in detail. The advantage of listing many ideas and then narrowing them down is threefold. First, many individuals discover that the last idea they think of is the most interesting. Second, a seemingly outlandish idea may trigger a more practical idea later; this creative process is a powerful tool. Third, the more options you write down, the easier it is to identify themes.

With so many career options to choose from, you can appropriately select a few to research in greater detail. You may initially need to examine all your options with your most important needs or preferences in mind. Then take time to explore the options that are most appealing.

Targeting Your Research

Here are some questions to help you decide what to research:

- How well does this option match your self-assessment information? Some people find it useful to create a decision-making chart that plots self-assessment highlights and career options. This visual representation easily allows comparisons between options and top needs.
- Is there a demand for this work, skill, or knowledge?
- What specific work options are there within the general career area? Are there many related but different jobs, or only a few?
- If you are employed, will this work option help your organization meet its business needs? How can your company help you learn this? What is in it for the company?

- If you are self-employed, have you identified a market for your product or service? Your research will need to focus on potential markets, customers, and competition for the product or service.
- Where, when, and how can you learn what you need to learn?

Finding the Information You Need

Here are some potential sources of the information you need:

- Activities, clubs, or groups
- Associations, organizations, or unions
- Books on careers or trends
- Coaches
- Computers
- Conferences
- Friends, or a friend of a friend
- Government, college, or private career centers
- Human resources consultants
- Information and job fairs
- Internet
- Libraries
- Magazines
- Newspapers
- People doing the work
- People hiring others to do the work
- Schools
- Supervisors

Looking to the Future

Watch for trends that may affect you. Look for new ideas, new points of view, and scientific and technological breakthroughs. Here are some tips for increasing your awareness of current trends and future possibilities.

READ, LISTEN, AND WATCH

- Review a variety of media sources.
- Review local, regional, and global news.
- Read nonfiction best-sellers.

- Subscribe to newsletters and association publications.
- Pay attention to trend reports.

RELATE
- Take note of the views of a variety of other people.
- Form a strong personal network.
- Join or monitor associations.
- Work with various clubs or groups.
- Attend conventions and trade shows.
- Talk to potential customers or employers.
- Visit schools and businesses, and ask for information.

REFLECT
- Observe your reaction to information.
- Note your assumptions and biases.
- Be aware of your needs, likes, and dislikes.
- Challenge yourself to take in new ideas.
- Use critical thinking to evaluate information.
- Use creative thinking to imagine new possibilities.

RESPOND
- Volunteer in new areas.
- Experiment.
- Try different things.
- Go different places.

"Future watching" will help you develop a vision of your own future. This view will be unique, one that guides you in your decision making regarding work, learning, and career development. It will help you shape your career in a way that ensures that you are prepared for tomorrow.

As you complete your research, remember that information can be biased. For example, schools are trying to promote their programs, so their career descriptions may be overly positive. People you talk to may be reacting to their personal experiences and how their work suits their own career preferences.

Using the Internet

The Internet contains a massive amount of information. Many people are unfamiliar with how to use this resource. Even those who do know a bit about searching the web often find the enormous number of sites overwhelming. There are a variety of search engines and directories you can use to do research. Most search engines have ways to refine and control a search to find the most relevant information.

It is worthwhile to develop an effective Internet search strategy. Depending on your learning preferences and time constraints, you may choose to

- Take a course about the Internet, either online or off
- "Surf"—many of the search engines have self-directed instructions for customizing or refining a search
- Get advice from an experienced "surfer," or observe an experienced researcher using the Internet
- Find a reference (book, magazine, list of web sites) or ask a reference librarian how to maximize your Internet research

Tips for Researching

Here are some additional tips to help you research that are specifically related to your natural way of doing things.

RESPONDERS

- Try acting and experiencing rather than collecting data up front.
- Do hands-on active research when possible, such as volunteering or "job shadowing." You will likely research as you go rather than doing it as a separate activity.

EXPLORERS

- Use your strengths to analyze trends or patterns.
- Increase your focus on the facts and details.

EXPEDITORS

- Use logical analysis to sort through information.
- Be careful not to narrow or complete your research too quickly.

CONTRIBUTORS
- Focus on using analytical skills as well as your personal approach to help you to critically analyze information.
- Use personal examples and experiences as information sources.

ASSIMILATORS
- Focus on identifying trends or patterns.
- Use a systematic search and information management strategy to collect and organize your data for review. Collect technical and reference information. Be careful not to become overwhelmed by details.

VISIONARIES
- Analyze trends or patterns; increase your focus on the facts and details. Start with the big picture and then focus in.
- Think of ways to link and transfer skills and preferences across disciplines. Research broad and diverse opportunities.

ANALYZERS
- Analyze trends or patterns; increase your focus on the facts and details.
- Use your critical, analytical skills as you research.

ENHANCERS
- Focus on using analytical skills as well as your personal approach to help you to critically analyze information.
- Use personal examples and experiences as information sources.

Your Research Plan

What work option would you like to research?

....

List five key pieces of information you need to know about this option. Use your self-assessment information as a guide to help you discover whether the work meets your most important preferences and needs.

What do you need to know?

....

....

....

....

....

Copy your option into the middle of the circle. Then think of possible information sources and list them on the spokes of the circle. Now you can collect your data.

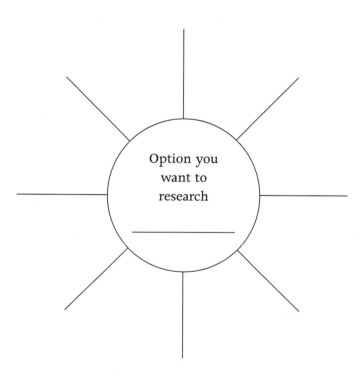

Option you want to research

DECIDE

Once you have some information about options, you can move into the decision-making stage of career shaping. It is helpful to examine your decision-making style and develop strategies to maximize your decision-making process. This will help you to make a well-informed and balanced decision.

You have clearly defined what makes a career personally satisfying, and you have considered and researched possibilities. Now you must choose an option and move ahead.

· 345 ·

Tips for Making Decisions

Here are some tips to help you make decisions that are specifically related to your natural way of doing things.

RESPONDERS

- You may prefer tentative decisions; try one of your options, or wait and see. Give yourself flexibility to maneuver and reevaluate decisions over time.
- Watch out for your preference to focus on short-term rather than long-term decisions.

EXPLORERS

- You may prefer tentative decisions; try one of your options, or wait and see. Give yourself flexibility to maneuver and reevaluate decisions over time.
- Make sure that you follow through on the details before you decide. You may make decisions based on a possibility and then later realize all is not what you thought.

EXPEDITORS

- Logical, analytical decision making is a strength for you. Make an effort to tolerate some ambiguity so you don't decide too soon.
- When deciding, you may see things as either black or white. Add a focus on personal values and the effects of your decisions on others.

CONTRIBUTORS

- You may tend to make decisions on the basis of personal values. Increase your focus on logical analysis.

• The effects of your decision on others may seem more important than your personal needs. Make sure you focus on what you need as you decide.

ASSIMILATORS

• Decision making tends to be a strength for you. Make an effort to tolerate some ambiguity so you don't decide too soon.
• You may tend to preserve the status quo rather than to choose change. Make sure that, if you do choose not to change, the consequences will not be negative.
• Watch out for your preference to focus on short-term rather than long-term decisions.

VISIONARIES

• Give yourself time to map out in your mind the long-term consequences of the decision.
• Make your decisions broad enough to allow you to take actions that will lead you in a general rather than a too specific direction.

ANALYZERS

• Logical, analytical decision making is a strength for you. Make an effort to tolerate some ambiguity so you don't decide too soon.
• When deciding, you may see things as either black or white. Add a focus on personal values and the effects of your decisions on others.

ENHANCERS

• You may tend to make decisions on the basis of personal values. Increase your focus on logical analysis.
• The effects of your decision on others may seem more important than your personal needs. Make sure you focus on what you need as you decide.

Decision-Making Style Checklist

There are two distinctly different decision-making styles: logical–analytical and values-based. These correspond to the personality type dichotomy of

Thinking (T) and Feeling (F) that you learned about in Chapter 2. As with all personality type differences, there is no good or bad decision-making style—only personal preferences.

Well-rounded decision makers can recognize and use their personal preferences and stretch themselves to appreciate and integrate alternative styles. Complete the following checklist to see whether you are incorporating aspects of both styles into your decision-making process.

When using logical–analytical decision making, I tend to
❑ Weigh the pros (benefits) and cons (disadvantages) of options
❑ Check that an option is reasonable
❑ Remain objective
❑ Analyze all the logical consequences and implications
❑ Look at the principles involved in the situation

When using values-based decision making I tend to
❑ Weigh options using my personal, subjective beliefs and values
❑ Assess the impact of my decisions on others
❑ Look at how the harmony of my environment will be affected
❑ Consider who will support me in my decisions
❑ Consider the likes, dislikes, and commitments of others

If you use one style much more than the other, you may want to consider incorporating preferences from the other style into your decision-making process.

Decision-Making Factors
When making a decision, no matter what your style preferences, you should take into consideration some key information.

SELF-ASSESSMENT DATA
Factors that you have defined as important or limiting are significant motivators for career decisions. Interests, skills, and values help you focus on finding

satisfying work. Constraints and lifestyle may limit or shape the where, when, how, and what of your career choices. Make sure you measure your choices against your self-assessment information.

FINANCES

Many people end up working at jobs they do not enjoy because of their lifestyle choices. Sometimes our possessions can trap us into financial obligations that limit our options. Taking a look at your wants and needs can help you decide whether you might be able to live more cheaply. There are two ways to have more money in your hands: make more and spend less.

When in career transition it is helpful (even essential!) to complete an itemized budget that lists monthly and yearly expenses. Financial information can help you rethink your options and plan more effectively. When you have completed your budget, you may wish to distinguish between what you *have* to spend and what you *choose* to spend. This can help you identify potential money-saving areas.

Often, in moving into a new career area, you will make less money, or will spend money in the short-term to meet your long-term goals. If you are financially unable to manage a career transition, you may be eligible for assistance through loans or other government programs. Check your local government employment agencies for information relevant to your region.

SIGNIFICANT OTHERS: ROLES AND RESPONSIBILITIES

Individuals must feel free to choose their own paths, but children, spouses or partners, parents, and friends also must be considered. Many couples find it helpful to plan their careers together. In times of career transition, restructuring family responsibilities may give rise to conflict. Discussions about family values and goals can help you and your family clarify expectations and contributions.

BUSINESS NEEDS

If you want to change careers within your organization, you will need to know how the change adds value to the organization and helps it meet its business needs. If you are self-employed, you will need to make a business plan. Your decision making should be directed toward your potential for success.

CHOOSING A CAREER PATH, NOT JUST A JOB

Try not to view a specific job as a career goal. Jobs are opportunities for learning; they are stepping-stones along a path. Focus on the underlying needs and preferences you meet by performing your job duties, rather than merely focusing on the job itself. Being able to shift from one position to another within a related field is especially important in today's work environment, where job security and long-term organizational commitments to staff are becoming a thing of the past. Once you have determined a career path, you can let it direct your choice of learning activities—and keep you motivated while completing them!

The learning activities from which you can choose are as diverse as the potential array of career and work choices. Most people develop new skills while working. If they do not, they may not stay employed for long. Others take courses while holding down various combinations of full- and part-time work. Still others start a business while working at another job to pay the bills.

TAKE ACTION

The last part of career shaping is putting your decision into action. This is where "the rubber meets the road": acting on and achieving more satisfying work. Summarizing what you have done so far will help you know what action you need to take. Focus your career needs by completing the summary that follows.

The most important things that will make a career satisfying for me are

....

....

....

I have decided that my career path lies in the area(s) of

....

....

....

Skills and knowledge that will help me move in this career direction are

....

....

....

Things I need to do are

....

....

....

The first thing I can do to start to shape my career is

....

....

....

Now is the time to take action to shape your career. Make time to complete the one thing you have chosen to start with, and then choose a second thing to do, and so on. Shaping your career path is an ongoing process. Generating options, researching, deciding, and taking action are things you will do throughout your life.

Tips for Taking Action

Here are some tips to help you take action—tips specifically related to your natural way of doing things.

RESPONDERS

- Shape your career by making changes that have immediate and practical applications. Use a step-by-step, active approach to move forward.
- Commit to a deadline to motivate yourself to follow through.

EXPLORERS

- Taking on several things at once can limit the time you have to follow through on each individual endeavor. Learn to set priorities.
- Take action when you feel inspired. Do not expect that you will work toward goals at a constant, steady pace. However, do not use this as an excuse to avoid action.

EXPEDITORS

- Use your organizational and planning ability to move forward. Taking action is a strength for you.
- Reflect as you go. Continue to take in information and modify your plan as you go, rather than moving ahead too quickly.

CONTRIBUTORS

- Make sure that your sense of responsibility and focus on meeting others' needs do not get in the way of working on your own career development.
- Use your organizational and planning ability to move forward. Taking action is a strength for you.

ASSIMILATORS

- Make a practical and detailed plan of what you want to accomplish, and follow it in a systematic, step-by-step manner.
- If sticking with the tried and true does not work, try something different.

VISIONARIES

- Keep your end goal in mind as a motivator. Focus on the specific small steps you need to take.
- First make your mental plan from start to finish. Then put it into action.

ANALYZERS

- Make a logical plan that allows some flexibility and maneuverability.
- Commit to a deadline to motivate yourself to follow through.

ENHANCERS

- Make sure your focus on meeting others' needs does not get in the way of working on your own career development.
- Find someone to support your action plan, and ensure that your action plan allows you to express your values.

Advantages of Career Shaping

Often our careers simply evolve naturally and change by chance. Opportunities and situations outside of our control appear, and we are triggered to make a change. Job loss, birth of children or children leaving home, change of marital status, and health challenges, for example, present opportunities to reassess our career path. For many of us, our first impulse is to quickly find new work, often doing the same thing we did before. This can seem like a fine solution if we are highly engaged in that type of work. Sometimes it is not possible or appealing, for various reasons, to continue with the same type of work. We may be proactively looking for new opportunities or choosing to get out of work that is not satisfying. Whatever the reasons for transition, it is a chance to reevaluate and move in new directions. Take time to shape your career and ensure that you can

- Become more aware of factors affecting work satisfaction
- Search for work that will use your natural way of working
- Have more control over the type of work you end up doing

- Effectively decide what information to learn and what skills to develop
- Have a focus for negotiation and discussion with leaders or supervisors
- Bring focus to your business plan and strategies
- Be better prepared for the changing future

Final Tips for Success

Here are a few key suggestions to help you shape your career. Feel free to add your own ideas and customize the list. With some effort, you will be able to find satisfying work that provides opportunities to use and develop your natural way of working.

- Take the time to assess what is really important to you.
- Find work that reflects your natural way of working.
- Continue to learn: take a course, learn a skill, try something new at work, volunteer.
- Get feedback from someone regarding how you are doing.
- Explore new options: write a proposal, create a new resume, compile a portfolio.
- Make realistic goals and deadlines that take into account your roles and responsibilities.
- Find someone to mentor you and encourage your career development.
- Reward yourself when you meet a goal.
- Make career shaping a lifelong activity.

References

Berens, L., and Isachsen, O. *A Quick Guide to Working Together with the Sixteen Types*. Huntington Beach, CA: Telos Publications, 1992.

Corlett, E. S., and Millner, N. B. *Navigating Midlife: Using Typology as a Guide*. Mountain View, CA: Davics-Black® Publishing, 1993.

Demarest, L. *Looking at Type in the Workplace*. Gainesville, FL: Center for Applications of Psychological Type, 1997.

Dunning, D. *Learning Your Way*. Red Deer, AB, Canada: Unlimited Learning Publications, 1998.

Hammer, A. L. *Introduction to Type® and Careers*. Mountain View, CA: CPP Inc., 1993.

Hirsh, S. K., and Kummerow, J. M. *LifeTypes*. New York: Warner Books, 1992.

Hirsh, S. K., and Kummerow, J. M. *Introduction to Type® in Organizations*. Mountain View, CA: CPP, Inc., 1998.

Isachsen, O., and Berens, L. *Working Together: A Personality Centered Approach to Management* (2nd ed.). San Juan Capistrano, CA: Institute for Management Development, 1995.

Kroeger, O., and Thuesen, J. *Type Talk at Work*. New York, Dell Publishing, 1992.

Kummerow, J. M., Barger, N. J., and Kirby, L. K. *WorkTypes*. New York: Warner Books, 1997.

Lawrence, G. *Looking at Type and Learning Styles*. Gainesville, FL: Center for Applications of Psychological Type, 1997.

Macdaid, G., McCaulley, M., and Kainz, R. *Atlas of Type Tables*. Gainesville, FL: Center for Applications of Psychological Type, 1995.

Martin, C. *Looking at Type and Careers*. Gainesville, FL: Center for Applications of Psychological Type, 1995.

Millner, N. B. *Creative Aging*. Mountain View, CA: Davies-Black Publishing, 1997.

Myers, I. B. *Introduction to Type®*. Mountain View, CA: CPP, Inc., 1998.

Myers, I. B., McCaulley, M. H., Quenk, N. L., and Hammer, A. L. *MBTI® Manual: A Guide to the Development and Use of the Myers-Briggs Type Indicator®*. Mountain View, CA: CPP, Inc., 1998.

Myers, I. B., with Myers, P. B. *Gifts Differing: Understanding Personality Type*. Mountain View, CA: Davies-Black Publishing, 1995.

Myers, K. D., and Kirby, L. K. *Introduction to Type® Dynamics and Development: Exploring the Next Level of Type*. Mountain View, CA: CPP, Inc., 1994.

Pearman, R. R., and Albritton, S. C. *I'm Not Crazy, I'm Just Not You*. Mountain View, CA: Davies-Black Publishing, 1997.

Quenk, N. L. *Was That Really Me? How Everyday Stress Brings Out Our Hidden Personality*. Mountain View, CA: Davies-Black Publishing, 2002.

Thomson, L. *Personality Type: An Owners Manual*. Boston: Shambhala Publications, 1998.

Tieger, P., and Barron-Tieger, B. *Do What You Are: Discover the Perfect Career for You Through the Secrets of Personality Type*. Boston: Little, Brown, 1995.

Index

Analyzers: adaptability of, 245–246; balancing approach used by, 250–251; challenges for, 270–273; characteristics of, 21, 243–244; communication style of, 247; decision-making tips for, 346; feedback for, 245, 271; following through by, 272; independent nature of, 246; insightful. *See* Insightful Analyzers; logical analysis, 244; natural work preferences of, 244–246, 248, 273–274; occupations that attract, 249–250; options for, 339; personality types of, 21; practical. *See* Practical Analyzers; prevalence of, 243; rapport building, 270 271; research tips for, 343; rules and regulations followed by, 247; self-assessments, 27, 248–249, 310–311; shortcomings of, 246–247; social norms followed by, 246

assessments. *See* self-assessments

Assimilators: balancing approach used by, 187–188; challenges for, 207–208; change effects on, 184–185, 207–208; characteristics of, 20; compassionate. *See* Compassionate Assimilators; decision-making tips for, 346; detail-oriented nature of, 181; information gathering by, 180–181; logical. *See* Logical Assimilators; natural work preferences of, 180–185, 209–210; occupations that attract, 186–187; options for, 338; overview of, 179–180; personality types of, 20; practical nature of, 184; prevalence of, 179; procedural approach of, 182–183; reliability of, 183–184; research tips for, 343; self-assessments, 26, 186, 310; self-confident nature of, 182; shortcomings of, 184–185; work focus of, 208

brainstorming, 336

career satisfaction, 7

career shaping: action taking, 349–350; decision making, 345–349; options, 335–339; research, 339–344

change: adapting to, 5–6; Assimilator's approach to, 184–185, 207–208; Explorer's approach to, 71–72; Insightful Contributor's approach to, 163; Insightful Expeditor's approach to, 130; Logical Explorer's approach to, 104; skills assessment, 319; Visionary's approach to, 214–215

communication skills: Compassionate Visionaries, 221–222; Explorers, 70–71, 78; self-assessment of, 319

Compassionate Assimilators: challenges for, 207–208; change effects on, 184–185, 207–208; conflict avoidance by, 195 196; detail-oriented nature of, 191; feedback for, 190; helping nature of, 189–190, 193; leadership role of, 194–196; learning approach used by, 197–198; natural work preferences of, 180–185, 189–191, 209–210; occupations that attract, 192–194; overview of, 188; prevalence of, 189; skills and valued activities for, 192; supportive nature of, 190–191, 195; team member role of, 196–197; work environment ideally suited for, 191; work focus of, 208; work relationships valued by, 190. *See also* Assimilators

Compassionate Explorers: advocate role of, 81, 84; attention to present moment, 101–103; challenges for, 98–103; change accepted by, 104; creative expression by, 81, 83; individualism valued by, 87; leadership role of, 84–86; learning approach used by, 79, 88; natural work preferences of, 80–81, 104–105; occupations that attract, 83–84; overview of, 79–80; patience of, 100–101; prevalence of, 80; rapport building, 81–82; skills and valued activities for, 83;

team member role of, 87; time and tasks management, 98–100; work environment ideally suited for, 82. *See also* Explorers

Compassionate Responders: big-picture focus of, 65–67; casual and personal nature of, 52; challenges for, 64–67; connecting with others, 47–48, 50–51; crisis management approach of, 52–53; decision-making approach of, 46; helping nature of, 46–47, 50; leadership role of, 52–53; learning approach used by, 54–55; long-term planning by, 64–65; natural work preferences of, 46–48; occupations preferred by, 49–52; overview of, 45–46; prevalence of, 46; self-expression, 48, 51; skills and valued activities for, 49; team member role of, 53–54; work environment ideally suited for, 49. *See also* Responders

Compassionate Visionaries: attention to present moment, 238–239; challenges for, 238–241; communication skills of, 221–222; description of, 219; feedback for, 227; flexibility of, 240; idea conceptualization by, 220–221; leadership role of, 226–227; learning approach used by, 228–229; natural work preferences of, 212–214, 216, 220–223, 241–242; occupations that attract, 224–226; overview of, 220; prevalence of, 220; self-expressive nature of, 223; skills and valued activities for, 224; team

member role of, 227–228; values of, 221–223; work environment ideally suited for, 224. *See also* Visionaries

Contributors: balancing approach used by, 148–149; challenges for, 170–173; characteristics of, 19; decision-making tips for, 345–346; feedback for, 144–145, 171–172; harmony created by, 143; insightful. *See* Insightful Contributors; logical decision making by, 170–171; natural work preferences of, 142–144, 146, 173–174; occupations that attract, 147–148; options for, 338; overview of, 141; personality types of, 19; personal needs unmet, 145; practical. *See* Practical Contributors; prevalence of, 141; rapport building by, 142; research tips for, 343; self-assessments, 25, 146–147, 310; self-expression by, 142–143; shortcomings of, 144–145; societal contributions by, 144; work environment ideally suited for, 143–144

decision making, 345–349

Enhancers: appreciation for others, 277; balancing approach used by, 282–283; challenges for, 302–305; characteristics of, 22, 275–276; decision-making tips for, 346; feedback for, 303–304; flexibility of, 278; harmonious nature of, 278–279; insightful. *See* Insightful Enhancers; natural work preferences of, 276–280, 305–306; occupations that

attract, 281–282; options for, 339; personal approach of, 276; personality types of, 22; personal needs unmet, 279, 302–303; practical. *See* Practical Enhancers; prevalence of, 275; research tips for, 343; self-assessments, 28, 280–281, 311; self-expression by, 277; shortcomings of, 279; values of, 276, 278

Expeditors: balancing approach used by, 115; challenges for, 134–137; characteristics of, 18–19; control relinquished by, 139; decision making by, 135–139, 345; decisive thinking of, 108, 111–112; empathizing and collaborating skills development, 134; insightful. *See* Insightful Expeditors; logical thinking of, 108, 138; natural work preferences of, 108–110, 137–139; occupations that attract, 113–114; options for, 338; organizational skills of, 138; overview of, 107; personality types of, 18–19, 107; practical. *See* Practical Expeditors; prevalence of, 107; research tips for, 342; self-assessments, 24, 113, 310; shortcomings of, 111–112; standards set by, 110; time and tasks management, 109–110; work environment ideally suited for, 109

Explorers: adaptability of, 71; attention to present moment, 101–103; balancing approach used by, 79–80; challenges for, 98–103; change initiated by, 71–72, 104; characteristics of, 18; communication skills of, 70–71, 78; compassionate. *See* Compassionate Explorers; decision-making tips for, 345; details not valued by, 74–75; entrepreneurship considerations, 104–105; flexibility of, 104; innovative thinking of, 70, 77; learning approach used by, 72; logical. *See* Logical Explorers; natural work preferences of, 70–73, 104–105; occupations that attract, 77–78; options for, 338; overview of, 69; patience of, 100–101; personality types of, 18, 69; prevalence of, 69; problem-solving abilities of, 70, 77; research tips for, 342; rules avoidance by, 73–74; self-assessments, 24, 76–77, 310; shortcomings, 73–76; time and tasks management, 98–100; variety of, 72–73; work environment ideally suited for, 73, 76

Extraverted type: characteristics of, 10; definition of, 10

extraverted ways of working: characteristics of, 17–19, 23–25; Contributors. *See* Contributors; Expeditors. *See* Expeditors; Explorers. *See* Explorers; preferences, 33; Responders. *See* Responders

feedback: Analyzer's approach, 245; Assimilator's approach, 190; Contributor's approach, 144–145, 171–172; Enhancer's approach, 292, 300

Feeling type: Assimilators. *See* Compassionate

Assimilators; characteristics of, 12; definition of, 12; Explorers. *See* Compassionate Explorers; Responders. *See* Compassionate Responders; Visionaries. *See* Compassionate Visionaries

growth, 6

Insightful Analyzers: challenges for, 270–273; characteristics of, 251, 262; creative nature of, 263; feedback for, 271; following through by, 272; ideas, 262–263; leadership role of, 267–268; learning approach used by, 269–270; long term focus of, 263, 267; natural work preferences of, 244–246, 248, 262–263, 273–274; occupations that attract, 265–267; prevalence of, 262; rapport building, 270–271; skills and valued activities for, 264; task-oriented nature of, 267–268; team member role of, 269; work environment ideally suited for, 264. *See also* Analyzers

Insightful Contributors: challenges for, 170–173; change, 163; creative energy of, 162, 166; feedback for, 171–172; goal-oriented nature of, 167; growth and development supported by, 162; leadership role of, 166–168; learning approach used by, 169–170; logical decision making by, 170–171; natural work preferences of, 162–164; occupations that attract, 165–166; organizational abilities of, 163–164; overview of,

161; prevalence of, 161; relationship building by, 162–163; skills and valued activities for, 165; team member role of, 168–169; work environment ideally suited for, 164. *See also* Contributors

Insightful Enhancers: challenges for, 302–305; characteristics of, 283–284; communication style of, 295–296; creative nature of, 295; feedback for, 300, 303–304; leadership role of, 298–299; learning approach used by, 301; natural work preferences of, 276–280, 294–296, 305–306; occupations that attract, 296–298; personal needs unmet, 302–303; prevalence of, 294; skills and valued activities for, 297; supportive nature of, 294–295, 299; team member role of, 300; work environment ideally suited for, 297. *See also* Enhancers

Insightful Expeditors: challenges for, 134–137; change initiated by, 130; decision-making approach of, 135–137; empathizing and collaborating skills development, 134; leadership role of, 127, 130–131; learning approach used by, 132–133; natural work preferences of, 126–127; occupations that attract, 129–130; overview of, 125–126; prevalence of, 125; skills and valued activities for, 128; systems and process improvements valued by, 126–127; team member role of, 131–132; work environment ideally suited for, 128. *See also* Expeditors

interests assessment, 327–330
Internet, 341–342
Intraverted type: characteristics of, 10; definition of, 10
intraverted way of working: Analyzers. *See* Analyzers; Assimilators. *See* Assimilators; characteristics of, 19–22, 26–28; Enhancers. *See* Enhancers; preferences, 177; Visionaries. *See* Visionaries
Intuitive type: Analyzers. *See* Insightful Analyzers; characteristics of, 11; definition of, 11; enhancers that prefer. *See* Insightful Enhancers; Expeditors. *See* Insightful Expeditors

job satisfaction, 5
Judging type: characteristics of, 13; definition of, 13

leaders: Compassionate Assimilators as, 194–196; Compassionate Explorers as, 84–86; Compassionate Responders as, 52–53; Compassionate Visionaries as, 226–227; Insightful Analyzers as, 267–268; Insightful Contributors as, 166–168; Insightful Enhancers as, 298–299; Insightful Expeditors as, 127, 130–131; Logical Assimilators as, 203–204; Logical Explorers as, 94–96; Logical Responders as, 60–62; Logical Visionaries as, 234–236; Practical Analyzers as, 257–259; Practical Contributors as, 157–159; Practical Enhancers as, 290–291; Practical Expeditors as, 122–123; skills assessment, 321

learning: Compassionate Assimilator's approach to,

197–198; Compassionate Explorer's approach to, 79, 88; Compassionate Responder's approach to, 54–55; Compassionate Visionary's approach to, 228–229; Insightful Analyzer's approach to, 269–270; Insightful Contributor's approach to, 169–170; Insightful Enhancer's approach to, 301; Insightful Expeditor's approach to, 132–133; Logical Assimilator's approach to, 205–206; Logical Explorer's approach to, 97–98; Logical Responder's approach to, 63–64; Logical Visionary's approach to, 237–238; Practical Analyzer's approach to, 261; Practical Contributor's approach to, 160–161; Practical Enhancer's approach to, 293; Practical Expeditor's approach to, 124–125; skills assessment, 321
lifestyle assessments, 330–331
Logical Assimilators: analytical techniques used by, 200; challenges for, 207–208; change effects on, 184–185, 207–208; leadership role of, 203–204; learning approach used by, 205 206; natural work preferences of, 180–185, 199–200; occupations that attract, 201–203; overview of, 188, 198–199; prevalence of, 198; rules and regulations followed by, 199; skills and valued activities for, 201; task-oriented nature of, 203–204; team member

role of, 204–205; thoroughness of, 199–200; work environment ideally suited for, 200; work focus of, 208. *See also* Assimilators
Logical Explorers: analytical nature of, 95; attention to present moment, 101–103; big-picture focus of, 89–90, 93; challenges for, 98–103; change accepted by, 104; flexibility of, 95, 104; independent and competent nature of, 90–91, 93–94; leadership role of, 94–96; learning approach used by, 97–98; logical thinking of, 89; natural work preferences of, 89–91, 104–105; negotiating skills of, 90; occupations that attract, 92–93; overview of, 88–89; patience of, 100–101; prevalence of, 88; problem-solving abilities of, 89–90, 93; skills and valued activities for, 92; team member role of, 96–97; time and tasks management, 98–100; work environment ideally suited for, 91. *See also* Explorers
Logical Responders: big-picture focus of, 65–67; challenges for, 64–67; characteristics of, 45; communication style of, 57; crisis management approach of, 60–61; interpersonal skills of, 62; leadership role of, 60–62; learning approach used by, 63–64; long-term planning by, 64–65; natural work preferences of, 56–58; negotiating, 56–57, 59; occupations that attract, 58–60; overview of, 55–56; prevalence of,

55; risk taking by, 57, 60; skills and valued activities for, 58; team member role of, 62–63; work environment ideally suited for, 58. *See also* Responders

Logical Visionaries: attention to present moment, 238–239; challenges for, 238–241; description of, 219; flexibility of, 240; leadership role of, 234–236; learning approach used by, 237–238; natural work preferences of, 212–214, 216, 230–231, 241–242; occupations that attract, 232–234; overview of, 230; plans implemented by, 231; prevalence of, 230; problem-solving abilities of, 230–231; skills and valued activities for, 232; task-oriented nature of, 235; team member role of, 236–237; work environment ideally suited for, 232. *See also* Visionaries

Myers-Briggs Type Indicator® instrument, 9

numerical data skills assessment, 321

Perceiving type: characteristics of, 13; definition of, 13
personal growth, 6
personality preferences, 14–16
personality type, 9. *See also* specific type
Practical Analyzers: challenges for, 270–273; characteristics of, 251–252; competency valued by, 259; detail-oriented nature of, 252–253; feedback, 271; following through by, 272; leadership role of,

257–259; learning approach used by, 261; natural work preferences of, 244–246, 248, 252–254, 273–274; occupations that attract, 255–257; physical dexterity skills, 253–254; prevalence of, 252; problem-solving abilities of, 253, 258–259; rapport building, 270–271; risk taking, 254; skills and valued activities for, 255; solutions-oriented nature of, 258–259; team member role of, 260; work environment ideally suited for, 255. *See also* Analyzers

Practical Contributors: challenges for, 170–173; community work involvement, 151–153; feedback for, 171–172; harmonious approach of, 158; leadership role of, 157–159; learning approach used by, 160–161; logical decision making by, 170–171; natural work preferences of, 151–154; occupations that attract, 155–157; overview of, 150; skills and valued activities for, 154; structured approach, 153; supportive nature of, 158; team member role of, 159–160; work environment ideally suited for, 154. *See also* Contributors

Practical Enhancers: attention to present moment, 285; challenges for, 302–305; characteristics of, 283–285; feedback, 292, 303–304; leadership role of, 290–291; learning approach used by, 293; natural work preferences of, 276–280, 285–287, 305–306; occupations that attract, 288–290; personal

contributions of, 285–286; personal needs unmet, 302–303; prevalence of, 284; problem-solving abilities of, 286–287, 290–291; self-expressive nature of, 286; skills and valued activities for, 287; team member role of, 292; work environment ideally suited for, 287. *See also* Enhancers

Practical Expeditors: challenges for, 134–137; decision-making approach of, 135–137; empathizing and collaborating skills development, 134; leadership role of, 122–123; learning approach used by, 124–125; natural work preferences of, 116–118; occupations that attract, 120–121; organizational abilities of, 121; overview of, 116; prevalence of, 116; results-oriented approach, 116–117, 120; skills and valued activities for, 119; structured environments, 117–118; team member role of, 123–124; work environment ideally suited for, 119; work ethic of, 118. *See also* Expeditors

problem-solving skills: Explorers, 70, 77; Logical Explorers, 89–90, 93; Logical Visionaries, 230–231; Practical Analyzers, 253, 258–259; Practical Enhancers, 286–287, 290–291; Responders, 36; self-assessment of, 321

research, 339–344
Responders: adaptability of, 37–38, 68; balancing approach used by, 44–45; big-picture focus of, 65–67; challenges for,

64–67; characteristics of, 17–18; compassionate. *See* Compassionate Responders; decision-making tips for, 345; entertaining nature of, 38–39; learning approach, 39–40; logical. *See* Logical Responders; long-term planning by, 64–65; natural work preferences of, 36–41, 67–68; occupations preferred by, 42–44; options for, 338; overview of, 35–36; personality types of, 17, 35; prevalence of, 35; problem-solving abilities of, 36; realistic approach used by, 37; research tips for, 342; "seize the day" mentality of, 38, 67; self-assessments, 23, 42, 309; shortcomings of, 40–41
results orientation skills assessment, 322

self-acceptance, 7
self-assessments: Analyzers, 27, 248–249, 310–311; Assimilators, 26, 186, 310; Contributors, 25, 146–147, 310; Enhancers, 28, 280–281, 311; Expeditors, 24, 113, 310; Explorers, 24, 76–77, 310; interests, 327–330; lifestyle, 330–331; natural way of working, 315–316; occupation-specific skills, 326–327; personality preferences, 14–16; pitfalls commonly associated with, 311–312; present knowledge, 312–314; Responders, 23, 42, 309; skills, 317–327; summary of, 331–333; values, 327–330; Visionaries, 27, 216–217, 310

Sensing type: Analyzers. *See* Practical Analyzers; characteristics of, 11; definition of, 11; Enhancers. *See* Practical Enhancers; Expeditors. *See* Practical Expeditors
skills assessment, 317–327

team members: Compassionate Assimilators as, 196–197; Compassionate Explorers as, 87; Compassionate Responders as, 53–54; Compassionate Visionaries as, 227–228; Insightful Analyzers as, 269; Insightful Contributors as, 168–169; Insightful Enhancers as, 300; Insightful Expeditors as, 131–132; Logical Assimilators as, 204–205; Logical Explorers as, 96–97; Logical Responders as, 62–63; Logical Visionaries as, 236–237; Practical Analyzers as, 260; Practical Contributors as, 159–160; Practical Enhancers as, 292; Practical Expeditors as, 123–124; skills assessment, 322
thinking skills assessment, 323
Thinking type: Assimilators. *See* Logical Assimilators; characteristics of, 12; definition of, 12; Explorers. *See* Logical Explorers; Responders. *See* Logical Responders; Visionaries. *See* Logical Visionaries

values assessment, 327–330
Visionaries: attention to present moment, 238–239; balancing approach used by, 218–219; challenges for, 238–241; change effects, 214–215; characteristics of, 21; compassionate. *See* Compassionate Visionaries; creative nature of, 213; decision-making tips for, 346; flexibility of, 240; ideas of, 213–214, 217; insightful approach of, 211–212; learning approach used by, 212–213; logical. *See* Logical Visionaries; natural work preferences of, 212–214, 216, 241–242; occupations that attract, 217–218; options for, 338; overview of, 211; personality types of, 21; prevalence of, 211; research tips for, 343; self-assessments, 27, 216–217, 310; shortcomings of, 214–215

working: extraverted ways of. *See* extraverted ways of working; intraverted ways of. *See* intraverted ways of working; natural way of, 16–17